104

D0084576

CROSS-CULTURAL MANAGEMENT

Cross Cultural Management Series

Series Editor:

Kwok Leung, *Professor of Management at City University, Hong Kong, China*

This series provides high quality research monographs and edited volumes that examine key issues in cross-cultural management such as workplace diversity, varieties of capitalism, comparative national performance, international joint ventures, and transnational negotiations. The series encompasses multidisciplinary perspectives and is aimed at an academic readership. The purpose of the series is to provide a global academic forum for the study of cross-cultural management.

Forthcoming title:

Management and Organization in Germany
Thomas Armbrüster
ISBN 0 7546 3880 4

This book describes how national and organizational culture are linked. This is shown through an empirical investigation. Patterns of organizational culture in Germany are then analyzed in the context of national culture and institutional structure. Three differentiating features of German organizations are identified. The book conveys and explains German organizational culture and modes of cooperation to readers from other backgrounds.

Cross-Cultural Management

Foundations and Future

Edited by

DEAN TJOSVOLD
Lingnan University, Hong Kong, China

KWOK LEUNG
City University of Hong Kong, China

ASHGATE

Published by
Ashgate Publishing Limited
Gower House
Croft Road
Aldershot
Hampshire GU11 3HR
England

Ashgate Publishing Company
Suite 420
101 Cherry Street
Burlington, VT 05401-4405
USA

Ashgate website: http://www.ashgate.com

British Library Cataloguing in Publication Data
Cross-cultural management : foundations and future
    1. International business enterprises - Management -
    Psychological aspects 2. Intercultural communication
    3. Psychology, Industrial 4. Ethnopsychology 5. Communication
    in management 6. Organizational behavior
    I. Tjosvold, Dean II. Leung, Kwok, 1958-
    658'. 049

Library of Congress Cataloging-in-Publication Data
Cross-cultural management : foundations and future / edited by Dean Tjosvold, and Kwok Leung
    p. cm – (Cross-cultural management)
    Includes bibliographical references and index.
    ISBN 0-7546-1881-1 (alk.paper)
    1. Industrial management – Cross-cultural studies. 2. Diversity in the
workplace – Management. 3. Multiculturalism. 4. Intercultural communication. I.
Tjosvold, Dean. II. Leung, Kwok, 1958- III. Series.

HD31.C75 2003
658.3'0089–dc21

2003052108

ISBN 0 7546 1881 1

Printed and bound in Great Britain by MPG Books Ltd, Bodmin, Cornwall

Contents

List of Figures

List of Tables

List of Contributors

Rabi S. Bhagat, Professor, University of Memphis, Memphis, Tennessee

Michael Harris Bond, Professor of Psychology, Chinese University of Hong Kong

Geert Hofstede, Professor Emeritus, Institute for Research on Intercultural Cooperation, Tilburg, the Netherlands

Susan E. Jackson, Professor, School of Management and Labor Relations, Rutgers University, USA.

Balaji Krishnan, Assistant Professor, University of Memphis, Memphis, Tennessee

Kwok Leung, Professor of Management, City University of Hong Kong, China

Mark F. Peterson, Professor of Management, Florida Atlantic University

B. Ram Baliga, Professor, Wake Forest University, Winston-Salem, North Carolina

S. Antonio Ruiz Quintanilla, Associate Director Professor, Department of Organization and Management, Aarhus School of Business

Randall S. Schuler, Professor, School of Management and Labor Relations, Rutgers University

Peter B. Smith, Professor of Social Psychology, School of Social Sciences, University of Sussex

Karen South Moustafa, Doctoral Candidate, University of Memphis, Memphis, Tennessee

David C. Thomas, Professor, International Management, Simon Fraser University

Dean Tjosvold, Chair Professor, Department of Management, Lingnan University, Hong Kong, China.

Harry C. Triandis, Professor Emeritus, UIUC Department of Psychology, Social-Personality-Organizational Division, University of Illinois, Urbana-Champaign

Rosalie L. Tung, Professor, International Business, Simon Fraser University

Introduction

Cross-Cultural Foundations: Traditions for Managing in a Global World

Dean Tjosvold

Kwok Leung

Each nation ought, not only to endeavour itself to excel, but from the love of mankind to promote, instead of obstruct the excellence of its neighbors (Adam Smith).

Cross-cultural management is rapidly becoming everyone's challenge. Expanding international trade and continued immigration flows mean that increasingly people of diverse cultures must work together. Companies from all parts of the world are forming joint ventures and strategic alliances to participate in the global marketplace (Jackson and Schuler). Immigration and birth rates are making European, North American, and Oceanic workforces more culturally diverse. In the United States, less that 60 per cent of new entrances into the job market are expected to be from the majority, white, native born Americans (Tung and Thomas). From the executive suites to the shop floor, people must increasingly be able to work across cultural boundaries.

Intense global competition requires this cross-cultural teamwork be highly productive and innovative. Organizations report that it takes years to develop effective teams even when people are from the same culture and work in one site. But now managers must develop teamwork with people distributed over different cultures, regions, and time zones, and do so quickly or lose out to more nimble rivals.

The underlying intellectual, economic, and technological dynamics seem too powerful to reverse the need to work across boundaries. Cross-cultural interdependence is the reality that we must face. Our choice is how we are going to understand, approach, and handle our cultural differences. Our ability to live and work across cultural boundaries will very much shape the quality of our lives and the success of our organizations. Indeed, effective relationships across cultures will affect whether globalization of the marketplace helps unite or divide nations against each other.

Progress has been made. Managers and researchers alike increasingly recognize the limitations of traditional organizational theories and management approaches that assume individual and cultural homogeneity. They want to move away from reliance on Western ideas and approaches to incorporate those from Asian and other cultures. They are moving away from "the one way to manage" and "one organization fits all". They are experimenting with new ways of organizing and managing that are effective for today and responsive to the diversity of employees. Imperialism is a dirty word.

But critiquing old ways is easier than building the new. How can leadership be carried out that respects the cultural diversity and individuality of employees yet results in high value for customers? How can diverse people become highly committed yet the organization retain a single-minded focus? Managers and employees worldwide need empirically developed ideas to make their cross-cultural teams and organizations productive. Leading and working as a team are never easy but doing so across cultures is particularly challenging. It is in the context of globalization that the field of cross-cultural management has emerged to guide the development of organizations that involve and inspire people of diverse values.

Cross-cultural management, as a young field, remains amorphous and fragmented. In this volume, pioneers in cross-cultural management review the foundations they have laid for understanding our diversity and improving professional practice and look to the future for important areas to develop. In so doing, 'Cross-Cultural Foundations: Traditions for Managing in a Global World' brings clarity and coherence to this burgeoning field, serves as a signpost for future advances, and constitutes a valuable resource for researchers, students, managers, and specialists. They can consider the fundamental theories and frameworks of cross-cultural management, identify key issues for further research, and deepen their understanding of applying cross-cultural management knowledge.

Cross-cultural management is a professional practice as well as research field. Trainers are often able to help people from diverse cultures work together effectively (Bond). International alliances must recognize and respond to the cultural values of all partners or risk failure (Jackson and Schuler). Human resource management practices that incorporate cross-cultural management knowledge involve and motivate diverse people, but imposing the practices of one group on others alienates (Tung and Thomas). There is no realistic alternative to effective cross-cultural management.

Identifying Cultural Differences

As the following chapters attest, cross-cultural management researchers have made important advances in understanding and documenting cultural differences. They have sought to know how societies differ in their characteristic ways of thinking, feeling, and acting. These cultural values are theorized to very much affect the outlook, approaches, and effectiveness of individuals and organizations.

Although there are commonalties in the genetic make-up of all people, families and societies very much shape the attitudes and goals of individuals, resulting in a rich array of differences. Not content with theorizing that there are cultural differences, researchers have developed frameworks and impressive data-bases for identifying and documenting value differences.

Consequences of Culture

Geert Hofstede's chapter, like several others in this volume, builds upon his work on the consequences of culture that laid the foundation for contemporary cross-cultural management. He has argued strongly that values very much shape the actions of individuals and the dynamics of organizations and are key to understanding and comparing societies. He has boldly and empirically developed a theoretical framework that identifies the central dimensions upon which values of societies can be compared.

Other chapters show their indebtedness to Hofstede's work. Gupta and House report the remarkable research program of the Global Leadership and Organizational Behavior Effectiveness (GLOBE). One hundred and fifty investigators have worked for a decade collecting data on cultural values and leadership practices and attributes from 18,000 managers in 62 societies, representing ten major geographical regions of the world! They have modified and added to Hofstede's framework by identifying nine value dimensions: performance orientation, assertiveness orientation, future orientation, humane orientation, institutional collectivism, family collectivism, gender egalitarianism, power distance, and uncertainty avoidance. They use these dimensions to distinguish societies and predict leadership approaches.

In addition to intellectual understanding, research on cultural values has important practical implications. Tung and Thomas indicate how cultural diversity very much impacts human resource management practices. Jackson and Schuler demonstrate the need for appropriate organizational and interpersonal practices and skills to manage cultural diversity in cross-boundary alliances.

Most fundamentally, research on value differences empirically demonstrates that peoples have their own ideals, aspirations, and ways of working and directly challenges the imposing of one's societies institutions and practices on another. More specifically, cross-cultural management research provides guideposts to differences. The research can provide "cultural markers" that identify how societies are similar and dissimilar and suggest the overall nature of organizations appropriate for the culture. Although people have their own individual characteristics and do not exactly replicate the modal values of their society, knowing the person's cultural background can be a first step to knowing him or her as an individual person and working together successfully.

Issues

Theorizing and research on identifying value differences on various dimensions has served as the foundation to cross-culture research and has provided many insights. Indeed, it is hard to imagine cross-cultural management without this emphasis. Although highly useful and dominant, we should also appreciate the limitations of this approach.

Cross-cultural management researchers have led the way in recognizing the important role of values on human behavior and societies. But the preeminence of values has been largely assumed rather than vigorously tested. Researchers have found correlations between values and individual actions and outcomes but much less work has identified the dynamics by which values have their theorized pervasive impact. The effects of cultural values may not be as generally significant as assumed (Oyserman, Coon, and Kemmelmeier, 2002). Fortunately, recent research has begun to examine directly the dynamics between values and behavior (Morris, Williams, Leung, Larrick, Mendoza, Bhatnagar, Li, Kondo, Luo, and Hu, 1998).

Social psychologists have concluded that attitudes have a complex relationship with actual behavior and that the more general the attitude, the less its apparent power to affect behavior (Fishbein and Ajzen, 1975). Smith argues in his chapter that in cross-cultural interaction diverse people do not simply act upon their own cultural values or adopt the values of others. Our own research suggests that Chinese values of harmony, relationships, and collectivism can result in open, constructive conflict as well as conflict avoidance (Leung, Koch, and Lu, 2002; Tjosvold and Sun, in press; Tjosvold, Leung, and Johnson, 2000). Much more research is needed to identify and document the dynamics between values, actions, and consequences.

Cross-cultural researchers have broken away from the confining methods of traditional psychological and management research and boldly compared societies. Hofstede's (1983) original study compared samples from 50 different societies! This method though assumes that the samples are generally representative and differ from each other largely in terms of their culture. Researchers are aware that these assumptions cannot be vigorously met; there is always at least some reason to believe that the observed differences are due to differences in the samples on such variables as chronological age and business experience, not culture.

Bhagat, Baliga, Moustafa, and Krishnan argue that too often differences are attributed to cultural values at the expense of technology and organizational culture. Wakabayashi proposes that culture has been over-used to explain management practices in Asia. How people differ in their values turns out to be an easy question to ask, but difficult to answer.

A less appreciated, but important limitation of comparing across cultures is that it restricts experimental research. Cultural values are defined as stable, long-term beliefs that can be measured and compared, not induced. But experiments would directly test and develop understanding of how cultural values have their effects. One approach is to do experiments on alternative ways that values can be applied and their effects within a culture (Leung and Su, in press; Tjosvold and Sun, 2001; Tjosvold, Hui, and Sun, 2000). This method can suggest how applying values and other conditions affect the consequences of values.

The documentation of cultural differences has profound practical implications on organizations and management. However, researchers have also suggested the limitations of this approach. Evidence about cross-cultural differences, even if they are reasonably accurate and timely, provide only general guidance. It cannot be assumed that the manager and employee exactly represent their "cultures" in that they have the same values as national samples. What drives behavior are the orientations of the specific individuals involved, not national averages. Knowing that one's partner as a Chinese probably has collectivist values does not directly identify the person's resources nor predict the behaviors that will promote the relationship (Bond).

Theorizing and research on cultural differences remain central to cross-cultural management. However, the contribution of this emphasis should not obscure its limitations. Indeed, Bond and Smith both argue that much more attention is needed directly on how diverse people interact and work together.

Cross-Cultural Interaction

Cross-cultural interactions are often complex and have the potential to communicate a disrespect for others' identity and values. Although there are often significant gains when people of diverse cultures work together, research is needed on how they are able to overcome barriers and collaborate effectively.

Traditional cross-cultural management research highlights potential value differences between people from diverse societies and can help them use reasonably accurate stereotypes to form their expectations of each other. Recent studies though suggest that diverse people do not simply act out their cultural values but continually adapt to each other.

Smith summarizes studies suggesting the limits of knowledge on cultural values for the understanding and practice of cross-cultural leadership. Japanese managers, for example, have been found to be more assertive with Canadian employees and indirect with Japanese subordinates (Rao and Hashimoto 1996). US employees of a Japanese firm evaluated a Japanese who had somewhat adapted his behaviour to US styles as more effective than those who did not adapt but thought one that acted very American was not genuine (Thomas and Ravlin 1995). Japanese managers have been found to adapt their behavior when negotiating with US Americans (Adair, Okumura, and Brett, 2001).

Bond argues for the need for a rich textual understanding of interaction between diverse people. Cross-cultural interactions tend to be more complex and problematic than within culture interactions. Identifying the behaviors such as respect and attentiveness that can help diverse people interact successfully would be both theoretically and practically valuable. In addition, research could examine the personality variables that give rise to these useful interaction behaviors.

Smith proposes that cultural values, even if they can specifically identified, are only one part of the situation in which diverse people work and interact and that the behavior of diverse people very much depends upon the specific situation as well as any impact of general values. The tasks and demands, the organization's climate and its intergroup relations, the particular aspirations of the individuals, and many other variables all impact interaction. Wakabayashi theorizes that external demands and internal functions very much affect the development and practices of managers in Asia.

Smith's chapter outlines event management theory and recent research that have begun to understand how diverse people adapt to each other as they respond to specific issues and use and limit their traditional ways of working. Diverse people negotiate how they will behave toward each other. Cultural values do not dictate their behavior. Managers and employees must deal with cultural differences as they act in specific settings with specific events. Research is needed to understand and help managers and employees with different cultural and national backgrounds find ways to work effectively together.

According to Bond, intercultural exchange is critical for enhancing cultural diversity. Managers do not simply act out of their national values nor just adopt the culturally endorsed approach of the employee. Managers must have the abilities and procedures to apply their knowledge of cultural values in sensitive, adaptive ways. They must develop methods so that employees understand them and feel motivated to get things done.

Tolerance and respect for differences are widely considered a moral obligation and necessity in the global age. Without mutual respect, people feel demeaned, turn away from each other and their goals, and spend their energy in ongoing hostilities or suppressing anger and bitterness. But accepting differences is much easier to say than to do. Decades of research suggest that people like those with similar attitudes and backgrounds (Byrne, 1971). Much more research is needed to help diverse people interact so that they feel accepted and respected.

Value of Cultural Diversity

Cultural diversity is not only a present reality but can be highly constructive. Tung and Thomas and Jackson and Schuler argue that cultural diversity can enhance people and promote organizational productivity. International assignments have become important management development opportunities.

Some studies directly support the value of cultural diversity. For example, diversity of perspectives and backgrounds have been found to improve the decision making of work groups and top management teams (Adler, 1997; Ely and Thomas, 2001). Diversity appears to provide groups with alternative views that can challenge assumptions, promote exploration of issues, and the creation of quality decisions as they strengthen relationships and commitment.

However, researchers have proposed that the diverse perspectives must be skillfully discussed before they are useful (Tjosvold, 1998). Studies are needed directly on the conditions and dynamics by which cultural diversity can contribute to relationships and effective collaboration.

Researchers have recently theorized that diverse people should develop a "third culture" that supports their enhancing interaction and makes diversity productive (Earley and Mosakowski, 2000). Diverse people combine their values and preferred methods to develop their own ways of working and interacting that they find enhancing and useful. This third culture would incorporate elements of all the participants' cultures but would not replicate any of them. Although an intriguing idea, much more research is needed to identify the processes of developing a "third culture" and documenting its consequences.

Diverse Perspectives for Cross-Cultural Management

Cross-cultural research needs a variety of voices, perspectives, and methods to advance our knowledge. The chapters reflect the contributions of psychologists, anthropologists, linguists, sociologists, international business and management specialists. Cross-cultural trainers, human resource managers, and other professionals have also all contributed.

Triandis describes the personal experiences and theoretical insights that shaped his ideas and development as a cross-cultural psychologist. His learning as an immigrant, interests in applied problems, and his intellectual adventuresomeness lay behind his making important contributions to the field. The personal convictions and desires to inform critical social and organizational issues are motivations for many cross-cultural researchers.

Peterson and Quintanilla argue strongly that comprehensive theory (etic) and local practices (emic) are both needed in cross-cultural research. Researchers should continually refer and explore specific experiences as they develop general and theoretical understanding. More specifically, theorists should talk with local practitioners and people from the "outside" should work with those on the "inside" to develop cross-cultural knowledge.

Cross-cultural research itself thrives on diversity. The field needs diverse points of views and backgrounds. Cross-cultural management should not be allowed to become its own self-contained area, closed off from other disciplines. It is true that theories developed in one culture cannot be assumed to apply in another but it is also true they should not be assumed not to apply. Knowledge regardless of where it is developed is needed to inform our understanding of cross-cultural management. It will take social scientists of all kinds as well as managers, trainers, and other professionals to combine their expertise and integrate their methods and ideas in order to continue to make progress in our vital, challenging field.

Our Distinctiveness, Our Commonness

An enduring debate is whether with rapid communication and the world marketplace cultures are converging (Inglehart and Baker, 2000). Are we becoming global citizens with similar beliefs, interests, and tastes? Perhaps differences in cultures are becoming less salient and an international culture more pervasive.

Evidence to support this hypothesis is apparent: The language and ways of western business are increasingly apart of the national life of countries around the world. Many products have world-wide appeal. Democratic governments, at least the practice of holding elections, are more popular. However, the adoption of some international ways does not mean that people are less local. People continue to demonstrate their commitment to their own ethnic and geographical groups (Inglehart and Baker, 2000). Unfortunately, our ways of showing local loyalties remain too often hostile and primitive.

The hypothesis that cultures are converging provokes an interesting debate but documenting its validity seems too demanding for our present social science methods. What seems more easily accepted is that our global world gives us greater opportunities to know each other and these opportunities reveal both our commonness and our distinctiveness.

We can not be sanguine that our greater opportunities to know each other will result in actual understanding and compassion and a feeling of world community. To do that, cross-cultural interactions have to be cooperative and open-minded. Closed-mindedness heightens hostility and rejection.

Each person is unique, each culture is distinct. But these differences need not be obstacles. They are natural and inevitable and add a richness to social and work lives. Our differences are what we have in common. How can we expect others to value and support our values and individuality if we do not value theirs? There is no realistic alternative to accepting and respecting our differences.

Positive Cultural Diversity

> The fact that a problem will certainly take a long time to solve, and that it will demand the attention of many minds for several generations, is no justification for postponing the study. And, in times of emergency, it may prove in the long run that the problems we have postponed or ignored, rather than those we have failed to attack successfully, will return to plague us. Our difficulties of the moment must always be dealt with somehow; but our permanent difficulties are difficulties of every moment (T. S. Eliot).

The imperative to value diversity and respect our differences, though always true, now has greater urgency. Organizations confront the necessity to capture the energy and ideas of all employees to meet the challenges of the intensely competitive marketplace. As organizations seek to participate in the global economy, individuals are increasingly asked to work with people with diverse values and nationalities. Technology brings us closer both to direct cooperation and to direct hostility. The global marketplace is an everyday reality where people around the world negotiate deals and make things happen. Our need to work across cultural boundaries has never been greater.

Positive diversity requires valuing and utilizing the full capabilities of all people throughout the organization. Positive diverse organizations communicate that people's values and backgrounds are known, accepted, and respected. They show that they are learning to value differences in their home organization as they reach out beyond their organizational and national boundaries to develop mutually enhancing relationships with partners and customers around the world.

If our organizations and societies do not become more diverse positive, we face the dangers of more fragmentation and disunity. But because we should become more cross-culturally effective does not mean that we will. Valuing diversity has too often been restricted to nice sounding statements and slogans in constitutions, mission statements, and after dinner speeches. Today's leaders face not only a diverse work force but a divided one. Many are suspicious of their leaders and each other. Employees want credibility from their leaders, but often feel they get little honesty. Good intentions are seldom the major obstacle; translating ideas into reality is much more formidable.

Although confidence may not be warranted, hope is essential. Knowledge about cultural differences and intercultural interaction provides an important foundation to value our diversity. *Cross-Cultural Management: Foundations and Future* can help managers and researchers develop their understanding and professional practice in working across cultural boundaries. It is our sincere hope that this volume will provide an important step toward a harmonious world epitomized by the Confucian adage: "All within the four seas are our brothers".

References

Adler, N. J. (1997). International dimensions of organizational behavior. Cincinnati: South-Western.

Adair, W. L., Okumura, T. & Brett, J. M. (2001). Negotiating behavior when cultures collide: The United States and Japan. *Journal of Applied Psychology*, **86**, 371-385.

Byrne, D. (1971). *The attraction paradigm*. New York: Academic Press.

Earley, P. C. & Mosakowski, E. (2000). Creating hybrid team cultures: An empirical test of transnational team functioning. *Academy of Management Journal*, **43**, 26-49.

Ely, R. J. & Thomas, D. A. (2001). Cultural diversity at work: the effects of diversity persecives on work group processes and outcomes. *Administrative Science Quarterly*, **46**, 229-273.

Fishbein, M., & Ajzen, I. (1975). Belief, attitude, intention, and behavior: An introduction to theory and research. Reading, MA: Addison-Wesley.

Hofstede, G. (1983). Dimensions of national cultures in fifty countries and three regions. In J. Deregowski, S. Dzuirawiec and R. Annis (Eds.), *Expiscations in cross-cultural psychology*. Lisse, Netherlands: Swets and Zeitlinger.

Inglehart, R., & Baker, W. E. (2000). Modernization, cultural change, and the persistence of traditional values. *American Sociological Review*, **65**, 19-51

Leung, K., Koch, P. T. & Lu, L. (2002). A dualisic model of harmony and is implications for conflict management in Asia. *Asia Pacific Journal of Management*, **19**, 201-220.

Leung, K., & Su, S. K. (In press). Experimental Methods for Research on Culture and Management. In B. J. Punnett and O. Shenkar (Eds.), *Handbook for international management research (2nd Edition)*. Cambridge, Mass.: Blackwell.

Morris, M. W., Williams, K. Y., Leung, K., Larrick, R., Mendoza, M. T., Bhatnagar, D., Li, J., Kondo, M. Luo, J. L., & Hu. J. C. (1998). Conflict management style: Accounting for cross-national differences. *Journal of International Business Studies*, **29**, 729-748.

Oyserman, D., Coon, H.M, & Kemmelmeier, M. (2002). Rethinking individualism and collectivism: Evaluation of theoretical assumptions and meta-analyses. *Psychological Bulletin*, **128**, 3-72.

Rao, A. & Hashimoto, K. (1996). Intercultural influence: A study of Japanese expatriate managers in Canada. *Journal of International Business Studies*, **27**, 443-466.

Thomas, D. C., & Ravlin, E. C. (1995). Responses of employees to cultural adaptation by a foreign manager. *Journal of Applied Psychology*, **80**, 133-146.

Tjosvold, D., & Sun, H. (in press). Openness among Chinese in conflict: Effects of direct discussion and warmth on integrated decision making. *Journal of Applied Social Psychology*.

Tjosvold, D., & Sun, H. (2001). Effects of influence tactics and social contexts: An experiment on relationships in China. *International Journal of Conflict Management*, **12**. 239-258.

Tjosvold, D. (1998). The cooperative and competitive goal approach to conflict: Accomplishments and challenges. *Applied Psychology: An International Review*, **47**, 285-313.

Tjosvold, D., Hui, C., & Sun, H. (2000). Building Social face and open-mindedness: Constructive conflict in Asia. C. M. Lau, K. S. Law, D. K. Tse, and C. S. Wong (Eds.) In Asian Management Matters: *Regional Relevance and Global Impact* (pp. 4-16). London: Imperial College Press.

Tjosvold, D., Leung, K., & Johnson, D. W. (2000). Cooperative and competitive conflict in China. In M. Deutsch and P. T. Coleman (Eds.) *The Handbook of Conflict Resolution: Theory and Practice* (pp. 475-495). San Francisco: Jossey-Bass.

Chapter 1

Forty-Five Years of Researching the Culture and Behavior Link: An Intellectual Autobiography

Harry C. Triandis

Since Bond has published my autobiography (Triandis, 1997) I will focus here on the intellectual aspects of my life. I will start by discussing how I got involved in the analysis of subjective culture. Then I will discuss studies about how to deal with diversity, especially in the workplace. Then, I will mention the development of two handbooks. Next, I will discuss my work on individualism and collectivism. Finally, I will make some general observations about my career.

I am a strong believer in multiple perspectives. Each culture is a worldview; its members look at reality somewhat differently from the way members of other cultures do. This view hit me when I was growing up in Greece, where in addition to Greek, I learned French, German, Italian, and English. I was fascinated by the differences I noted among the speakers of these languages.

When I went to Canada to study I was able to observe these differences even better. For example, my fellow students were not as close to their parents as I was, an attribute that I learned later differentiates many collectivist from individualist cultures (Triandis, 1995). Many of my Canadian fellow students did not feel embarrassed about discussing negative aspects of their family life with me, whereas I would have been embarrassed to do so. I found them very easy to meet, yet there were many aspects of their personal life that they did not want to talk about. By contrast, Greek fellow students were more difficult to meet, but if one became their friend, they discussed many aspects of their personal life. It is as if, in individualist cultures, family life is an open book, but personal life is private, while in collectivist cultures personal life is not private within the ingroup, but family life is private when interacting with out-groups. It took many years before I did actually measured these tendencies (Triandis, 1995).

My life as a psychologist has always been a mixture of applied and theoretical perspectives. I never thought of myself as an applied psychologist only, though I have been associated with the International Association of Applied Psychology since 1961, and was its President from 1990-94. Much of the work I did on cultural patterns, such as the analysis of subjective culture (Triandis, 1972), and on individualism and collectivism can be seen as theoretical, but it had definite applications, such as to cross-cultural training (Triandis, 1994, Chapter 10).

I think that most of the time I started from an applied problem, and to understand the phenomena that underlie it I had to develop theory. For example, in the 1960s, Admiral Zumwalt, who was Chief of Naval Operations, wanted to make "every sailor an ambassador." This is perfectly understandable, since the USA had bases all over the world, and the sailors frequently did not behave correctly from the perspectives of the host countries. Thus, in 1962 a group of us in Illinois received funding from the Navy to study how to make every sailor an ambassador – a practical problem. The problem was divided into four parts: I was to identify ways to study cultures. Fred Fiedler was to study how leadership might be used in making each sailor an ambassador. Charles Osgood was to study how communication might be used for that purpose; Larry Stolurow was to study how the information generated by the other members of the team could be converted to training programs for the sailors.

This generated the idea of culture assimilators – training materials that consist of critical incidents followed by four or five explanations about why a behavior described in the incident is "correct" or "wrong" from the point of view of the host culture. After a sailor picks one of the explanations as the potentially correct one, feedback is given concerning whether the explanation is correct or incorrect. If correct, a paragraph or more of cultural information about the similarities and differences between US-mainstream culture and the host culture provides some insight about the differences between the cultures. After a sailor has worked through 100 such episodes, he has a fairly good understanding of the major differences between his culture and the other culture. Validation of these assimilators (Fiedler, Mitchell, and Triandis, 1971) provided encouraging results. For example, those who have been trained feel more relaxed about their assignment abroad (Mitchell, Dossett, Fiedler, and Triandis, 1972). However, problems do arise (Weldon, Carlston, Rissman, Slobodin, and Triandis, 1975). For instance, those who get trained sometimes "freeze" when they interact with members of other cultures, because they are too worried that they will make mistakes. Nevertheless, the culture assimilator has become a standard method of cross-cultural training (Brislin and Bhawuk, 1999). It has been shown to increase the making of 'isomorphic attributions' (Triandis, 1975), where the trainee learns to use similar attributions, and thus assign the same meaning to a behavior, that members of the host culture give to that behavior.

In short, my task in that project was to find out how to analyze cultures. This resulted in the analysis of subjective culture (Triandis, 1972).

Analysis of Subjective Culture

People in each culture have characteristic ways of viewing the human-made part of the environment. That is what we call their "subjective culture." The ideas, theories, the political, religious, scientific, aesthetic, economic, and social standards for judging events in the environment are human-made and shape the way people view their environment. To analyze their subjective culture, the first step was to identify key terms that are used frequently in the host culture, and do not have a monoleximic (single word) equivalent in other cultures. In short, the task is to discover the culture-specific (emic) ways of cutting the pie of experience. In other words, How do people categorize experience in each culture?

Since I knew most about Greece, I did most of the work in Greece, but I also worked with colleagues in India and Japan (Triandis, 1972). For example, a key term in Greece is "philotimo." This literally means "love of honor." However, it really means "I act as members of my ingroup expect me to act." This idea is very collectivist. Greece in the 1960s was collectivist, and the differences in behavior toward members of the ingroup and outgroup were striking.

In Greece I collaborated with Vasso Vassiliou, who was making marketing surveys. She used representative samples of the two largest cities (almost half the population of the country). In such surveys she slipped-in questions for the analysis of subjective culture. For example, when asked, "what are you like?" Greeks were very likely to say that they were "philotimos." But the probability of giving that response was very high if they were recent arrivals from the provinces, i.e. had a rural background. The longer they had lived in the cities the less likely they were to give that response (Vassiliou and Vassiliou, 1966; Vassiliou and Vassiliou, 1973). Later we learned that collectivism was generally higher in rural than in urban settings, except when the urban settings had ethnic neighborhoods as is often the case in the USA (Vandello and Cohen, 1999). Ethnic neighborhoods are collectivist.

Another way to talk about the first step in the analysis of subjective culture is to discuss categorization. All humans categorize. But the categories that they use are not always similar. For example, even when a simple term like "red" is used, what members of one culture call "red" is not identical to what members of other cultures call "red" (Triandis, 1964a). It is true that the focal red is more or less the same, but the boundaries of what is red are not. In fact, there are cultures that do not even have a word for red. Such cultures have only words for white and black. However, if a culture has a color word then red is likely to be it. More complex color names can be found, as cultures have more and more words for colors. Thus, Berlin and Kay (1969) showed that there is a progression from red, to yellow-green, then to both yellow and green, and then to blue, brown, and finally purple, pink, orange, and gray. If simple color names do not have identical meanings across cultures, imagine what happens to more complex words like "democracy!"

One of the ways to study a category is to find instances of the category and ask people in the culture whether the instance belongs or does not belong to the category. For instance, "Is the regime in Nigeria a democracy?" Another way to study the category is to use the antecedent-consequent meaning method (Triandis, 1972, Chapter 7). Participants are asked to complete sentences of the form "If you have __, then you have democracy DEMOCRACY" and "If you have DEMOCRACY, then you have __". You take the responses that are most frequently given by members of different cultures and present them with the above mentioned antecedents and consequents in a multiple choice format. In that study we used one antecedent that was common across our samples (etic) and one emic antecedent from Greece, India, Japan, and the USA. We then looked at the frequencies with which our samples from these cultures selected the various antecedents. We did the same for the consequents. That study produced an enormous body of information (20 concepts had 30 antecedents and 30 consequents, i.e. 1200 "findings").

Data of that kind can be used to corroborate hunches one has about a particular culture. The key idea is convergence. One does not believe any one cultural difference. It is only when several differences converge that one begins to pay attention to them. The particular data were used by Hofstede (1980, 2001), to support his findings on individualism and collectivism.

In addition to studying the meaning of key terms, that study examined stereotypes, values, role perceptions, and the meaning of social behaviors. Triandis (1972, Chapter 9) compared Greek and American cultures. "Reality in Greece is impregnated with social considerations, whereas in America it is focused on the individual." (p. 299). Traditional Greek social behavior depends on whether the other person is a member of the ingroup or of the outgroup. Greeks obey ingroup authorities and undermine outgroup authorities.

Stereotypes can be used as estimates of cultural differences, because when two cultures are different on some attribute the greater the difference the more likely it is that both the autostereotypes (e.g., how Greeks see Greeks) and the heterostereotypes (e.g., how Americans see Greeks) will reflect that difference. When the auto- and hetero-stereotypes agree there is reason to think that a real difference is present. For instance, Americans saw Greeks as "inefficient," and Greeks saw Americans as "efficient." Furthermore, Greeks saw Greeks as "inefficient." Then, the probability is high that there is a cultural difference on "efficiency." Americans perceived Greeks as "suspicious" which makes sense when one considers that Greeks treat outgroups differently from ingroups.

An examination of the geography and history of Greece was used to explain the emergence of the particular Greek subjective culture. Role perceptions reflected cultural differences in the way people act toward ingroup and outgroup members. For example, Greeks were very positive and intimate in ingroup roles (e.g., father-son), but not in outgroup roles (landlord-tenant), while Americans were relatively positive in outgroup roles.

Greeks (relative to Americans) were oversensitive to criticism, and tended to blame their own mistakes on others. This is the kind of information that is most useful for supervisors of Greeks, and can be used in cross-cultural training.

The chapter argued that the principle of "fairness" is equivalent to the principle of "philotimo." In America people try to be fair to others, but the more similar the other person is in beliefs, race, religion, and social class, the more does a person try to be fair. In traditional Greece one is philotimos when dealing with ingroup members, but in dealing with outgroup members it is perfectly okay to be aphilotimos (the opposite, e.g., to cheat). The American ingroup is large; the Greek ingroup is small (family, friends, friendly guests, and people who are concerned with my welfare).

Misunderstandings across cultures occur when people give different meaning to social behavior. The associations of specific social behaviors give clues to such misunderstandings. For instance "to advise" is seen as closely linked to "gives love" in Greece, but not so much in the USA. "To enjoy working for" is a very positive emotion in Greece, which implies going out of your way to help, support, stand for, etc. It is not so positive in the USA. But to enjoy working for the traditional Greek needs a supervisor who will treat him like a father, will be responsive to his special needs, and so on. "To invite to dinner" Greeks see as more formal than do Americans.

This type of work was later done with African-Americans (Triandis, 1976b), and Hispanic-Americans (Triandis, Marin, Lisansky, and Betancourt, 1984). For instance, we found that African-Americans who had never had a job were very different from African-Americans with jobs. The former tended to distrust their social environment. We called this "ecosystem distrust." Hispanics tend to see social behavior as being more positive and less negative than is true for European-Americans. We called this the "simpatia" script, because people who want to be simpatico would behave that way.

An important part of the analysis of subjective culture was a model that linked it to social behavior. The key elements of that model (Triandis 1964b, 1977, 1980) included elements of subjective culture such as self-definitions, role perceptions, norms, and also behavioral intentions, habits, and facilitating conditions.

Briefly, the probability of an act is a function of behavioral intentions (I) and habits (H), multiplied by facilitating conditions (F).

$$P = (I + H) F$$

Behavioral intentions are conscious processes that depend on social factors, such as perceived self-definitions, norms, and roles, the affect toward the behavior (would I enjoy doing this or find it disgusting?), and the perceived utility of the behavior. Utility is a function of the sum of the products of the probabilities of the perceived consequences of the behavior multiplied by the value of each consequence. Habits are unconscious processes that depend on the previous repetitions of the behavior. A concert pianist is not paying attention to every note. It is only when learning the piece that she pays attention to each note and has the behavioral intention to play it. After the piece has been learned the note is played automatically. Facilitating conditions depend on self-efficacy (can I do that?) and the situation. For instance, if the situation does not contain the tools necessary to do the act (say, a piano), obviously the behavior will not occur.

This theory has been too complex to test in its entirety. In the future, as out technology develops and permits tests of such complex theories, it might be tested. It has been tested, however, in part. For example, Godin and his associates (e.g., Godin, Maticka-Tyndale, Adrien, Manson-Singer, Willms, and Cappon, 1996) and Verplanken and his associates (e.g., Verplanken, Aarts, Knippenberg, and Knippenberg, 1994) have published a number of studies that were supportive. Lee (2000) obtained support with data from several cultures. A review by Ouellette and Wood (1998) is also relevant.

People who have very different subjective cultures will have much trouble communicating, and generally getting along. I turn now to the question of how to deal with diversity, which is a broad topic that includes the matter of interpersonal communication and satisfactory relationships.

Dealing with Diversity

When we reviewed the literature (Triandis, Kurowski, and Gelfand, 1994) on diversity in the workplace, we organized it according to a model that was an extension of Allport's contact hypothesis. Allport thought that for contact to be effective in reducing animosity, it had to be equal-status. The model says that equal status is not enough. Many attributes in addition to status should be similar. It uses the concept of "culture distance" and argues that where there is culture distance there is culture shock (Ward, Bochner, and Furnham, 2001).

A key construct is perceived similarity. If people must interact, and they see each other as similar the consequence is little or no culture shock. But if they see each other as dissimilar then there is a high probability of culture shock.

Of course, perceived similarity reflects real similarity. The more cultural distance (Triandis, 1994, p. 33) there is the greater the probability that people will see each other as dissimilar. Culture distance is an aggregate of differences in language, social structure, religion, life style (e.g., income), and values.

My dissertation (Triandis, 1959, 1960) established that cognitive dissimilarity is related to poor communication and low levels of interpersonal attraction. I measured cognitive similarity by examining (a) the similarities in the kinds of categories that people used to think about jobs and people, and (b) the way they rated these categories on semantic differentials. When people used very different categories or rated the categories very differently they failed to communicate. I used a task that required people to identify a particular photograph, so I had an objective measure of whether they did or did not communicate. When they did not communicate they disliked each other.

Clearly, culture distance will be related to different ways of thinking and hence to low attraction. One effort in culture training is to train people to know how members of other cultures think, so they can anticipate communication difficulties. If they know about such difficulties they might be able to compensate and overcome them.

If two groups have had a history of conflict, they will see each other as dissimilar. If they know a good deal about each other they will see each other as more similar. The better they know each other's languages the more they are likely to see each other as similar. The more equal their status the more they will see each other as similar. The more they have superordinate goals (goals that one group cannot reach without the help of the other group) the more they will see each other as similar.

If they do see each other as similar, and they do interact, they will experience the interaction as rewarding. The interaction will be especially rewarding if there are superordinate goals and authorities approve of the intergroup contact. Rewarding interactions will result in positive attitudes toward the other group. The greater the rewards the more they will interact. The more they interact the more they will develop social networks that overlap (common friends and the like). The more they develop social networks that overlap the less likely it is that they will show ethnic affirmation (my culture is better than your culture).

The more they know about each other, the more likely it is that their stereotypes will be accurate and valid (Triandis, and Vassiliou, 1967). Valid stereotypes are called sociotypes. Stereotypes have many dimensions (uniformity, intensity, direction, and quality) (Triandis, Lisansky, Setiadi, Chang, Marin, and Betancourt, 1982). Thus it is possible for a stereotype to be valid on one dimension but not on other dimensions. Sociotypes should be valid on all dimensions.

The more interaction, the more sociotypes are likely to be used. The more they interact and use sociotypes the more they will make isomorphic attributions (see above). If they make isomorphic attributions they will have a sense of control over the social situation. When that happens they will try to accommodate to each other. In some cases the accommodation will be so enthusiastic that they will overshoot and take positions that are even more like the positions of the other group than is the other group's position. Also, the more of a sense of control they have the less culture shock they will experience when working with people from other cultures.

But if they perceive each other as dissimilar all the variables mentioned above are reversed, so that there is much culture shock.

When two groups come in contact, one or both of these groups change their positions on important issues. That is an aspect of acculturation. Acculturation is especially likely when a minority group is in contact with a majority group. Acculturation can take three forms: accommodation, overshooting or ethnic affirmation (my culture is better than yours is).

Since accommodation of minorities to majority cultures is the more typical pattern, it is possible to use acculturation indices to study cultural differences. The greater a cultural difference the more likely it is that some shift (either accommodation or overshooting) will be observed. Examining such shifts as a function of acculturation can tell us that cultural differences do in fact exist. When more than two groups are involved, we can get converging information about cultural differences among the groups (Triandis, Kashima, Shimada, and Villareal, 1986).

To study the relationships among the variables of the model we need to get culture-specific information about how each group sees the other groups. Triandis, Kurowski, Techtiel, and Chan (1993) suggested how one might extract the emics of diversity. Each cultural group has its own way of thinking about other groups, based on its history and experiences with the other group. Intensive interviews with each cultural group extracted these emics. Then the emics of all groups were presented to samples from all the groups. These samples provided judgments of the extent a particular way of looking at intergroup situations was valid. Cultural differences were identified that contrasted how the various groups thought about each other.

An especially important aspect of intergroup relationships is the social distance that each group feels toward the other groups. What factors, such as race, social class, religion, quality of spoken English, and so on determine social distance? The measurement of social distance had to be emic (appropriate for each culture), but the construct itself is etic. Indians may show social distance by making sure that a person of a lower caste does not touch their earthenware, while Americans may show it by rejecting a person from their club or neighborhood. This resulted in studies of social distance in Greece and the USA (Triandis and Triandis, 1962), and Germany, Japan, and the USA (Triandis, Davis, and Takezawa, 1965). Generalizing beyond social distance, I examined the way people thought about social behavior more generally (Triandis, 1964). Five dimensions were identified, one of which was social distance. It is important to distinguish among these dimensions. For instance, two of the dimensions were "showing respect" and "friendship." We found, with a representative sample of Athens, Greece, that Respect is a positive function of the other person's status but Friendship is a negative function of the other person's status (Triandis, Vassiliou, and Tomashek, 1966). Triandis (1967) provided a summary of this literature. I also argued that some social behaviors are universal (Triandis, 1978).

Development of Handbooks

By 1972 a good deal of cross-cultural information was available. Allyn and Bacon, Publishers, asked me if I wanted to edit a handbook. Development of this handbook turned out to require an enormous amount of correspondence with more than 50 people. Many authors did not deliver their chapters on time, and were slow in revising. The job was much more time-consuming than I had expected. It was published eight years later (Triandis, 1980-81). But Lee Cronbach stated that this handbook established cross-cultural psychology as a separate discipline within psychology.

When the publishers asked about a second edition I refused, but was happy to see that John Berry was willing to do it and did a very good job (Berry, 1997).

In the mid-1980s Marv Dunnette, who was developing the second edition of his *Handbook of Industrial and Organizational Psychology,* asked me to do a chapter on culture. I sent him the first draft in 1986. The typical delays in the production of handbooks required several revisions of that chapter, to incorporate the latest publications. By 1992 the topic of cross-cultural management had become so popular that Marv asked me to edit a whole volume of the handbook with him. Thus was produced Triandis, Dunnette and Hough (1994).

Individualism and Collectivism

In 1978 I reviewed Hofstede's (1980) book in manuscript form for SAGE Publications. Of course, I recommended publication, but I also realized that the dimension of individualism and collectivism he talked about was useful in describing the differences I had observed between traditional Greeks and Hispanics on the one hand, and European-Americans on the other hand. This led to 20 years of research on the cultural syndrome (Triandis, 1996) of individualism and collectivism.

In collectivist cultures people use the group as the unit of analysis; in individualist cultures they use individuals as the unit of analysis. In the former cultures people think of themselves as interdependent with their in-groups (family, co-workers, tribe, co-religionists, country, etc.). In the latter people see themselves as autonomous individuals who are independent of their groups (Markus and Kitayama, 1991). In the former cultures people give priority to the goals of their in-group rather than to their personal goals (Triandis, 1990); they are more likely to use in-group norms to shape their behavior than personal attitudes (Abrams, Ando, and Hinkle, 1998). Furthermore, they are more likely to conceive of social relationships as communal (Mills and Clark, 1982). In the latter cultures, people analyze social situations as described by exchange theory (are the costs of staying in this relationship lower than the advantages I get from this relationship?) (Triandis, 1995). Collectivist cultures generally have languages that do not require the use of "I" and "you" (Kashima and Kashima, 1998). People in collectivist cultures feel more positively about "us" and negatively about "them" than do people in individualist cultures.

There are many kinds of collectivist cultures. For example, Korea and the Israeli kibbutz are both collectivist cultures, but they are different from each other. Thus, we need to use additional attributes to distinguish among the different kinds of collectivist and individualist cultures (Triandis, 1995). One of the major ways in which cultures differ is the vertical-horizontal dimension. People who emphasize the vertical dimension are especially concerned with hierarchy; those who are horizontal are concerned with equality (e.g., one-person one vote).

Horizontal individualists (HI) want to be unique and do their own thing. Vertical individualists (VI) want to be unique but also to be "the best." They get upset when somebody tells them that they are just average (Weldon, 1984). American student samples show self-enhancement. That is, when they are asked to compare themselves to the average student on some desirable trait they see themselves as much better than the average student. For example, they claim that they are better drivers than 90 per cent of college students. When we average such responses we discover that they average much more than 50 per cent, which is a mathematical impossibility.

Horizontal collectivists (HC) merge with their groups, but vertical collectivists (VC) accept their insignificance in relation to their group and its authorities, and are willing to submit to the group, and sacrifice themselves for the benefit of the group. Vertical Collectivism is correlated around .40 with Right Wing Authoritarianism.

We should not think that people are collectivists or individualists across all situations. The situation is very important. Rather, people have some probability of being collectivists across situations. For example, Triandis, Chen and Chan (1998) used scenarios followed by responses that had been pre-tested to be HI, VI, HC, or

VC. Then they computed the per cent of the time that a person selected one of these four responses to be the best course of action across 16 different scenarios. By summing the individual responses within each culture they obtained an estimate of the attributes of the culture.

Triandis, Carnevale, et al (2001) obtained such data from 8 cultures. As an example, the profiles of the German and Hong Kong samples respectively were as follows: HI 43 per cent and 25 per cent HC 27 per cent and 36 per cent; VI 20 per cent and 20 per cent; VC 10 per cent and 19 per cent. These percentages are based on large samples, so a difference of 2 per cent is significant at p < .001.

In short, people are not "stamped in" with a collectivism or individualism label. Rather, depending on the situation, they are sometimes VI, VC, HI or HC. But in collectivist cultures they are more likely to be HC and VC, in individualist cultures they are more likely to be HI or VI.

One of the important points of this research was the need to distinguish levels of analysis. When one measures, say 30 values, and correlates the data across 50 cultures, that is the cultural level of analysis. When one correlates the values within culture, with let us say 100 individuals, one has data at the individual level. It is important to keep the two levels separate, because relationships that are positive at one level can be negative at the other level. We introduced the terms idiocentric and allocentric (Triandis, Leung, Villareal, and Clack, 1985) to correspond at the individual level of analysis to the terms individualism and collectivism at the cultural level.

Our research found that in every culture there are both allocentrics and idiocentrics, but in different proportions. In collectivist cultures there are about 60 to 80 per cent allocentrics; in individualist cultures about 60 to 100 per cent idiocentrics. The percentages vary because being upper social class, having migrated, having a high level of education, financial independence, and exposure to other cultures, and to American-made mass media increase idiocentrism. Participation in organized religion, large families, lower social class status, less education, old age, fixed residence, little exposure to other cultures and much interaction with ethnocentrics result in more allocentrism.

Cultural information predicts diverse behaviors, but the correlations are relatively low. By now more than 100 differences have been found in empirical studies. A few will be mentioned bellow. Collectivism predicts high levels of conformity (Bond and Smith, 1996). Individualists prefer situations with many choices (Iyengar and Lepper, 1999) and want to have the freedom to choose. Collectivists write novels in which the heroes do their duties (Hsu, 1983) rather than have fun. Changing the self to fit into the situation (Diaz-Guerrero, 1979) is typical of collectivists; changing the situation to fit the person is typical of individualists. Little or no social loafing is observed among collectivists who work with in-group members (Earley, 1989). Individualists show a good deal of social loafing.

In addition to individualism and collectivism, cultures differ in a very large number of ways. Here are some additional dimensions that contrast cultures:

Complexity Some cultures (hunters and gatherers) are relatively simple, and other cultures (information societies) are relatively complex. Cities are more complex than villages. The size of settlements is one of the best ways to index cultural complexity (Chick, 1997).

Tightness In tight cultures there are many rules, norms, and ideas about what is correct behavior in different kinds of situations; in loose cultures there are fewer rules and norms. In tight cultures also, people become quite upset when others do not follow the norms of the society, and may even kill those who do not behave as is expected. In loose cultures people are tolerant of deviations from normative behaviors. Thus, conformity is high in tight cultures. Tightness is more likely when the culture is homogeneous and relatively isolated from other cultures, so that consensus about what is proper behavior can develop. Cosmopolitan cities are loose, except when they have ethnic enclaves, which can be very tight; small communities are relatively tight.

Triandis (1994) has suggested that individualism emerges in societies that are both complex and loose; collectivism is found in societies that are both simple and tight. Carpenter (2000) found empirical support for the links between tightness and collectivism and looseness and individualism. Theocracies or monasteries are both tight and relatively poor; Hollywood stars live in a culture that is both complex and loose. English speaking countries are individualistic; the rest of the world is more or less collectivist, especially the economically less developed parts of the world.

Active-passive cultures. In active cultures individuals try to change the environment to fit them; in passive cultures people change themselves to fit into the environment. The active are more competitive, action-oriented, and emphasize self-fulfillment; the passive are more cooperative, emphasize the experience of living, and are especially concerned with getting along with others. In general individualist cultures are more active than collectivist cultures.

Universalism-particularism In universalist cultures people treat others on the basis of universal criteria (e.g., all competent persons regardless of who they are in sex, age, race, etc. are acceptable employees). In particularist cultures people treat others on the basis of who the other person is (e.g., I know Joe Blow and he is a good person, so he will be a good employee). In general individualists are more universalist and collectivists are likely to be particularists.

Diffuse-specific Diffuse cultures respond to the environment in a holistic manner (e.g., I do not like your report means I do not like you). Specific cultures discriminate different aspects of the stimulus complex (e.g., I do not like your report says nothing about how much I like you). Collectivists are often more diffuse; individualists are often more specific and analytic (Nisbett, Peng, Choi and Norenzayan, 2001).

Ascription-achievement People may judge others primarily on the basis of ascribed attributes, such as sex, race, nationality, village where born, family membership, etc. These are attributes people are born with. By contrast, other people in other cultures judge others primarily in terms of achieved attributes, such as skill, publications, awards. In general collectivists give ascribed attributes more weight than achieved attributes, while individualists emphasize achieved more than ascribed attributes, though people in all cultures use both kinds of attributes in judging others.

Instrumental-expressive People in some cultures sample more heavily attributes that are instrumental (e.g., get the job done) or expressive (e.g., enjoy the social relationship). In general individualists are more instrumental and collectivists are more expressive.

Emotional expression or suppression People may express their emotions freely, no matter what the consequences, or they may control the expression of emotion. Collectivists around the Mediterranean are quite expressive, while collectivists in East Asia are quite controlling. In general in collectivist cultures people suppress negative emotional expressions within the ingroup, but are very free to express negative emotions in relation to out-groups. In individualist countries this difference is not as sharp.

Paralinguistic behaviors include the proper distance between the bodies in conversation, whether one can touch or not touch, and what parts of the body can be touched, the orientation of the body in conversation, the level of loudness when speaking, and what gestures are in frequent use. There are cultural differences in such behaviors. There is no evidence that these differences are related to individualism and collectivism.

Nisbett (2003) summarizes a great deal of information, supported by extensive recent empirical work, that extends the framework I presented above. It shows that major differences between the West and the East include:

- In the West objects are judged in isolation; in the East in context
- In the West A and not-A cannot be true at the same time. In the East they can, depending on context
- In the West A stays more or less the same across time, while in the East it changes over time
- In the West thinking is linear; in the East good leads to bad which leads to good, hence it is circular
- In the West thinking is analytic; in the East holistic
- In the West categorization is done by attributes, in the East by relationships (for instance, given cow, grass, and hen, and asked "Which two go together?", in the West people say hen and cow, in the East cow and grass)
- In the West learning nouns is easier than learning verbs; in the East it is the other way around
- There is more field independence in the West and more field dependence in the East
- Contradiction is anathema in the West and tolerated in the East

- Emphasis on creativity, the new and on debate is high in the West and emphasis on the old, the common, and on harmony is high in the East
- In the West persons are seen to remain the same while the environment is seen as changing; in the East the environment is more or less stable and persons learn to fit in
- In the East people are especially sensitive to the feelings and attitudes of others
- In the West during communication people assume a transmitter orientation and in the East a receiver orientation
- Behavior is perceived to be a function of inside factors such as beliefs or personality in the West, and outside factors, such as group memberships or obligations in the East
- People make the fundamental attribution error more in the West than in the East
- Matter is conceived as consisting of atoms in the West and is viewed as a continuous substance (a field) in the East.

Some Thoughts about Cultural Differences

The concepts of individualism and collectivism link with the question of how modernization affects a culture. My answer has been that cultures are very complex entities. Modernization changes some aspects of culture toward individualism, but other aspects remain collectivist. Furthermore, no culture is perfect. All cultures have defects, because they have developed to adjust to one kind of ecology, and environments change, and cultural lag prevents cultures to become optimal for the new ecology. Bohannan (1995) talks about "cultural traps" that occur when cultures persist in using elements that are no longer adaptive. Furthermore, there are individual differences and a culture that fits well an allocentric would not fit well an idiocentric person.

Moreover, it is important to realize that all humans are ethnocentric, i.e. they use their own culture as the standard for evaluating other cultures. Humans also differ in ethnocentrism, with authoritarians more ethnocentric than non-authoritarians. Thus, when we judge cultures we need to keep in mind this reality and compensate for it.

In such evaluations it is important to keep in mind that some elements of culture are so fundamental that when they are challenged it is especially difficult to evaluate the other culture positively. For example, in monotheistic religions people pay a lot of attention to cognitive consistency, and to the beliefs that people have. But in polytheist religions there are many truths, and some of them are contradictory. The view that the opposite of a great idea is also a great idea was stated by the Danish physicist Neils Bohr (Nobel Prize, 1922), but it is not part of the way of thinking of most people in monotheistic religions. Furthermore, judging people by their beliefs is not so common in India as it is in monotheistic regions. In

South and East Asia people are judged more by what they do than by what they believe.

Indians live with contradictions. One can be a "meat eating vegetarian" simply because one eats meat when others eat meat, otherwise one eats vegetables. This situational and context-based view of the world is foreign to people in monotheistic regions of the world, and they get very upset when people use such logic. People in Asia generally use context more than Europeans do. For example, the history of the topic is part of the way of thinking about the topic to a greater extent in Asia than in Europe. When fundamental ways of thinking are challenged, it requires a great deal of effort to look at another culture positively.

Applications of Cultural Differences

In addition to cross-cultural training, knowing about cultural differences has many applications. For instance, one can examine how differences in culture affect negotiation behavior (Davis and Triandis, 1971), the meaning of work and non-work (Triandis, 1973; Hulin and Triandis, 1981), and organizational communication (Triandis and Albert, 1987). In educational settings it is important for pupils to learn about each others' cultures (Triandis, 1976a).

Retrospect

When I first started working in cross-cultural psychology, and later on individualism and collectivism, the topics were not popular. Deciding on whether to put them on the map required considerable soul searching. I remember worrying that I might stir Harry Hui in the wrong direction by suggesting that he develop a valid method for the assessment of individualism and collectivism for his dissertation. What if this is a dead end? Will it ruin his career? The concepts of individualism and collectivism are so vague, maybe they will never be important topics of study. I suppose I persisted because I had already seen the utility of the constructs when I compared my experiences in Greece and Canada. Thus, my progress was to some extent a matter of luck.

References

Abrams, D., Ando, K., & Hinkle, S. (1998). Psychological attachment to groups: Cross-cultural differences in organizational identification and subjective norms as predictors of workers' turnover intentions. *Personality and Social Psychology Bulletin*, **24**, 1027-1039.

Berlin, B. & Kay, P. (1969) *Basic color terms*. Berkeley, Cal. University of California Press.

Berry, Jo. W. (1997). *Handbook of cross-cultural psychology*. (Second Edition, in three volumes). Boston: Allyn & Bacon.

Bohannan, P. (1995) *How culture works*. New York: Free Press.

Bond, R. A. & Smith, P. B. (1996). Culture and conformity: A meta-analysis of studies using Asch's (1952b, 1956) line judgment task. *Psychological Bulletin*, **119**, 111-137.

Brislin, R. W., & Bhawuk, D. P. S. (1999). Cross-cultural training: Research and innovations. In J. Adamopoulos & Y. Kashima (Eds.) *Social psychology and cultural context*. (pp. 205-216). Thousand Oaks, CA: Sage.

Carpenter, S. (2000). Effects of cultural tightness and collectivism on self-concept and causal attributions. *Cross-Cultural Research*, **34**, 38-56.

Chick, G. (1997). Cultural complexity: The concept and its measurement. *Cross-Cultural Research*, 31, 275-307.

Davis, E. E., & Triandis, H. C. (1971). An exploratory study of black-white negotiations. *Journal of Applied Social Psychology*, **1**, 240-262.

Diaz-Guerrero, R. (1979) The development of coping style. *Human Development*, 22, 320-331.

Earley, P. C. (1989). Social loafing and collectivism. A comparison of the U.S. and the People's Republic of China. *Administrative Science Quarterly*, **34**, 565-581.

Fiedler, F. E., Mitchell, T. R., & Triandis, H. C. (1971). The culture assimilator: An approach to cross-cultural training. *Journal of Applied Psychology*, **55**, 95-102.

Godin, G., Mticka-Tyndale, E., Adrien, A., Manson-singer, S., Willms, D., & Cappon, P. (1996). Cross-cultural testing of three social cogntive theories: An application to condom use. *Journal of Applied Social Psychology*, **26**, 1556-1586.

Hofstede, G. (1980, 2001, Second Edition) *Culture's consequences*. Thousand Oaks, CA. Sage.

Hsu, F. L., K. (1983). *Rugged individualism reconsidered*. Knoxville: University of Tennessee Press.

Hulin, C. L. & Triandis, H. C. (1981). Meaning of work in different organizational environments. In P. C. Nystrom & W. H. Starbuck (eds.) *Handbook of organizational design*. pp. 336-357. New York: Oxford University Press.

Iyengar, S. S.& Lepper, M. R. (1999). Rethinking the value of choice: A cultural perspective on intrinsic motivation. *Journal of Personality and Social Psychology*, **76**, 349-366.

Kashima, E. S. & Kashima, Y. (1998) culture and language: The case of cultural dimensions and personal pronoun use. *Journal of Cross-Cultural Psychology*, **29**, 461-486.

Lee, J.(2000). Adapting Triandis's model of subjective culture and social behavior relations to consumer behavior. *Journal of Consumer Behavior*, **9**, 117-126.

Markus, H. and Kitayama, S. (1991). Culture and self: Implications for cognition, emotion and motivation. *Psychological Review*, **98**, 224-253.

Mills, J. & Clark, M. S. (1982). Exchange and communal relationships. In L. Wheeler (Ed.) *Review of personality and social psychology*. (Vol. 3, pp. 121-144) Beverly Hills, CA: Sage.

Mitchell, T. R., Dossett, D. I., Fiedler, F. E., & Triandis, H. C. (1972). Culture training: Validation evidence for the culture assimilator. *International Journal of Psychology*, **7**, 97-104.

Nisbett, R. E. (2003). *The circle and the line*. New York: Free Press.

Nisbett, R. e., Peng, K. , Choic, I. & Norenzayan, A. (2001). Culture and systems of thought: Holistic versus analytic cognition. *Psychological Review*, **108**, 291-310.

Ouellette J. A. & Wood, W. (1998), Habit and intention in everyday life: The multiple processes by which past behavior predicts future behavior. *Psychological Bulletin*, **124**, 54-74.

Triandis, H. C. (1959). Cognitive similarity and interpersonal communication in industry. *Journal of Applied Psychology*, **43**, 321-326.

Triandis, H. C. (1960). Cognitive similarity and communication in a dyad. *Human Relations*, **13**, 175-183.

Triandis, H. C. (1964a). Cultural influences upon cognitive process. In L. Berkowitz (ed.) *Advances in experimental social psychology*, (pp. 1-48). New York: Academic Press.

Triandis, H. C. (1964b). Exploratory factor analyses of the behavioral component of social attitudes. *Journal of Abnormal and Social Psychology*, **68**, 420-430.

Triandis, H. C. (1967). Towards an analysis of the components of interpersonal attitudes. In Carolyn and Muzafer Sherif (Eds.) *Attitudes, ego-involvement and change*. Pp. 227-270. New York: Wiley.

Triandis, H. C. (1972). *The analysis of subjective culture*. New York: Wiley.

Triandis, H. C. (1973). Work and non-work: Intercultural perspectives. In M. D. Dunnette (Ed.) *Work and non-work in the year 2001*. Pp. 29-52. Monterey CA: Books/Cole.

Triandis, H. C. (1975). Culture training, cognitive complexity and interpersonal attitudes. In R. Brislin, S. Bochner, & W. Lonner (Eds.) *Cross-cultural perspectives on learning*. (pp. 39-77). Beverley Hills CA: Sage.

Triandis, H. C. (1976a). *The future of pluralism. Journal of Social Issues*, **32**, 179-208.

Triandis, H. C. (1976b). *Variations in black and white perceptions of the social environment*. Urbana: University of Illinois Press.

Triandis, H.C. (1977) *Interpersonal behavior*. Monterey: Brooks/Cole.

Triandis, H. C. (1978). Some universals of social behavior. *Personality and Social Psychology Bulletin*, **4**, 1-16.

Triandis, H. C. (1980). Values, attitudes and interpersonal behavior. In H.E. Howe and M.M. Page (Eds.) *Nebraska Symposium on Motivation*, 1979, (pp. 195-260). Lincoln, Nebraska. University of Nebraska Press.

Triandis, H. C. (1980-81). *Handbook of cross-cultural psychology*. (First Edition, in 6 volumes). Boston: Allyn & Bacon.

Triandis, H. C. (1990). Cross-cultural studies of individualism and collectivism. In J. Berman (Ed.) *Nebraska Symposium on Motivation*, 1989. (pp. 41-133) Lincoln, Nebraska: University of Nebraska Press.

Triandis, H. C. (1994). *Culture and social behavior*. New York: McGraw-Hill.

Triandis, H. C. (1995). *Individualism and collectivism*. Boulder, CO: Westview Press.

Triandis, H. C. (1996). The psychological measurement of cultural syndromes. *American Psychologist*, **51**, 407-415.

Triandis, H.C. (1997). Raised in a collectivist culture, one may become an individualist. In M. H. Bond (Ed.) *Working at the interface of cultures: eighteen lives in social science*. (pp.38-46) London: Routledge.

Triandis, H. C. & Albert, R. (1987). Cross-cultural perspectives on organizational communication. In F. M. Jablin, L. L. Putnam, K. H. Roberts, & L. W. Porter (Eds.) *Handbook of organizational communication*. Pp. 264-295. Beverly Hills, SAGE.

Triandis, H. C. & Triandis, L. M. (1962). A cross-cultural study of social distance. *Psychological Monographs*, **76**, No. 21 (Whole No. 540).

Triandis, H. C. & Vassiliou, V. (1967). Frequency of contact and stereotyping. *Journal of Personality and Social Psychology*, **7**, 316-328.

Triandis, H. C., Chen, X. P., & Chan, D. K-S. (1998) Scenarios for the measurement of collectivism and individualism. *Journal of Cross-Cultural Psychology*, **29**, 275-289.

Triandis, H. C., Davis, E. E. & Takazawa, S. I. (1965). Some determinants of social distance among American, German, and Japanese students. *Journal of Personality and Social Psychology*, **2**, 540-551.

Triandis, H. C., Dunnette, M. D., & Hough, L. M. (1994). *Handbook of industrial and organizational psychology*. (Second Edition, Volume 4). Palo alto, CA: Consulting Psychologists Press.

Triandis, H. C., Vassiliou, V. & Thomashek, E. K. (1966). Social status as a determinants of social acceptance and friendship acceptance. *Sociometry*, **29**, 396-405.

Triandis, H. C., Kurowski, L, & Gelfand, M. (1994). Workplace diversity. In H. C. Triandis, M. Dunnette, and L. Hough (Eds.) *Handbook of industrial and organizational psychology* (Second Edition, Volume 4, pp. 769-827) Palo Alto: CA: Consulting Psychologists Press.

Triandis, H. C., Kashima, Y., Shimada, E., & Villareal, M. (1986). Acculturation indices as a means of confirming cultural differences. *International Journal of Psychology*, 21, 43-70.

Triandis, H. C., Kurowski, L., Tachtiel, A., & Chan, D. K. (1993). Extracting the emics of diversity. *International Journal of Intergroup Relations*, 17, 217-234.

Triandis, H. C., Leung, K., Villareal, M. & Clack, F. L. (1985). Allocentric vs. idiocentric tendencies: Convergent and discriminant validation. *Journal of Research in Personlaity*, 19, 395-415.

Triandis, H. C., Marin, G., Lisansky, J., & Betancourt, H. (1984). Simpatia as a cultural script of Hispanics. *Journal of Personality and Social Psychology*, 47, 1363-1375.

Triandis, H. c. , Lisansky, J., Setiadi, B., Chang, B., Marin, G., & Betancourt, H. (1982). Stereotyping among Hispanics and Anglos: The uniformity, intensity, direction, and quality of auto- and heterosterotypes. *Journal of Cross-Cultural Psychology*, 13, 409-426.

Triandis, H. C., Carnevale, P. Gelfand, M., Robert, C., Wasti, A. Probst, T., Kashima, E., Dragonas, T. Chan, D, Chen, X. P., Kim, U. deDreu, C., van de Vliert E., Iwao, S., Ohbuchi, K-L. & Schmidt, P. (2001). Culture, personality and deception: A multilevel approach. *International Journal of Cross-Cultural Management, 1,* 73-90.

Vandello, J. A. & Cohen, D. (1999). Patterns of individualism and collectivism across the United States, *Journal of Personality and Social Psychology*, 77, 279-292.

Vassiliou, G. & Vassiliou, V. (1966). Social values as a psychodynamic variable: Preliminary explorations of the semantics of philotimo. *Acta Neurologica et Psychiatrica Hellenika*, 5, 121-135.

Vassiliou, V. G., & Vassiliou, G. (1973). The implicative meaning of the Greek concept of philotimo. *Journal of Cross-Cultural Psychology*, 4, 326-341.

Verplanken, B., Aarts, H., van Knippenberg, A. & van Knippenberg, C. (1994). Attitude versus general habit: Antecedents of travel mode choice. *Journal of Applied Psychology*, 24, 285-300.

Ward, C., Bochner, S., & Furnham, A. (2001). *The psychology of culture shock.* Philadelphia, Taylor & Francis.

Weldon, E. (1984). Deindividuation, interpersonal affect, and productivity in laboratory task groups. *Journal of Applied Social Psychology*, 14, 469-485.

Weldon, D. E., Carlston, D. E., Rissman, A. K., Slobodin, L., & Triandis, H. C. (1975). A laboratory test of effects of culture assimilator training. *Journal of Personality and Social Psychology*, 32, 300-310.

Chapter 2

The Universal and the Specific in 21st Century Management*

Geert Hofstede

Introduction

The essence of management is that it is about people. Since human nature has not changed in the past centuries and is unlikely to change in the present, the process of management will basically remain the same. It differs less from period to period than from country to country. A French management researcher who compared three technically identical subsidiaries of a French aluminum corporation in France, the USA and the Netherlands has shown management processes on the shop floor to be dramatically different in the three cases, managers and subordinates in each country following traditions that were already in place two centuries ago. Technological innovations did not change these traditions. Technology will change some practices of organizations but not many others which rest on values embedded in the surrounding society and transferred from generation to generation.

Management theories were developed in the West, mainly in Britain and the USA. These theories were based on Western individualistic assumptions, which do not necessarily apply for the majority of the world's population in other continents. The present century is expected to bring alternative theories for these other parts of the world. These will leave room for more collectivist values, and for an orientation on the long term rather than the short.

For those involved in managing across cultures, meta-theories stressing the relativity of any single cultural orientation will become more accepted, but dilemmas will continue to exist. An example of such a dilemma is coping with the economic and cultural dynamics of corruption.

* This is a revised, updated and extended version of an article in "Management in the Twenty-First Century", special issue of "Organizational Dynamics", Volume 28 no.1, Summer 1999, pp.34-43.

The Perennial Nature of Management Problems

Do management processes change over time? Is there anything new about management in this 21st century? Most of the popular literature suggests that management processes do change over time: One should always follow the latest trends. At the same time, most of the same popular literature implicitly assumes that management processes are universal and can be applied across the world. Today's management fads, say privatization, or Total Quality Management, apply anywhere, whether in North America, France, Brazil, Russia, Thailand or China. If they don't work somewhere this is not the fault of the principles on which they are based but of the people who implement these principles.

Against these alleged popular assumptions I will defend the opposite viewpoint: *That management processes basically have changed little over time, and that this will remain so. They differ less from period to period than from part of the world to part of the world, and even from country to country.* So management in the 21st century will not be basically different from management in the 20th. In fact, similar management problems have existed as long as human societies have existed. Examples of management problems, even if they were not called that, can be found all over the world's literature, from the oldest sources onwards.

What is management? I prefer the general definition of "getting things done through other people". Or more specifically "coordinating the efforts of people towards common goals". The "other people" involved may be subordinates, clients, customers, suppliers, authorities, or the public in general. Important is that *management is always about people.* Jobs in which no other people are involved are technical, not management. Because management is always about people, its essence is dealing with human nature. Since human nature seems to have been extremely stable over recorded history, the essence of management has been and will be equally stable over time.

A case study may illustrate this. A group of refugees, about ten thousand strong, follow their charismatic leader in search of a safe haven. A powerful friend sends a consultant to help them. The consultant notices that the leader tries to handle all problems and conflicts of his people himself. People queue up before his office and although he is overworked himself, he still cannot handle all the business. So the consultant has a private talk with the leader, and tells him to structure his organization by delegating authority: To nominate able men as managers of thousands, hundreds, fifties and tens. Candidates should be selected not only on their leadership abilities but also on their character: They should be law-abiding, truthful, and not driven by material gain. The management structure should resolve all daily issues at the lowest possible level; only the big and difficult issues should be brought before the leader. He should focus on strategy; on dealing with the supreme authority, on establishing new rules and laws and teaching these to the people, on showing them the way to go and the work to be done. The case states that the leader listens to the consultant and carries out the re-organization, which is a success; and the consultant returns home.

Asian readers may think that this referred to the Long March of Chairman Mao. The refugees in this case, however, were Jews and their leader was called Moses, who led them from Egypt to Palestine. The Supreme Authority was God, and the consultant, Jethro, was Moses' father-in-law, which definitely helped in making Moses listen to him. The case is codified in the book Exodus, of the Old Testament of the Bible (Exodus 18:13-27). It is one of the oldest source books of Western Civilization, recognized by Jewry, Christianity and Islam alike. The migration is supposed to have taken place in the 12th century BC, over 3,000 years ago.

The case shows many elements that look very modern. We see the important role of the management consultant. His advice deals with managerial stress, delegation of authority, management by exception, and span of control. New and charismatic leaders even today try to do too much themselves. The consultant turns Moses into a Chief Executive with a strategic task; he should stay out of operational details. The selection criteria for the appointment of middle managers are also specified: They should be male, able, God-fearing, truthful, and free from greed. Jethro here gets into what we would now call "agency theory".

All of this happened at the dawn of human civilization. Many problems in modern management are not so modern at all; they are basic human dilemmas, and every generation anew has had to cope with them.

National Traditions in Management: D'Iribarne

Because management is about people, it is part of the culture of the society in which it takes place. Culture is "the collective programming of the mind that distinguishes the members of one group or category of people from another". The core element in culture is formed by values. Values are "broad tendencies to prefer certain states of affairs over others". They are about what is evil and what is good, dirty and clean, immoral and moral, irrational and rational. Relationships between people in a society are affected by the values that form part of the collective programming of people's minds in that society. So management is subject to cultural values. Cultural values differ among societies, but within a society they are remarkably stable over time. This is why I claim that management processes, which are embedded in a culture, differ from society to society but within each society show strong continuity.

The historical stability of the national component in management has recently been convincingly demonstrated by the French management researcher Philippe d'Iribarne. In the 1980s he did in-depth interviews in three production plants of a French-owned aluminum company, one in France, one in the USA and one in the Netherlands. The plants were technically identical, but employee-manager and employee-employee relations on the shop floor differed dramatically between them. D'Iribarne in his book identifies three different "logics" - philosophies - that control the interpersonal interactions at the sites: *Honor* in France, the *fair contract* in the USA and *consensus* in the Netherlands. These philosophies represent patterns of thinking, feeling and acting distinguishable in the histories of these three societies for centuries.

In France, d'Iribarne refers to the *Ancien Régime* (the 17th and 18th century monarchy before Napoleon) and he cites Montesquieu (1689-1755), in particular his book *The Spirit of the Laws*, written in 1748, as a suitable authority on present-day French management. The most important feature is that France was and still is a class society - d'Iribarne even compares it to the caste society of India. Within the plant, different classes meet. There are at least three levels: The *cadres* (managers and professionals), the *maîtrise* (first-line supervisors) and the *non-cadres* (the levels below). Within each of these there are further status distinctions, such as between higher and lower cadres and between skilled craft workers and production personnel. The relationship between the classes is governed by antagonism; in one of my own courses for French managers a participant once remarked "Cadres think in terms of efficiency; non-cadres in terms of protest". At the same time, a sense of respect prevails for the honor concomitant to each class. The system is profoundly hierarchical, yet the kinds of orders a supervisor can give are constrained by a need to respect the honor of the subordinates, which implies their autonomy for certain tasks. And there is no evidence at all that the French are about to change the class nature of their society. It is deeply embedded in their institutions, in their family structure, in their educational system, and in their political landscape.

In the USA, on the contrary, everybody is supposed to be equal; the relationship between management and workers is contractual. Within the limits of the contract, managers can give orders and subordinates will carry them out. Paradoxically, while this system is basically less hierarchical than in France, American management can get away with demanding things from their workers that in France would be impossible. In practice some people are still more "equal" than others, and the freedom of the contract may be that of the free fox in the free chicken-pen. D'Iribarne bases the US practices on the country's immigrant past, on the heritage of the *Pilgrim Fathers* and other 17th and 18th century (white) settlers. As there was no traditional aristocracy like in France, the immigrants developed a middle class society seeking a free association of equal citizens, related by contractual agreements. D'Iribarne calls them "pious merchants". As "merchants" they hold their contracts to be holy; if necessary, they will ruthlessly enforce them. The "pious" element is the simultaneous need for moral rectitude, inspired by the religious communities to which the settlers have a strong need to belong. In the shop floor situations observed by d'Iribarne both elements, contractual and moral thinking, are amply represented. As a foreign observer, d'Iribarne is astonished about the extent to which the daily practice of employer-employee relations is influenced by endless rules that should guarantee "fairness".

D'Iribarne finds he shares the surprises of the French traveller Alexis de Tocqueville (1805-1859) in his 1835 book *Democracy in America*. De Tocqueville was struck by the individualism and egalitarianism he found in America. About the relationship between masters and servants in the USA, as opposed to France, de Tocqueville wrote: "The masters, from their side, only demand that their servants faithfully and rigorously execute their contract; they do not ask for their respect; they expect neither their love nor their devotion; it suffices them to find them punctual and honest". As partners to a contract, employer and employee were and are more equal in the US than in the French system. At the same time, according to William Graham Sumner (1840-1910), the founder of American sociology, they were also quite antagonistic: He remarked that to say that employer and employee "are partners in an enterprise is only a delusive figure of speech". With the start of the new millennium, there is no evidence that the Americans are about to change their ways towards less litigation about contractual relationships, or towards less moralism; in fact, many Americans believe in a historical necessity for the rest of the world to eventually become like them.

Management processes in the Netherlands, as d'Iribarne describes them, are again of a different nature. Management is less based on orders and more on consensus: On convincing the other, subordinate or superior, about what should be done. This calls for a lot of talking, either person-to-person or in meetings. In the Dutch aluminum plant, d'Iribarne is struck by everybody's respect for facts, which he finds stronger than either in France or in the USA; in France status and power often prevail over facts; Americans often want facts to yield to moral principles. The Dutch, like the Americans, have their pious merchant ancestors; they were the founders of the Republic of the Seven United Provinces (1579-1795). In the Dutch case, however, relationships have always been based on compromise rather than on contract. The Republic was born from a revolt against the Spanish overlords. In order to survive, the former rebels learned to cooperate across religious and ideological lines. The Dutch tradition has room for contracts as well, but negotiations may be re-opened the day after conclusion, if new facts emerge. Employer-employee relations in the Netherlands need not be antagonistic, contrary to the French and the US case. The Dutch consensus in a way resembles the well-known Japanese consensus, but it has very different ancestral roots. Japanese consensus is based on group interest, on collectivist integration within the work group and the enterprise. Dutch consensus is based on the concern for individuals' quality of life, which should not be harmed by avoidable conflicts with other individuals. To date, the Dutch "polder" consensus model has been resilient to influences of international business and of European integration.

D'Iribarne combines solid knowledge of contemporary practices of management in the three countries with profound historical insight. He refutes a superficial belief in the universality of management fads by showing how life in each country follows a line of historical continuity, which affects many facets of society, of which management is one.

Culture and Technology in Management: Values and Practices

But, you may object, the Pilgrim Fathers did not produce aluminum. Of course not; the technical content of the management processes has changed completely, and it keeps changing today. Just think of the influence different forms of electronic communication have had on management processes. But I would argue that these are changes to which the French dictum applies "*Plus ça change, plus ca reste la même chose*": The more things change, the more they stay the same (attributed to Alphonse Karr, 1808-1890). That means that there are different orders of change.

When studying manifestations of culture, in general and in management, it is useful to distinguish *values* from *practices*. Values, as defined earlier in this article, are broad tendencies to prefer certain states of affairs over others. These are invisible except in their effects on people's behavior. Practices, on the contrary, are visible to an observer. They are ways of behaving as well as artefacts. Practices are more superficial and easier to change than values. Values are cultural and resilient against technological influences. Practices can be purely social, purely technical, or mixed (socio-technical). Management deals with all three. D'Iribarne studied technically identical plants so the purely technical component in its management was kept constant, which made the social and socio-technical influences stand out clearly. Technology keeps changing but it normally affects only management practices, not the underlying values. People in different countries use the same computer programs but the purposes to which they put them vary according to the programming of their minds, not of their computers.

In the past decades I was involved in two large research projects on cultural differences: The first on different national cultures within the same multinational organization (IBM) and the second on different organizational cultures across a variety of public and private organizations within the same nations (Denmark and the Netherlands). The first project showed that *national* cultures affected mainly people's *values*, which were considerably different from country to country in spite of the similarities in job practices among IBM employees in similar jobs. The second project, which compared otherwise similar people in different *organizations* within the same countries, showed considerable differences in *practices* but much smaller differences in values. Cultural differences at the country level resided mostly in values, less in practices (as long as we compared otherwise similar people). At the organizational level, "culture" differences consisted mostly of different practices, not of different values. Using the word *culture* for both levels suggested that the two kinds of culture are identical phenomena but this was clearly false. A nation is not an organization, and the two types of "culture" are of a different kind.

This conclusion from our research contradicts a popular notion about "corporate culture" which assumes, following Peters and Waterman's classic *In Search of Excellence*, that shared values represent the core of a corporate culture. We found empirically that shared (perceptions of) practices should be considered the core of an organization's culture. In our cross-organizational study, employees' values differed more according to nationality, age and education than according to their membership in the organization *per se*. The difference between Peters and Waterman's and our findings can be explained from the fact that the former collected statements by the leaders, while we interviewed and surveyed all levels in our organizations. We have thus assessed to what extent leaders' messages had come across to members. The values of founders and key leaders undoubtedly shape organizational cultures, but the way these cultures affect ordinary members is through shared practices. Founders/leaders' values become members' practices.

The fact that organizational cultures are shaped by management practices and not by cultural values, explains why such cultures can, to some extent, be managed. Values, as I defined them, are shaped early in our lives, through family, school and peers. After the age of ten such values are firmly imprinted and hardly changeable. Employers cannot change the values of their employees. The only way in which they can affect them is through selecting and promoting employees with the desired values, if candidates are available. If in order to change organizational cultures employers had to change their employees' values, theirs would be a hopeless task. Precisely because organizational cultures reside mainly in more superficial practices they are *somewhat* manageable.

Asian Management Theories for the 21st Century

While I argued that management in the 21st century will not be basically different from management in the 20th, I do expect a breakthrough in the development of theories of management, which will become more adapted to national cultural value systems in different parts of the world.

The study by d'Iribarne, described previously, covered matched cases in three countries in considerable detail. My own cross-national study (Hofstede,1997) provided information from matched samples in over 50 countries, but obviously with less depth. The two approaches are complementary; mine is more quantitative, d'Iribarne's more qualitative. I provided a skeleton for the countries he studied, and he provided the flesh. The skeleton I proposed is a worldwide structure in cultural differences among countries.

This structure consists of four largely independent dimensions on which each country could be assigned a relative position. Initially it was based on comparing similar people in different national subsidiaries of IBM (Hofstede, 1980); later on, these results were replicated on cross-country samples of managers, country elites, employees of other organizations, airline pilots and consumers (Hofstede, 2001); still more recently on civil servants (Mouritzen and Svara, 2002) and employees of a multinational bank (van Nimwegen, 2002). Moreover, the dimensions correlate with published quantitative results of other cross-country studies; the new edition of my scholarly book lists more than 400 significant contributions to multiple regression (Hofstede, 2001, Appendix 6).

One of these dimensions is *Individualism versus Collectivism*. Individualism stands for a society in which the ties between individuals are loose: Everyone is expected to look after her/himself and her/his immediate family only. The opposite, Collectivism, stands for a society in which people from birth onwards are integrated into strong, cohesive in-groups, which throughout their lifetime continue to protect them, in exchange for unquestioning loyalty. All Western countries in my research scored individualist, Asian, African and Latin American countries collectivist. The most individualist scores out of 53 countries and regions were found for the USA, Australia, Britain, Canada and the Netherlands, in this order.

The Individualism/Collectivism dimension is the only of the four on which worldwide shifts have been noticeable in the past decades. There is a relationship between cultural Individualism and economic affluence. Wealthier countries score more individualist, but countries that became wealthier also became more individualist, a process visible in recent years in Asia, like in Japan, South Korea and Thailand. Old people in these countries, for example, are less automatically taken care of by their families than they used to be. Nevertheless, while affluence thus increases individualism, it does not make Asian countries as individualist as Western countries. Even when Western countries like Scotland or Sweden were still quite poor, they were already individualist. Increasing or decreasing affluence reduces but does not eliminate differences in Individualism/Collectivism among parts of the world.

Management as a concept originated in Britain. Adam Smith in his 1776 book *The Wealth of Nations* used the words "manage", "manager" and "management" when discussing the functioning of joint stock companies. Over 100 years later management was promoted to a separate field of study in the USA, in particular by Frederick W. Taylor in his books *Shop Management* (1903) and *The Principles of Scientific Management* (1911). Both Britain and the USA were already strongly individualist societies, and all theories of management that were developed subsequently betray their individualist roots. They are based on assumptions about the behavior of detached individuals; on values that are not shared by the vast majority of the world's population. Few management textbooks deal, for example, with the role of employee loyalty to employers, of employers' responsibility towards employees and their families, and of family and/or ethnic loyalties among employers and/or employees.

Collectivism is a facet of culture in most of the world and organizations in collectivist societies are managed according to the values of those societies. However, the remarkable growth of certain non-Western economies, especially in East Asia, such as South Korea and Taiwan, in the last third of the 20th century was not due to their collectivism. Other non-Western economies, equally or more collectivist, for example Pakistan and Venezuela, grew hardly at all. What distinguished the Asian growth economies from others was their long-term orientation.

Long versus Short Term Orientation was not one of the four original dimensions I had identified, but on the basis of research in the 1980s by Professor Michael Bond from Hong Kong and his collaborators, I added it as a fifth dimension (Hofstede and Bond, 1988). Long Term Orientation means focusing on the future. It implies a cultural trend towards delaying immediate gratification by practicing persistence and thriftiness. Its opposite, Short Term Orientation, means focusing on the past and present, by respecting tradition and by a need to follow trends in spending even if this means borrowing money. This dimension set the economically most successful Asian countries apart from those in the rest of the world, in the sense that these countries scored Long-Term and the others medium or Short-Term. The most long-term oriented countries were China, Hong Kong, Taiwan, Japan and South Korea, in this order. All Western countries showed a medium to short-term orientation. African countries, but also, for example, Pakistan and the Philippines scored short-term. Scores on this dimension were strongly related to the countries' economic success in the 25 years since world markets opened up, from 1965 to 1990. Countries scoring Long-Term, in which thriftiness was valued, had in fact higher savings rates than countries scoring Short-Term (Read, 1993). More savings meant more money for productive investment. The Asian crisis of recent years does not mean a shift on this dimension, but is due to a lack of institutional and political reforms, which lag behind the economic development.

Since 1998 Asian countries have their own Asia Academy of Management History has shown that leading economies also take a lead in selling ideas to other parts of the world; we have seen this happening in the cases of Britain, the USA. and Japan. In our 21st century this is likely to lead to an emancipation of management theories from their Anglo roots and to a proliferation of theories applicable to countries in Asia and maybe elsewhere in the world.

Equal/Unequal, Tough/Tender and Rigid/Flexible in Management

The three other dimensions along which I found national cultures to differ are Power Distance (large versus small), Masculinity versus Femininity, and Uncertainty Avoidance (strong versus weak).

The different management philosophies of France, the USA and the Netherlands which d'Iribarne identified can be associated with Power Distance and Masculinity/Femininity. Power Distance is the extent of inequality in a society: Less powerful members of institutions and organizations within a country expecting and accepting that power is distributed unequally. Among the 53 countries and regions around the world for which I was able to compute a Power Distance Index, France ranked 16th from the top, that is well above average, and the USA and the Netherlands 38th and 40th, respectively, both below average. These positions confirm the inequality in the French system and the relative greater equality in the two other countries.

The dimension of Masculinity (versus Femininity) distinguishes tough societies focusing on performance, assertiveness and material success from tender societies in which people focus on relationships, modesty and quality of life. Among the same 53 countries and regions the USA scored 15th highest on Masculinity, well above average; France 35th, somewhat below average, and the Netherlands 51th, extremely feminine. This dimension explains the toughness with which contractual relations in the USA are enforced versus the Dutch concern for consensual relationships; French relations within the "honor" system are also less tough.

France also scored considerably higher on Uncertainty Avoidance (13th) than the Netherlands (35th) and especially the USA (43th), but this difference is less evident in d'Iribarne's analysis. Uncertainty Avoidance is the extent to which the members of a culture feel threatened by uncertain or unknown situations: It opposes rigid towards more flexible cultures. It implies a need for structure and absolute truths, and a feeling that "what is different, is dangerous". An important aspect of the level of Uncertainty Avoidance in a society is the amount of trust between citizens and authorities. Weak Uncertainty Avoidance stands for citizen competence, that is a belief that ordinary citizens are able to influence their authorities, and some degree of mutual trust between them. Strong Uncertainty Avoidance implies that decisions should be left to experts; citizens and authorities mutually distrust each other. Latin, Mediterranean, Central and East-European countries tended to score above average on Uncertainty Avoidance, along with Japan, South Korea and Pakistan. Nordic and Anglo countries as well as most other Asian and below-Sahara African countries scored average or below.

Theories for Managing across Cultures

The viewpoint that management problems remain the same over time, but that their solutions differ from country to country, is not necessarily popular in an age in which business is supposed to be globalizing. Global business looks for global management solutions. I believe that businesses and other cross-national organizations are and will remain less global than management authors pretend they are and their leaders would like them to be. Businesses have home countries that stand for values that are functional, even essential, for their effectiveness and corporate identity. Supra-national organizations without a home country, like various UN agencies, suffer from poor efficiency and effectiveness.

Multinational organizations, private, public, and non-governmental, stand for values that originated in their home country and that will not be shared equally with their employees and managers from other national origins. Coming back to the distinction between values and practices made above, multinational organizations are kept together by shared practices, not by shared values. Philippe d'Iribarne once remarked that international cooperation consists of doing things together, even if each partner does them for a different reason.

Values are specific to national cultures, never universal. If there is one moral principle that can be offered as a candidate for a *universal* value and as a must for organizations aspiring to be global, it is the principle of moderation: *Seeking a Middle Way*. This principle is independently found in the teachings of three contemporaries who revolutionized human thinking in the 5th Century B.C: Buddha, Confucius and Socrates. The rationale of the Middle Way is that any virtue becomes a sin when extended too far. Fields of application of this principle can be chosen at will: Merging, privatization, outsourcing, downsizing, just-in-time management, total quality management, teleworking, lobbying, executive compensation and whatever other fads the present millennium may have in store for us.

Working internationally demands partly different skills and attitudes from working in the home country. A multicultural perspective implies restraint in passing judgment; the ability to recognize that in different environments, different rules of the same game may apply. Success at home is often based on a strong drive and quick and firm opinions. These very qualities may make a person less qualified for an international position.

International managers need to be context-sensitive. Narrow specialists may be needed at times for solving technical problems abroad, but they should be shipped back as soon as possible. International managers need a broad interest and an eagerness to absorb new information, including language, history, geography, religion, literature and art.

National cultural differences have become a topic in all textbooks of International Management, and virtually all textbooks of Management in general, but the way they are treated is often superficial. The problem is that, if taken serious, the cross-cultural view implies that question marks may have to be placed in all other chapters in the books. "This is what we taught you, but seen from another cultural angle *it ain't necessarily so*". And much of culture cannot be learned from a book, anyway. Our 21st century will need a lot of creativity from persons developing theories and teaching practices for cross-cultural management.

A Cross-Cultural Challenge: the Economic and Cultural Dynamics of Corruption

One example of a dilemma in cross-cultural management, which no theory can resolve, is the balance between private interests and the goals of the organization. In his 1776 book Adam Smith already raised the issue to what extent joint stock companies could function well. He doubted whether their managers, hired persons who were not owners, could be trusted with other people's money. Later the British economist John Stuart Mill (1806-1873) echoed the same concern. Recently, agency theory has produced quantitative models trying to show the extent to which self-interested agents will represent their principals' interest. "Trust" as a management concept has also gained new popularity, for example as a condition for successful strategic alliances.

Corruption is a taboo in the management literature, but in view of its frequency and consequences it deserves to be squarely addressed. Official and unofficial side payments to "agents" occur in many situations throughout the world. What is called "corruption" is partly a matter of definition. We speak of corruption when those in power use illegal means to get the collaboration of authorities, or to enrich themselves. But what to say about the US. practice of lobbying, and of its levels of Chief Executive compensation, which, although formally legal, rest on similar motives? In Japan, China and many other cultures the giving of gifts is an important ritual, and the borderline between gift giving and bribing is diffuse. To a purist even tip giving can be considered a form of bribing.

Since 1995 Transparency International, a non-governmental organization located in Berlin, Germany, issues a yearly Corruption Perception Index (CPI) on the

Internet. The CPI was developed by Johann Graf Lambsdorff, an economist at the University of Göttingen, Germany, and combines information from up to 12 different sources in business, the press and the foreign services. The 2001 CPI covers 91 countries; the index runs from 10.0 (entirely clean) to 1.0 (entirely corrupt). The countries perceived as cleanest in the 2001 list are Finland, Denmark, New Zealand and Iceland on a par with Singapore (in this order), and those perceived as the most corrupt are Bangladesh, Nigeria, Indonesia on a par with Uganda, and Azerbaijan on a par with Bolivia, Cameroon and Kenya.

In order to understand why some countries were rated more corrupt than others, I have analysed the statistical relationships between 2001 CPI scores and economic and cultural indexes. As an economic index I used the 1998 Gross National Product per capita, published in the World Bank's 1999-2000 World Development Report. As cultural indexes I used the country scores on the four dimensions identified in my IBM research: Individualism, Power Distance, Uncertainty Avoidance and Masculinity.

Across 49 countries for which all indexes were available, CPI depended primarily on wealth. Seventy-three per cent of the differences in CPI could be predicted from a country's wealth, or rather from its poverty. Under conditions of poverty, acquiring money in unofficial ways is not just a matter of greed; it may be a matter of survival. Officials, police and teachers in poor countries are often so ill paid that without side payments they cannot feed their families.

Poverty, however, did not fully explain all the differences among countries. Power Distance and Masculinity added to the prediction of corruption perceptions. Adding Power Distance as a factor we could increase the share of CPI differences predicted to 77 per cent: Large Power Distances increased perceived corruption. The influence of Power Distance points to the influence of checks and balances in a society on the use of power. Large power distances in a society mean fewer checks and balances and stronger temptation for power holders to illegally enrich themselves. Enlightened rulers can impose checks where traditional culture does not provide them. Examples are high Power Distance countries Singapore and Hong Kong, which the Transparency International list classifies as reasonably "clean". This reflects the iron hands of Senior Minister Lee Kuan Yew in Singapore, and of the ICAC (Independent Commission Against Corruption) in Hong Kong.

Adding Masculinity we could further increase the share of CPI differences explained to 79 per cent. Countries with masculine cultures were perceived to have more corruption than countries with feminine cultures. Masculinity stands for assertive behavior and a need to show off among leaders, but also for a need to admire among followers; Its opposite pole, Femininity, stands for modesty among leaders and jealousy among followers. The first stimulates corrupt behavior, the second limits it.

More insight into the reasons for corruption is gained when we split the countries into rich and poor. From the 49 countries for which we had complete data, 24 had a 1998 GNP per capita over 10,000 $ and 25 below 10,000 $. In this way all European Union and other Western and a few Asian countries were counted as rich; all Latin American, African and most Asian countries were classified as poor.

Across the 24 wealthy countries, the level of perceived corruption was not related to their GNP/capita. All seem to have reached a level of affluence where corruption is no longer economically motivated. Instead, 65 per cent of the (considerable) country differences in CPI could be explained by a combination of Uncertainty Avoidance and Power Distance. Uncertainty Avoidance means that citizens consider themselves incompetent and are felt to be incompetent by authorities; in this case there are fewer checks on abuse of authority - and there is more suspicion of such abuse. The influence of large Power Distance was discussed above.

Across the 25 poor countries, the level of perceived corruption was also no longer related to their GNP/capita. This time a smaller part of differences in corruption perceptions could be explained by societal values, and the explaining variables were different: Masculinity and Collectivism (low Individualism) emerged as explaining factors. Together they accounted for 34 per cent of the differences. The need to conspicuously assert oneself by showing material wealth (Masculinity), and the need to support one's own in-group members as opposed to out-group members (Collectivism) evidently play a more important role in motivating corrupt practices in poor than in wealthy countries.

In 1984 the US/German researcher Michael H. Hoppe collected new scores on the same dimensions, this time from members of the political, business and scientific elite in 18 mostly wealthy countries contacted via the Salzburg Seminar, a US-founded international conference center in Salzburg, Austria. If instead of my country scores for these four dimensions, which date from IBM personnel around 1970, I use the scores from Hoppe's elites, their Power Distance index scores alone correlate with the 2001 Corruption Perception Index with r=.90 (p<.001), which means differences in Power Distance explain eighty-one per cent of the differences in perceived corruption among these 18 countries. Power Distance in this case measured how these members of national elites described their own values; the CPI on the other hand measured how their country was perceived by others. The power values of the elites in 1984 allowed predicting the perceived corruption in their countries, 17 years later, with astonishing accuracy.

To Lord Acton, a 19th century British politician turned Cambridge professor, we owe a famous aphorism: "Power tends to corrupt, and absolute power corrupts absolutely". Prevailing values with regard to power will continue to differ between countries. Therefore, corruption will remain a key dilemma to cross-cultural management, which no agency theory or other management fad can resolve. The dilemma touches upon basic ethics. Corruption is bad for societies, but many multinational companies can increase their profits by bribing officials in client countries. What will get priority, profits or social responsibility? This choice in itself is influenced by values, that is by culture.

References

d'Iribarne, P. (1989), *"La logique de l'honneur: Gestion des entreprisese et tradtions nationales"* (in French). Paris: Éditions du Seuil.

d'Iribarne, P. (1997), "The usefulness of an ethnographic approach to the international comparison of organizations", in *International Studies of Management and Organization*, 26, 4, 30-47.

de Tocqueville, A. (1991), [1835]. *Democracy in America*. Edited by R. D. Heffner. New York: New American Library.

Hofstede, G. (1980) "Motivation, Leadership and Organization: Do American Theories Apply Abroad?" in *Organizational Dynamics*, 9, 1, Summer, 42-63.

Hofstede, G. & Bond M.H. (1988), "The Confucius Connection: From Cultural Roots to Economic Growth" in *Organizational Dynamics*, 16, 4, Spring, 4-21.

Hofstede, G. (1997), *Cultures and Organizations: Software of the Mind*. New York: McGraw-Hill.

Hofstede, G. (2001), *Culture's Consequences: Comparing values, behaviors, institutions and organizations across nations*. Thousand Oaks CA: Sage.

Hoppe, M.H. (1998), "Validating the Masculinity/Femininity Dimension on Elites from 19 Countries", in G. Hofstede (Ed), *Masculinity and Femininity: The Taboo Dimension of National Cultures*. Thousand Oaks CA: Sage.

Mouritzen, P.E. & Svara J.H. (2002), *Leadership at the Apex: Politicians and Administrators in Western Local Governments*. Pittsburgh PA: University of Pittsburgh Press.

Peters, T & Waterman, Jr. R.H. (1982), *In Search of Excellence: Lessons from America's Best-Run Companies*. New York: Harper & Row.

Read, R. 1993. *Politics and Policies of National Economic Growth*. Ph.D. Dissertation, Stanford University, Stanford CA.

Smith, A. (1979) [1776]. *The Wealth of Nations*. Edited by A. Skinner. Harmondsworth, Middlesex: Penguin.

Sumner, W.G. (1906), *Folkways*. Boston: Ginn & Company.

Taylor, F.W. (1903),*Shop Management*. New York: Harper & Bros.

Taylor, F.W. (1911), *The Principles of Scientific Management*. New York: Harper & Bros.

Transparency International (Annually). *Corruption Perception Index (CPI)*, on-line. Internet: *http://www.gwdg.de/~uwvw/icr.htm*

van Nimwegen, T. (2002), *Global Banking, Global Values: The In-House Reception of the Corporate Values of ABN AMRO*. Ph.D. Dissertation, Nyenrode University. Delft Neth.: Eburon.

Chapter 3

Cross-Cultural Social Psychology and the Real World of Culturally Diverse Teams and Dyads

Michael Harris Bond

"Why do my subjects make such a fuss about the differences among themselves?" asked the Khan. "Because, majesty, some differences make a difference", replied Marco. "But which differences make a difference?" said the Khan. "In truth, Majesty, any difference can make a difference and some differences make all the difference", Marco observed. "What sort of difference?" the Khan persisted. "The difference between life and death", sighed Marco.
(With apologies to Italo Calvino)

Some Personal Puzzles, Earned in the Trenches of our Discipline

"…but I said 'if you please we will commit ourselves to this void, and see whether Providence is here also".
(William Blake, The Marriage of Heaven and Hell)

I work and otherwise live in an increasingly diverse life-space, and span progressively greater cultural divides in my daily exchanges. The nature of these exchanges is likewise mutating as communication technologies enlarge our modes of interfacing (Soderberg and Holden, 2002). This is a truism for us in 21st century academics, but also for those in business, politics, refugee resettlement, space flight, disaster relief, religious propagation, and military peacekeeping. I welcome this historical sea-change, since I have made a now 30 year professional investment in the field of cross-cultural social psychology. It has always seemed to me that we few in this discipline are ideally positioned to use our accumulated knowledge in advising others how better to function across increasingly numerous and politicized lines of cultural difference.

There is a now a considerable cottage industry of academic-practitioners, governmental advisors, business consultants, teacher trainers, social work counselors, and the like addressing this cultural issue. Many are members of organizations like the Society for Intercultural Education, Training and Research, dedicated to improving the delivery of intercultural resources to persons working at cultural interfaces. These educators contribute to our inter-cultural social cohesion by sensitizing their clients to cultural difference, by striving to reduce divisive prejudice, and by facilitating more productive exchanges across cultural lines. This is essential and laudable work

But, how do such trainers exercise an impact on their clients? Having delivered such courses myself and having listened to others do so, I believe that we achieve some progress by modeling cultural openness and accommodation ourselves, by humanizing others from different cultural heritages for our audience, and by legitimizing cultural practices as a cause of behavioral difference. We derive many of our examples from the research base of cross-cultural social psychology (Smith and Bond, 1998), and these inputs may also help by alerting our audience to variations in cultural norms and by suggesting more appropriate behavioral routines when our clients interact with others from different cultural backgrounds. We believe that we increase the cultural mindfulness (Gudykunst, 1998) of participants and change the relevant behaviors of trainees who then become cultural change agents within their own organizations.

The beliefs of us trainers, however, probably reflect our own cultural optimism, tolerance and social complexity, reinforced by the same qualities characterizing the typical participants in cross-cultural training. There is rarely any measurement of change in the cross-cultural interactions of any course participants. One consequence of this failure to assess is that we as inter-cultural researchers do not push ourselves to find out which behaviors make a salutary difference in the inter-cultural encounter. I am still puzzled about what these crucial exchanges might be. The need to identify these critical behaviors is important, given the frequent observation that people's inter-cultural behaviors typically do not vary from their intra-cultural offerings.

To date, cross-cultural social psychologists have been more concerned to demonstrate differences between two cultural groups on some social-cognitive variable of theoretical interest (see Smith and Bond, 1998, ch.5). Where we have addressed inter-cultural concerns, our typical approach has been to assess stereotypes or prejudice on paper-and-pencil measures of internal, psychological reactions (see Smith and Bond, 1998, ch.7). In order to justify our work, we have tended to highlight differences at the expense of commonalities, and downplayed the considerable overlap across cultural groups in the phenomena measured. We have generally failed to provide textured analyses and comparisons of interpersonal exchanges that lead to the outcomes of group success and member satisfaction. Nor have we explored the social factors that shape these exchanges and that probably vary in importance across cultures.

Our current level of development is understandable, but lamentable. We know little enough about member exchanges in dyads and groups, how they build into types of dyadic and group process, and how different levels of these dyadic and group processes combine to affect group performance and member attainment of goals. In consequence, "When it comes to training teams, little exists to guide human resource practitioners who must design training systems. In fact, empirically based prescriptions, guidelines, and specifications are virtually nonexistent for team training." (Cannon-Bowers, Tannenbaum, Salas, and Volpe, 1995, p. 333). We know even less about how culture affects the interpersonal processes that constitute the woof and warp of dyadic or group life and that must be interwoven to counteract their lurking potential for fragmentation (see Smith and Bond, 1998, ch. 6). I hope that this essay will nudge us in the field to address this practical issue in more useful ways.

If my premise and point of departure seem sensible, then we intercultural practitioners, busy "giving psychology away to the public", need to ask, "What behaviors must my trainees increase or decrease in order to improve their inter-cultural outcomes?" My puzzle has been to understand within what theoretical framework may these salutary changes operate when our trainees return to their various fields of inter-cultural play and work? What is a general approach to interpersonal relations within which the issue of cultural differences may be embedded?

More specifically, how do groups function, what issues must groups address in order to meet their performance objectives, and how must differences be accommodated and exploited by a group to avoid implosion, enhance performance, and meet its members' diverse objectives? The same questions could be asked of dyads. These are academic issues of considerable intrigue; our teasing out answers could be of practical moment, however, since they would guide interventions by trainers.

"Philosophers have interpreted the world differently; the problem is to change it". (Karl Marx)

Social Life as Resource Exchange

"Always do right. That will gratify some of the people and astonish the rest". (Mark Twain)

As a social psychologist, I work from the premise that our behaviors constitute our reality in the minds and hearts of others. Cooley may be right when he avers that, "Imaginations which people have of one another are the solid facts of society." What, however, produces those imaginations? I submit that it is an orchestrated exchange of resources (Foa, 1971) from one person to another in a dyadic or group setting. These exchanges occur within a normative framework informed by the cultural backgrounds of the interactants. These exchanges may be conceptualized along the two-dimensional integration of social behavior proposed by Wiggins and Trapnell (1996) with consequences for the "imaginations" that we then carry of one another. These imaginations may themselves be organized along the five fundamental dimensions of person perception that have emerged from a legacy of social psychological research in many cultural settings (Bond, 1994) and which Hogan (1996) argues has an evolutionary basis.

The dyadic encounter. Tam and Bond (2002) have explored how friendship or disaffection develops among same-sex, same culture roommates assigned to room together in their first year at university. This "forced encounter" is the basis of many of life's relationships, including those often occurring inter-culturally in task settings. Our question was to connect the emergence of communion or alienation between these former strangers to the character of the behavior exchanges between them across their first three to six months together.

Two constellations of behavior were identified, beneficence and restraint. Beneficence refers to proactive integrative, helpful behaviors, like including the other in dinners, shopping and other social events; praising the other; smiling in their presence; using the other's nickname, etc. Restraint refers to behaviors that avoid doing harm or invading the privacy of the other, such as not disturbing the other when s/he is working; keeping the room tidy and clean; not boasting in his/her presence. Not surprisingly, those relationships characterized by higher levels of these two types of behavior were associated with deeper communion or friendship three months after the relationship began.

These behaviors are the very stuff and substance of interpersonal exchanges. Regrettably, as McArthur and Baron (1983) have pointed out, social psychological documentation of these socially powerful behaviors has suffered because of our fascination with cognitive processes, like person perception, attribution, and perceived similarity. The consequence is that we often do not know which behaviors lead to which sorts of interpersonal consequences along the key dimensions of affiliation versus alienation and dominance versus subordination (Wiggins and Trapnell, 1996). Consequently, we are often at a loss when asked to advise people about what behaviors they should be evincing to manage what type of impression (Giacalone and Rosenfeld, 1991) or make up what type of face (Brown and Levinson, 1987), especially across cultural lines.

It is probable that many of these behaviors have the same sort of psychological and relational impact regardless of the interactants' culture; some may differ. It is these differently construed behaviors that provide some of the "critical incidents" used in constructing culture assimilators (Bhawuk, 2001). These behaviors often receive disproportionate attention in cross-cultural training, and may not be crucial relative to the "culture-general" behaviors that form the foundation of communion and hierarchy in any culture. Many cross-cultural interactants will be forgiven their occasional inter-cultural gaffes if their credits of beneficence and restraint are sufficiently high!

Close examination of cross-cultural marriages suggests how these over-sights may be effected. Fontaine (1990) notes that partners in successful mixed marriages often make cultural attributions for their partner's puzzling, unusual or impolite behavior. Instead of attributing objectionable behavior to their partner's personality, it is ascribed to his or her cultural background. Fontaine argues that this cognitive *"trompe l'oeil"* externalizes the cause of the behavior, rendering it forgivable and thereby protecting the relationship. Many persons engaged in cross-cultural interactions accept the premise that one's culture shapes one's behavior and are often well informed about the different cultural practices of their fellow interactant. The fact that he or she comes from a different culture is usually salient to them. Otherwise critical incidents are thus rendered less "critical" by attributing their cause to these various cultural differences. There is no experimental research on inter-cultural attributional activity, so we do not know whether its consequences will always be so benign. Nonetheless, it seems likely that "forgiving because of culture" often occurs, making cross-cultural interactions less fraught and centrifugal.

Cross-cultural trainers in particular need to know what behaviors constitute credits across cultural lines. The research we have provided comes mostly from the study of communication which has focused on single behavior domains, e.g., passing compliments, engaging in communication repairs, etc., in short-term encounters (see Smith and Bond, 1998, ch. 6). Inter-cultural encounters are often long-term, and without an early exit option, so that the broader profile of an interactant's behavioral offerings will become relevant. In this regard, it is instructive to note Ruben and Kealy's (1979) finding that the best predictor of host-national rated cross-cultural effectiveness for Canadian technical experts overseas was their rated effectiveness at "communication of respect" to their compatriots during pre-departure training. Research on inter-cultural and intra-cultural behavior repeatedly shows that persons do not vary their behavior as a function of inter-acting across cultures (see e.g., Black and Porter, 1991; Pekerti and Thomas, in press). We may thus assume that pre-departure behavioral profiles predict post-arrival performances. So, persons behaving in thoughtful, courteous ways here were effective there, presumably because their behavioral profile there was similarly integrative. It would be instructive and helpful, however, to know just what those behaviors are.

The group encounter. Cannon-Bowers et al. (1995) have made individual task competencies and team competencies key components in their model predicting team performance. These competencies become highlighted depending on the nature of the tasks and the work being undertaken by the team. One becomes valued as a team member to the extent that one commands a profile of competencies conducing to effective team performance. As an example of this logic, Leung and Bond (2001) have been exploring the communication behaviors of group members with one another and relating these behaviors to the basic social outcome measures of likeability and rated task competence (Bales, 1950). Communication behaviors signaling attentiveness to the other were associated with ratings of both likeability and task competence. Those who show more attentiveness towards others have personalities characterized as restrained, helpful, intelligent, emotionally stable, and hard-working.

In this study, we may discern a model for group relations that anchors the attractiveness and perceived productivity of a group member to measurable aspects of a member's communications, which themselves derive from their different personality profiles. It is the capacity to communicate in certain ways that facilitates the coordination task that is so essential to a group's functioning. As McGrath, Arrow, and Berdahl (1999) put this issue:

> ...coordination of understandings allows for the recognition of differences and the sometimes taxing process of finding connections that link and make sense of apparently incompatible views. When this process works, the outcome is high 'integrative complexity (p. 11).

Successful groups develop this "integrative complexity", but its achievement is in part the result of identifiable communications exchanged among members endowed with the personality skills underpinning these communicative competencies. Persons commanding other task-and work-relevant competencies would receive the same social endorsements of liking and high performance ratings.

Again, this study involved members of the same cultural group, as does most research into group process. So, the question arises about how the equation changes when members from different cultural groups must interact. It is probable that many of the same personal competencies are required when working effectively with those from different cultures as is required when working effectively with co-culturalists. So, for example, Ng and Bond (2002) found that groups of Hong Kongese performed better if their group evidenced higher levels of task focus. The group characteristic of task focus itself was related to the total level of its members' self-ratings on the personality variables of helpfulness and [negative] openness. These qualities of personality could well be important in predicting group performance in multi-cultural settings, also. The work of Rubin and Kealey (1979) mentioned earlier found that "communication of respect" by technical trainers to their co-nationals during pre-departure training predicted their success at training host nationals when placed overseas. Helpfulness as a personality attribute may well encapsulate many of the behaviors signaling "communication of respect", in which case there would be nothing distinctive about the role of personal helpfulness in facilitating inter-cultural interactions relative to intra-cultural interactions. Consistent with this argument is the finding that the adaptation of Turkish migrants to Dutch society is facilitated when they are higher in the Big Five trait of agreeableness Arendt-Toth, 2002). Agreeableness may be a social resource sustaining and buffering any kind of interpersonal coordination, cross-cultural as well as intra-cultural.

Some personality attributes may assume a special importance in multi-cultural groups. For example, second-language skills are an obvious new element in some inter-cultural coordination tasks (Du Babcock, Babcock, and Lai, 1995). Of course, language skills in one's native language are also required in mono-cultural groups, with a whole set of linguistic accommodations (Gallois, Franklyn-Stokes, Giles, and Coupland, 1988) to be made and common ground (Clark and Brennan, 1991) to be developed in order to achieve effective outcomes. Whether the intra-cultural and inter-cultural linguistic and social skills are different either in kind or degree, however, has yet to be established. One could well imagine that articulate, fluent extroverts are a group resource in many group tasks, and may be just those persons likely to acquire second-language skills during an overseas posting.

Some would argue that prejudice (Gudykunst and Bond, 1997) and its obverse, tolerance (Berry and Kalin, 1995), are distinctively important issues in inter-cultural interactions. This contention, too, is debatable. Prejudice has many targets, including persons of different gender, education levels, professional training, and so forth, as well as cultures and nationalities. There is evidence that prejudiced persons generalize across these various targets (Altemeyer, 1988), so that a person who rejects foreigners will also reject out-group targets within his or her own cultural group.

Further, the disposition to be prejudiced is related to the universal (McCrae and Costa, 1997) trait dimension of openness to experience (Trapnell, 1994). To the extent that prejudice, or its foundation trait, openness, results in divisive behaviors undercutting cooperation, it may well operate equally in intra-cultural as well as inter-cultural groupings. Consistent with this reasoning, Schmitz (1996) has found that higher openness in personality predicts smoother acculturation for immigrants. Demonstrations of this acculturation/adaptation could then enhance cross-cultural cooperation by increasing trust of the outsider by host nations (Thomas and Ravlin, 1995).

> "In such business, action is eloquence"
> (Shakespeare, Coriolanus, Act 3, Sc. 2, L. 75).

Cross-Cultural Interaction as another Form of Adaptation

> *"Plus ca change, plus c'est la meme chose"*
> (French adage).

Throughout our life course, we must interact with new others who present us with affordances and constraints in attaining our basic human goals of survival, social inclusion, and status (Hsu, 1971). Within the limits imposed by our own cognitive skills, interpersonal resources, and ideal self-concept, we learn to influence others to cooperate and coordinate with us in achieving our goals. Effective social living requires that we master the rules of exchange and procedure required for us to attain our goals with others while preserving those relationships necessary for future exchanges. Much of this interpersonal coordination and exchange is normatized and scripted by the role prescriptions of our culture, requiring little by way of on-line processing and negotiation skills.

Working with persons from different cultures can complexify these processes. As Anderson (1994) puts it, "Cross-cultural adaptation is a commonplace process of learning to live with change and difference--in this instance, a changed environment and different people, different norms, different standards, and different customs." (p. 299) Cross-cultural interpersonal adaptation thus becomes "a lengthy series of adjustments, each involving a motive to achieve an outcome, a thwarting of that desired outcome, the production of varied new responses to achieve that outcome, until satisfaction is achieved." (Smith and Bond, 1998, pp. 269-270) So, working with cultural others becomes a trial-and -error process where the procedural ground rules adopted by the others may have changed, and the willingness of these others to provide the new-culture learner with feedback on his or her performance may be less. The new-culture learner will struggle to figure out a way forward without alienating these others by increasing their coordination costs relative to the benefits he or she provides for them. This is a daunting task! Anderson concludes:

How any of us responds at any moment depends on our current appraisals of the stimulus situation. These appraisals in turn depend on both personal and situational factors.... The pattern and strength of our motivations, our current emotional state, commitments, beliefs and expectations, the degree of our interaction with host country inhabitants, and the relative power of our personal resources, for instance, all have an influence on the coping responses that are chosen. They interact with such features of the situation as its novelty, imminence, potency, or uncertainty to induce selection of a particular response to a particular stimulus at a particular time (p. 314).

Considerable personal resources are required to meet this recurring challenge. These resources, however, are required for any life-transition within one's own culture as well, such as making a job change, adjusting to the death of a spouse, or moving to a new neighborhood; inter-cultural tasks are not qualitatively different than those faced by people within their culture of origin. Furthermore, those who engage in inter-cultural exchanges are often self-selected, and possess high levels of motivation and resourcefulness when facing these challenges – exchange students, migrant workers, and even illegal immigrants are not typical members of their cultures of origin! Often they provide skills and services that are in high demand by members of the receiving culture, compensating for the coordination costs that may be involved in interacting with them instead of with cultural insiders. Additionally, the role prescriptions of the work settings where most inter-cultural interactions occur may be very similar across cultural groups, thereby easing any cross-cultural transition (McAuley, Bond, and Kashima, 2002). It is not surprising then that success rates for overseas business placements are very high, despite persistent assertions by cross-cultural trainers to the contrary (Harzing, 1995).

All these considerations contextualize the process of inter-cultural interactions, embedding them within the general adaptation process faced by all people throughout their lives. They, too, require the delicate trade-off between costs and benefits characterizing any interaction. Member personality resources, such as emotional stability (Ward, 1996), openness (Schmitz, 1996), interpersonal agreeableness (Rubin and Kealy, 1979), task competencies, and language skills will result in some dyads or groups succeeding better than others. So, too, will social supports, like the host nation's level of human rights observation (Humana, 1986), organizational policies which assist inter-cultural interactants through difficult moments and prevent the "easy exit option" and press diverse teams to confront their process dynamics (see e.g., Distefano and Maznevski, 2000; Watson, Kumar, and Michaelson, 1993), and interpersonal involvement across cultural lines in common-fate outcomes, where it is in the interest of both parties to help one another to succeed. The presumed vulnerability of cross-cultural interactions must be assessed relative to intra-cultural interactions using all these factors contributing to group or dyadic outcomes.

> "Well, it's still the same old story
> A fight for love and glory
> A case of do or die

The fundamental things apply..."
(Herman Hupfeld, 'As Time Goes By').

An Emerging Agenda for Research on the Success of Inter-Cultural Interactions

"...the art of research is that of making a problem soluble by finding out ways of getting at it – soft underbellies and the like"
(Peter Medawar, advice to a young scientist).

The preceding reflections arise as a result of our adding chapters on cross-cultural communication and outcomes to prior chapters on cross-cultural differences in various types of social behavior when writing Social psychology across cultures. In reading for these chapters, we became aware that those researchers charting these many differences were making little contact with those researchers and practitioners applying their work to improve interactions across cultural lines. This seems lamentable. I submit that psychological research in general and cross-cultural psychology in particular will benefit from addressing praxis, and propose the following questions to help focus our designs more productively:

Does Culture affect Inter-Cultural Outcomes?

An inter-cultural interaction involves two or more persons cooperating to complete a task that may be characterized along many dimensions (Steiner, 1972). This interaction may be extended over time, depending on a host of personal, social, and organizational considerations. These are the same considerations that inform intra-cultural interactions. The quality of the outcome in either type of interaction may well be determined by the same factors. The "culture derivedness" of the outcome in the inter-cultural case needs to be established, not presumed.

An obvious way to tease out culture is to compare equivalent intra-cultural groups with intercultural groups. Very few studies contrast intra-cultural groups or dyads with inter-cultural groups or dyads. The work of Watson et al. (1993) is an exception, but is most revealing in both what it found and in what it did not examine. These researchers determined that inter-cultural task groups in business school could outperform intra-cultural groups on a certain type of intellectual performance by the latter stages of the groups' life. What is often not noted about this research is that each group was coached on improving its process issues throughout the academic term. I expect that it was this mandated coaching that made the difference, forcing and enabling the inter-cultural groups to confront and repair their coordination issues (see also Distefano and Maznevski, 2000).

In a cultural climate that legitimizes, even exalts, cultural diversity, there will be a reluctance to challenge the behavior of one's group members from different cultures. In consequence, group members will block themselves from addressing issues necessary for the group's development of "integrative complexity'. As McGrath et al. (1999) put this matter;

Cooperation and conflict drive the establishment, enactment, monitoring, and modifying of a network of relations among members, tasks, and tools...the smooth connections of cooperation and the friction of conflict enable the group to pursue group projects and address changing member needs while continuing to evolve and adapt (p. 1).

All effective groups must develop this "integrative complexity", but the perceived cultural variation in the group itself may block members from doing so. Our socialized reluctance to confront difference may be even greater when we are together with those from manifestly different cultures. Many will adopt a dysfunctional "cultural correctness", perhaps derived from our concerns not to create experiences of "race-based rejection" (Mendoza-Denton, Downey, Purdie, Davis, and Pietrzak, in press) for apparent other-culture members. A mandated requirement from a superior authority, be that a graduate school teacher or organizational policy, can overcome that reluctance. In fact, such a mandate may be necessary in some cultural settings to force people from different cultural settings to engage in the group reflection necessary to promote integrative complexity. Once this reluctance is overcome, what Earley and Gibson (2002, pp. 112-113) have called a "hybrid" group culture can be fashioned. That hybrid culture may facilitate task completion by releasing the benefits of member diversity and enhanced group process (Ng and Bond, 2002).

Note that this cultural issue had nothing to do with the member capacities, personality profiles or the like of the group members that may arise from their different socialization experiences in different cultures of origin. There was no information on what these individual qualities were in Watson et al. (1993), nor how they differed between the intra-cultural and inter-cultural groups. What we do know is that the process of the inter-cultural groups improved and I suspect that this improvement only happened because of the interventions made by Watson et al. throughout each group's life to confront its group functioning.

What many cross-cultural practitioners would like to have is more detail about how Watson et al. (1993) intervened to effect such positive confrontation of the coordination issues arising from coordination across cultural lines (see p. 595). Perhaps, however, it was the fact of intervention itself that made the difference.

How does Culture Affect Inter-Cultural Outcomes?

Intervention may make a difference with some inter-cultural groups or dyads, just as it will do with some intra-cultural groups or dyads. With or without intervention, though, we are left grappling with the fundamental question of just what is it about these groups or dyads – the personality of their members, their emergent group process, the inter-group organizational structure within which they function, and the normative social climate concerning cultural diversity within which they function (see Earley and Gibson, ch. 4) that conduces to their success or failure in meeting individual and unit goals. It is these contributing factors to interpersonal outcomes that we must understand and measure, not the "culture" of the participants.

Merely knowing their culture of origin will be a poor proxy measure of each member's resource portfolio. For one thing, the persons who interact across cultural lines are usually atypical members of their cultural groups with respect to modal cultural personalities. More importantly, we will still need to know how dyads or groups composed of members from cultures however similar or different actually function to achieve member and unit goals, or not (see e.g., Elron, 1997).

The perceived cultural identity of the group or dyad participants may make a difference in shaping these outcomes. A history of inter-cultural hostility, resentment, revenge on the one hand, or of amity and cooperative struggle against a common enemy on the other may predispose members so identified to work cooperatively of antagonistically together. This kind of cultural influence, however, will be translated into behavioral exchanges among the participants which then lead to differing dyadic or group processes impacting on the outcomes (Ng and Bond, 2002). It is these behavioral exchanges we must chart and translate into outcomes.

If groups can wend their way through the negative consequences of such "surface-level" diversity, they may begin to confront the coordination challenges posed by their "deep-level" diversity ((Harrison, Price, and Bell, 1998). Again, our research focus at this stage of a group's interaction must be to connect these deep-level characteristics of members to the behavioral exchanges by which the work of the group is done.

Focus on Behavior

There are theoretical and practical reasons for attending to individual behaviors in the group and dyadic encounter: theoretically, behaviors are the public building blocks for the social and interpersonal constructions we fashion about our groups and about their members (McArthur and Baron, 1983). Those constructions sustain the interactions that promote processes enabling social units to facilitate goal attainment for individuals and their social units. If we wish to change the nature and quality of those constructions, and enhance their process, we need to understand what behaviors link to those constructions and those processes.

Those behaviors may be construed as resource exchanges, adding to or subtracting from others' security or independence, inclusion or status. Rules about resource exchange fall into the area of justice concerns, and these concerns, if mismanaged, can have destructive consequences in any culture (Tedeschi and Bond, 2001). Broadly speaking, we must all coordinate our performances with those of relevant others in order to achieve the outcomes that we need to sustain life. We are dependent upon the contributions of others for the success of our projects and learn a multitude of influence tactics to sustain their continued inputs. The legitimacy of tactic use is culturally mandated for the roles we are playing in any encounter, so that acceptable equity is maintained in the exchange process.

Dysfluencies inevitably arise during these complex and sustained interactions. Our interaction partners have additional projects that distract them from contributing their time, energy and tools to our joint task. When we attempt to influence a greater resource allocation to our joint project, they may consider that we are behaving illegitimately and retaliate rather than comply (Tedeschi and Bond, 2001). In the course of task performance, our interaction partners may come to believe that we are failing to provide the social rewards and material inputs required for an equitable exchange.

Interpersonal encounters are at risk when inequities are construed to have occurred. Depending on the strength of social forces acting for cohesion, members may exit in various ways. Individuals differ in their skill at detecting such exits by others, in the value they attach to further engagement with the other, and in their ability to confront such disengagements in a procedurally fair way. Although there are cultural differences in such justice issues (Leung and Morris, 2001), they are not great and allow for considerable variability across individuals within the same culture. So, the issue in inter-cultural dyads will not be to know the cultural style of persons from the other culture as much as to monitor the interpersonal exchanges of one's particular group members, ever vigilant to emerging equity issues.

These equity issues are relevant to intra-cultural encounters, of course, and skill in their management is probably a fundamental component of social intelligence in any culture (Salovey and Meyer, 1990). My position, however, is that such concerns arise out of behavioral exchanges construed as resource transactions. It is these transactions that construct the conceptions we develop about one another, which drive our interpersonal processes, which produce our unit outcomes, which in turn shape how we conceptualize our relationships and our unit. We must learn what those behavioral exchanges are if we wish to intervene and change dyadic or group outcomes, be they intra-cultural or inter-cultural.

Recent work by Leung and Tong (2002) is most welcome in this regard. Applying a justice framework to inter-cultural negotiations, they argue that it is important to discover "whether justice concepts are operationalized similarly (i.e., manifested by similar behaviors and practices) across cultures." (p. 2) They point out that justice must be "enacted", so "information about justice rules and criteria is insufficient in guiding people how to act fairly in a foreign culture and in facilitating intercultural negotiation by reducing the perception of injustice." (p. 7) To facilitate such inter-cultural negotiations, they propose the concept of "justice yardsticks", i.e., "operational definitions of justice criteria. Justice yardsticks are applied to evaluate acts of an actor, his/her attributes, or output that he/she generates to arrive at a justice judgment." (p. 10) These yardsticks apply to the fundamental areas of distributive, procedural, interactional, and informational justice and are hypothesized to vary in theoretically meaningful ways as a function of culture.

Importantly for present purposes, justice yardsticks are more proximal to behavior than the previously studied justice rules and criteria. A research focus on their application to enactments will facilitate the development of user-friendlier inputs for inter-cultural training. An escalating focus on behavior in all areas of cross-cultural social psychology will likewise result in findings that attract a wider audience of persons whose mandate is to apply knowledge about cultural differences.

"Practice is the only test of truth".
(Deng Hsiao Ping)

Conclusion

These reflections emerge out of my experience in writing a textbook summarizing our disciplinary progress in doing social psychology across cultures. In assessing the yield, I consider that we have contributed little by way of usable knowledge to practitioners whose mandate is to facilitate interactions across cultural lines.

Our colleagues in business studies have done considerably better, perhaps because they are pushed by their consumers' demands for relevance. Consequently, they push themselves to think strategically about how to marry theory with practice (see e. g., Latham, 2002). They look more carefully at how outcomes get done, focusing more attentively on behavior, an even more difficult and sobering focus when working across cultural groups.

This attention to behavior is welcome, since it provides fodder for teaching our clients what to do more and what to do less in order to facilitate their cross-cultural exchanges, either in dyads or in groups. I hypothesize that many of these effective behaviors exercise much the same social impact within a given culture as they do across cultures. Successful interactions probably look much the same regardless of the cultural backgrounds of the persons involved. That assertion is testable, although rarely tested, and I propose that more behaviorally focused research be done to compare inter-cultural interactions with intra-cultural interactions. Perhaps there are some distinctive qualities of effective cross-cultural persons, inter-cultural exchanges, and culturally diverse groups. Comparative, behaviorally focused research will help us decide.

Note

I wish to express my appreciation for the various inputs made towards writing this paper by thoughtful, informed, and judicious inputs from Ritchie Bent, Chris Earley, Kwok Leung, Romie Littrell, Andy Tomas, and Dean Tjosvold.

References

Altemeyer, B. (1988), *Enemies of freedom: Understanding right-wing authoritarianism*. San Francisco, CA: Jossey-Bass.

Anderson, L. E. (1994), A new look at an old construct: Cross-cultural adaptation. International Journal of Intercultural Relations, 18, 293-328.

Arendt-Toth, J. (2002), The adaptation of Turkish immigrants in the Netherlands. Unpublished doctoral dissertation, Tilburg University.

Bales, R. F. (1950), Interaction process analysis. Cambridge, MA: Addison-Wesley.

Berry, J. W., & Kalin, R. (1995), Multicultural and ethnic attitudes in Canada: An overview of the 1991 national survey. Canadian Journal of Behavioral Science, 27, 301-320.

Bhawuk, D. P. S. (2001), Evolution of culture assimilators: Toward theory-based assimilators. International Journal of Intercultural Relations, 25, 141-163.

Black, J. S., & Porter, L. W. (1991), Managerial behaviors and job performance: A successful manager in Los Angeles may not succeed in Hong Kong. International Journal of Business Studies, 22, 99-113.

Bond, M. H. (1994), Trait theory and cross-cultural studies of person perception. Psychological Inquiry, 5, 114-117

Brown, P. and Levinson, S. (1987), Politeness: Some universals in language use. Cambridge, England: Cambridge University Press.

Cannon_Bowers, J. A., Tannenbaum, S. I., Salas, E., & Volpe, C. E. (1995), Defining competencies and establishing team training requirements. In R. A. Guzzo, Salas, E. and associates (Eds.), Team effectiveness and decision making in organizations (pp. 333-380). San Francisco, CA: Jossey-Bass.

Clark, H. H., & Brennan, S. E. (1991), Grounding in communication. In L. B. Resnick, J. M. Levine, & S. D. Teasley (Eds.), Perspectives on socially shared communication (pp. 127-149). Washington, DC: American Psychological Association.

Distefano, J. J., & Maznevski, M. (2000), Creating value with diverse teams in global management. Organizational Dynamics, 29, 45-63.

Du Babcock, B., Babcock, R.D., Ng, P. and Lai, R. (1995), A comparison of use of L1 and L2 in small-group business decision-making meetings. Research Monograph 6, Department of English, City University of Hong Kong.

Elron, E. (1997), Top management teams within multinational corporations: Effects of cultural heterogeneity. Leadership Quarterly, 8, 393-412.

Earley, P. C., & Gibson, C. B. (2002), Multinational work teams: A new perspective. Manwah, NJ: Lawrence Erlbaum.

Foa, U. G. (1971), Interpersonal and economic resources. Science, 171, 345-351.

Fontaine, G. (1990), Cultural diversity in intimate intercultural relationships. In D. Cahn (Ed.), Intimates in conflict: A communication perspective (pp. 209-224). Hillsdale, NJ: Erlbaum.

Gallois, C., Franklyn-Stokes, A., Giles, H., & Coupland, N. (1988). Communication accommodation in intercultural encounters. In Y. Y. Kim, & W. B. Gudykunst (Eds.), Theories in intercultural communication (pp. 157-185). Newbury Park, CA: Sage.

Giacalone, R. A., & Rosenfeld, P. (Eds.) (1991). Applied impression management (pp. 195-215). Newbury Park, CA: Sage.

Gudykunst, W. B. (1998), Bridging differences: Effective intergroup communication (3rd ed.). Thousand Oaks, CA: Sage.

Gudykunst, W. B., & Bond, M. H. (1997), Intergroup relations across cultures. In J. Berry, M. Segall, and C. Kagitçibasi (Eds.), Handbook of cross-cultural psychology (pp. 119-161). Needham Heights, MA: Allyn and Bacon.

Harrison, D. A., Price, K. H., & Bell, M. P. (1998), Beyongd relational demography: Time and the effects of surface- and deep-level diversity on work group cohesion. Academy of Management Journal, 41, 96-107.

Harzing, A-W. (1995), The persistent myth of high expatriate failure rates, International Journal of Human Resource Management, 6, 457-475.

Hogan, R. (1996), A socioanalytic perspective on the five-factor model. In J. S. Wiggins (Ed.), The five-factor model of personality: Theoretical perspectives (pp. 163-179). New York: Guilford Press.

Hsu, F. L. K. (1971), Psychological homeostasis and jen: Conceptual tools for advancing psychological anthropology. American Anthropologist, 73, 23-44.

Humana, C. (1986), World human rights guide. London: Pan.

Latham, G. (2001), The reciprocal transfer of learning from journals to practice. Applied Psychology: An International Journal, 50, 201-211.

Leung, K., & Morris, M. (2001), Justice through the lens of culture and ethnicity. In Sanders, J., & Hamilton, V. L. (Eds.). Handbook of justice research in law (pp. 343-378). New York, NY: Kluwer Academic/Plenum Publishers.

Leung, K., & Tong, K. K. (2002), Justice across cultures: A three stage model for intercultural negotiation. Unpublished manuscript, City University of Hong Kong.

Leung, S. K., & Bond, M. H. (2001), Interpersonal communication and personality: Self and other perspectives. Asian Journal of Social Psychology, 4, 69-86.

McArthur, L. Z., & Baron, R. M. (1983), Toward an ecological theory of social perception, Psychological Review, 90, 215-38.

McAuley, P., Bond, M.H., & Kashima, E. (2002), Towards defining situations objectively: A culture-level analysis of role dyads in Hong Kong and Australia. Journal of Cross-Cultural Psychology, 33, 363-380.

McCrae, R. R., & Costa, P. T. (1997), Personality trait structure as a human universal. American Psychologist, 52, 509-516.

McGrath, J. E., Arrow, H., & Berdahl, J. L. (1999), Cooperation and conflict as manifestations of coordination in small groups. Polish Psychological Bulletin, 30, 1-14.

Mendoza-Denton, R., Downey, G., Purdie, V., Davis, A., & Pietrzak, J. (in press). Sensitivity to status-based rejection: Implications for African-American students' college experience. Journal of Personality and Social Psychology.

Ng, I. W. C., & Bond, M. H. (2002), Personality, group process and group performance: A group level analysis. Manuscript submitted for publication.

Pekerti, A., & Thomas, D. C. (in press). Communication in intercultural interaction: An empirical investigation of idiocentric and sociocentric communication styles. Journal of Cross-Cultural Psychology.

Ruben, B. D., & Kealey, D. J. (1979), Behavioral assessment of communication competency and the prediction of cross-cultural adaptation. International Journal of Intercultural Relations, 3, 15-47.

Salovey, P., & Meyer, J. D. (1990), Emotional intelligence. Imagination, Cognition and Personality, 9, 185-211.

Schmitz, P. G. (1996), Acculturation: The relevance of open-mindedness as a moderator variable. Paper presented at the 13th Congress of the International Association of Cross-Cultural Psychology, Montreal, July.

Smith, P. B, & Bond, M. H. (1998), Social psychology across cultures (2nd ed.). London: Prentice Hall International.

Soderberg, A-M, & Holden, N. (2002), Rethinking cross cultural management in a globalizing business world. International Journal of Cross-Cultural Management, 2, 103-121.

Steiner, I. D. (1972), Group process and productivity. New York: Academic Press.

Tam, B. K. Y., & Bond, M. H. (2002), Interpersonal behaviors and friendship in a Chinese culture. Asian Journal of Social Psychology, 5, 63-74.

Tedeschi, J. T., & Bond, M. H. (2001), Aversive behavior and aggression in cross-cultural perspective. In R. Kowalski (Ed.), Behaving badly: Aversive behaviors in interpersonal relationships (pp. 257-293). Washington, DC: APA Books.

Thomas, D.C., & Ravlin, E.C. (1995), Responses of employees to cultural adaptation by a foreign manager. Journal of Applied Psychology, 80, 133-46.

Trapnell, P. D. (1994), Openness versus intellect: A lexical left turn. European Journal of Personality, 8, 273-290.

Ward, C. (1996). Acculturation. In D. Landis, & R. S. Bhagat (Eds.), Handbook of intercultural training (2nd ed.) (pp. 124-147), Thousand Oaks, CA: Sage.

Watson, W.E., Kumar, K., & Michaelsen, L.K. (1993), Cultural diversity's impact on interaction process and performance: Comparing homogeneous and diverse task groups. Academy of Management Journal, 36, 590-602.

Wiggins, J. S., & Trapnell, P. D. (1996), A dyadic-interactional perspective on the five-factor model. In J. S. Wiggins (Ed.), The five-factor model of personality: Theoretical perspectives (pp. 88-162). New York: Guilford Press.

Chapter 4

Meeting the Challenge of Cultural Difference

Peter B. Smith

Meeting the Challenge of Cultural Difference

Many years ago, social scientists were already outlining a self-evident truth concerning difference: 'Every man is in certain respects like all other men, like some other men and like no other man' (Kluckhohn and Murray, 1948). If we leave to one side these authors' failure to consider women worthy of inclusion, their formulation encapsulates some of the difficulties to be faced as we seek ways of best handling cultural differences. Human beings in general clearly have a great deal in common with one another. Selected populations, such as those to be found among the ranks of middle and senior level managers have even more in common with one another. Yet it often proves to be the differences between them that stand in the way of effective collaborative working.

The aspirations of many social scientists to be first and foremost scientists has sidelined the exploration of these differences. The culture of psychology in particular has been one in which the prevalent assumption has been that generalisations about universals are what should be most highly esteemed. This has led to neglect of variability and difference. This can occur through reliance on samples restricted to single nations and atypical samples within them, such as students. Alternatively, it can occur through neglect of important sources of variability within one's samples and treatment of that variability as 'error variance'. My own development as a researcher has reflected these priorities. Early work focused upon very distinctive samples of managers working within a single nation. In the eighties, I became interested in Japanese managers and this led me gradually toward a widening focus on comparative studies of managers. Most recently, I have become aware of the growing practical importance of work relationships across cultural boundaries, and this chapter focuses upon some ways in which we can address this issue more directly.

Psychologists have long addressed aspects of difference through the study of personality. Here too, the predominant emphasis has been upon identifying the universal dimensions along which personalities may vary. Indeed, substantial evidence has been accumulated that personality in many parts of the world varies along five principal dimensions (McCrae and Costa, 1997). Progress in this direction might suggest to some that interactions between persons from different cultures could be understood by a detailed examination of the personality structures of those involved, or by examining the prevalence of different personality types in different cultures. Suppose one could show for instance that rather more Americans than Hong Kong Chinese score high on extraversion, it should be possible to predict some of the things that will occur when Americans negotiate with Hong Kong Chinese. In this case, we even have evidence that Americans and Hong Kong Chinese agree that these differences in typical personality do in fact exist (Bond, 1986). This type of thinking achieved a certain popularity among 'culture and personality' theorists in the mid-twentieth century (Piker, 1998). I have also found that managers who find difficulty in working with someone from another culture rather often attribute the problem to 'personality differences'. However, there are two reasons why we should take a more complex view of cultural difference. Firstly, we now have a clearer understanding of different levels of analysis. Secondly, we can better distinguish the relationship between universals and their contextual expression.

Levels of Analysis

A major step toward conceptualising cultural difference was achieved by the publication of Hofstede's (1980) study of IBM managers around the world. His focus has been consistently upon differences between nations rather than between individuals. It may not always be ideal to equate nations with cultures, but the core of his contribution is contained in the notion that individuals are socialised within distinctive contexts and that this 'collective programming of the mind' is what defines particular cultures. Someone who later becomes a manager may be born with particular personality predispositions. However, the way in which he or she learns to express these dispositions will be fashioned by the family, the educational systems, the work teams and the organisational systems in which he or she subsequently participates. Even at one particular point in an individual's life history, their basic personality may find expression in different ways, in response to the culturally-defined expectations that prevail in the specific settings in which they engage. Thus, to predict behaviour in a given setting one needs to choose an appropriate level of analysis. Hofstede's focus on predicting only culture-level phenomena is for the most part sustained in his recent development of the same data base (Hofstede, 2001). Those influenced by his project have rather often used his country scores to try to predict individual behaviours, thereby failing to grasp what can and cannot be done with his country scores. It is indeed often the case that what we need is an explanation of the behaviour of a small sample of individual managers, rather than of a nation as a whole. In that sense, Hofstede's exclusive focus on culture-level explanations may have led us away from what is most practically useful (Bond, 2002). Indeed, Hofstede himself does occasionally lapse into individual-level interpretations based on culture-level scores (Smith, 2002). However, the lasting benefit to me of Hofstede's perspective has been the awareness of the importance of choosing the right level of analysis in studying managerial behaviour cross-culturally.

Universals in Context

A fierce debate among personality psychologists over the past several decades has concerned the degree to which behaviour is a product of personality or a product of the specific situations in which one is present. As with some other long-running debates, there may be no definitive answer to the question posed, because the question is posed in the wrong way. As outlined in the previous section, behaviour will always be a function both of the individual and of the cultural context. However, this reformulation of a debate that is initially cast in terms of 'either/or' into a resolution as 'both/and' is particularly useful to cross-culturalists. Research into cross-cultural aspects of organizational behaviour has often focussed upon whether or not certain phenomena are universal. For instance, is value-based or transformational leadership always effective (House, Hanges, Ruiz-Quintanilla et al., 1999), does teamwork enhance performance (Earley, 1993; Earley and Gibson, 2002) and do people respond to equity-based reward systems (Leung, 1997)?

The perspective of the Japanese psychologist Misumi has strongly influenced the stance I take towards such questions. Misumi (1985) has been primarily a theorist of leadership. He proposes that leadership always has both 'general' functions and 'specific' functions. The general functions are twofold: to get the task done and to maintain work team relationships, in order that the task can continue be accomplished. These are universals, inherent in almost any definition of leadership. However, Misumi differs from the emphases of most Western leadership researchers in asserting that the specific ways in which these two functions are best accomplished will vary according to every specific situation. Thus effective leadership is both universal and highly situation specific, not one or the other. If one wants to emphasise the universal aspect, one would do best to define a measure of leadership that is worded in rather general terms, whereas the specific aspect would be brought out by very detailed questions about moment to moment behaviours. In a study of electronics assembly plants in Hong Kong, Japan, UK and USA, Smith, Misumi, Peterson, Tayeb and Bond (1989) used both general and specific items. The specific and the general items correlated with each other in different ways at the different locations, but the general items predicted some effectiveness measures at all locations (Smith, Peterson, Misumi and Bond, 1992).

While Misumi's model was formulated in relation to leadership, it has much broader potential for the avoidance of sterile debates about universality versus cultural specificity. By phrasing measures in general terms, we can (if we wish to do so) make it likely that we will conclude that some aspect of organizational behaviour is universal. By using locally distinctive terms, we can favour an indigenous perspective.

Redefining the Problem

So far it has been argued that in understanding cross-cultural aspects of management, we should choose the right level of analysis and attend to specifics as well as universals. How does this affect what we should do next? Firstly, we should scrutinise carefully the cultural 'maps' of the world that have guided cross-culturalists over the past decade or two. Secondly, we should consider more closely the nature of the specific cross-cultural contexts within which managers and organisational employees work.

The principal map of the world that has guided cross-culturalists has been that provided by Geert Hofstede. Indeed, even that map has been only partially scrutinised. While Hofstede identified four dimensions of cultural variation, most investigators have chosen to contrast nations that he found to be individualistic (particularly USA) with those that he found to be somewhat more collectivistic (principally Japan and Hong Kong). When differences have been found, these differences are then interpreted in terms of individualism and collectivism. In other words, continuing with the metaphor, when investigators drew samples from USA and Japan, they assumed that they were in fact in the locations specified by Hofstede's map. However, Hofstede's map was drawn on the basis of co-ordinates provided by IBM employees 35 years ago. The business world is undergoing rapid change. To be more sure of where one is, the modern investigator needs his or her own compass. They need to locate their samples by measuring the samples' own stance toward individualism, collectivism or whatever other values are considered relevant. We have other more recent maps, suggesting that the cultural differences surveyed by Hofstede are indeed still there (Schwartz, 1994; Smith, Dugan and Trompenaars, 1996; Smith, Peterson and Schwartz, 2002), but all that such maps can do is to provide indications of culture-level differences. National cultures are not by any means homogeneous and we still need to know what is the orientation of the particular individuals who have been sampled within a given study.

Having said this, culture-level maps remain useful. They provide a ready source of hypotheses as to the types of difference in managerial practices and organisational responses that may be expected in different parts of the world. They can also be used to make sure that our stereotypes about particular nations become more accurate. For instance, we can dispose of the widespread and incorrect belief that because Communist ideology favoured collectivism, therefore managers in former Soviet bloc countries will think in collectivist ways. We can also use these maps as part of programmes of training in cross-cultural awareness of all those engaged in multicultural aspects of business. Knowing what is the range of ways that managers handle their work, and knowing how one's own particular style fits onto the overall map are useful antidotes to ethnocentric thinking.

A second and in many ways crucial point is that there is a divergence between the information that cultural maps provide and the actual working circumstances that are increasingly prevalent. Maps tell us about differences between the average values of managers or organization members drawn from particular nations, and they are used to predict the behaviours of members of those nations. The assumption most typically and implicitly made is that these predictions about how employees from a particular nation will behave will hold true regardless of who they are actually working with. However, in contemporary business settings, it is quite frequently the case that I shall be working with persons who are not from the same national culture as myself. My contact with them may be long-term and face-to-face, or it may be transient or be mediated by e-mail or video-conferencing. I am not at all likely to behave in the same way in all these different settings. To put it another way, I am not likely to be a very effective manager if my behaviour is in fact invariant across all these types of situations.

Few researchers have investigated whether managers behave differently in the presence of those from other nations. Those who have done so have found quite marked differences. Rao and Hashimoto (1996) studied Japanese managers who had either Japanese or Canadian subordinates. With Canadian subordinates, they reported behaving more assertively, using more appeals to reason, made more threats and more appeals to higher authority. With Japanese subordinates, they made more frequent use of indirect forms of influence. Thomas and Ravlin (1995) showed videotapes of a Japanese supervisor to U.S. employees of a Japanese firm. Those who saw a tape where the supervisor had somewhat adapted his behaviour to US styles evaluated him as more effective than those who saw a tape where he had not. However, the Japanese supervisor who behaved in a totally American way was perceived as not genuine. Thus effective behaviour is not simply a matter of slavishly imitating the behaviours found in the others' culture. These two studies suggest that cultural maps may provide rather inaccurate guides to how managers actually behave in cross-national settings. Cross-cultural effectiveness will not simply be a matter of holding an accurate stereotype of how persons from another nation often behave, nor of reproducing that behaviour. It will entail knowledge of how one's own habitual behaviours are perceived by persons from particular other cultures, and skill in adapting these behaviours in ways that do convey intended messages. Given that at least one of the parties involved is likely not to be speaking their first language, this is no easy task. Cross-cultural psychologists have made extensive studies of the adaptations to intercultural contact made by long-term immigrants (Berry and Sam, 1997). However, the applicability of the models developed by Berry and others to short or long-term expatriate managers has been little explored.

In studying managers working cross-nationally, it is important to stay within the guidelines suggested above. In other words, we shall learn little by trying to identify universals of cross-cultural effectiveness. We shall learn more by identifying specific situations within which cross-cultural working occurs and examining how those situations are handled. In the next section of this chapter, two studies are reviewed that took this perspective.

Cross-Cultural Event Management

In an attempt to move the focus of leadership research toward a closer focus on the interaction between leaders and situations, Smith and Peterson (1998) proposed an 'event management' theory of leadership. In brief, what they proposed was that leaders are faced with an unending stream of work events, whose meaning is initially ambiguous. By drawing on a variety of sources of internal and external sources of guidance, leaders then determine how best to handle each event, sometimes very quickly and almost automatically, at other times only after protracted thought and consultation. The majority of studies completed that have used this perspective have involved comparisons of samples of managers from different nations (Smith, Peterson and Schwartz, 2002). Here we are concerned only with two studies that focused upon cross-national working.

Joint Venture Hotels

The first of these concerned Chinese middle-level managers working within joint venture hotels in the mid-nineties (Smith, Wang and Leung, 1997). Each of these managers was collaborating directly with a non-Chinese manager working at the same location. In almost all cases the non-Western manager was the superior of the Chinese manager. Preliminary interviews identified nine recurring work events that were seen as potentially problematic. These comprised the following:

- Ways of making decisions
- Ways of allocating tasks
- Punctuality
- Conduct of meetings
- Bonus payments
- Procedures for appointing middle managers
- Poor work by subordinates
- Work co-ordination
- Language problems

A questionnaire was then constructed which described two alternative ways of handling each event. For example, for task allocation, the alternatives were that responsibility should either be assigned to individuals or to teams. Chinese respondents were asked which way of handling each event they preferred, and whether this type of event had been a problem to them. If they responded that they had experienced problems, further ratings were then requested as to how much they had relied on a variety of different ways of handling each problem event and how well the events had in fact been handled. Among the 144 respondents, the frequency of reported problem events varied substantially, depending upon the nationality of their expatriate superior. Among 82 local managers with a superior from Hong Kong or Taiwan, 38 per cent of all work events were reported as problematic. Among 27 local managers with a superior from Japan, 58 per cent of events were rated problematic. Among 35 local managers with a Western superior, 60 per cent were problematic.

The local managers were next asked to rate how effectively each event had been handled and how much they had relied on seven possible ways of handling the problem events. These were:

- Following the usual policies and procedures
- Seeking to avoid differences
- Taking advice from other Chinese
- Using the overseas manager's approach
- Using indirect influence
- Talking directly
- Relying on widespread beliefs

The results showed that six of the events were rated as better handled where the superior was a Western manager. Ratings were lowest where the superior was Japanese. However care is needed in interpreting these differences: the ratings refer only to problematic events, and problem events arose less frequently where the superior was from Hong Kong or China. Thus we should say that where problems did arise, they were resolved better when there was a Western manager.

The main interest of these results lies in the relationship between how respondents reported that problem events had actually been handled and what they said was the most effective way to handle events. The ways of handling events that were reported as being used most frequently were those that are most consistent with traditional Chinese culture, namely using indirect influence and relying on widespread Chinese beliefs. However, the ways that were rated most effective were quite different. There was some variance between events, but the most significant predictors of effectiveness were reported to be following the overseas manager's approach, direct talk and following usual policies and procedures. Regression analyses also revealed significant interactions, indicating that respondents found different ways effective with superiors from different locations. For instance, direct talk was seen as ineffective with Japanese supervisors, but not with others.

This study provides a clear illustration of managers struggling with how best to handle cultural difference. On the one hand they had a cultural awareness of the ways of handling events that was most effective with partners from various different cultural backgrounds. On the other hand, their own reported behaviours showed no correlation with this awareness. They had not learned the cultural flexibility that was detected among Japanese managers in the study by Rao and Hashimoto (1996). In some ways, the results of the hotel study are unsurprising. The data were collected at a time of very rapid change in China, and other data collected from the managers who were sampled indicated that they were at that time still evaluating their current work situation relative to prior experiences in Chinese state enterprises (Leung, Smith, Wang and Sun, 1996). More recently, their attention has become much more focussed upon emulating their joint venture expatriate partners (Leung, Smith and Wang, in press). They have learned better how to work with difference.

Belarus Joint Ventures

A further study within joint ventures was completed more recently in Belarus, using similar methods (Smith, Yanchuk and Sekun, 2001). In this case, a survey was first undertaken of 338 managers working in indigenous Belarus organisations. The methods used were the same as those employed in the multination event management project (Smith, Peterson and Schwartz, 2002). This showed that, in common with the neighbouring nations of Poland, Slovakia and Ukraine, prevailing ways of handling work events involve very strong reliance on one's superior (Smith, Kruzela, Groblewska et al., 2000). In fact, management in these nations appears to involve stronger reliance on superiors than in any of the other 47 nations that have been sampled.

The joint venture study involved both quantitative and qualitative data collection. Initial interviews indicated the need for some adaptation of the questionnaire used in China. The first seven work events were retained and a new set of six ways of handling work events was constructed. Joint venture enterprises in Belarus are mostly rather small, but quite numerous. The questionnaire was completed by 172 Belarus employees, who were working within 75 different joint venture organizations. Joint venture partners were predominantly Poland, Germany, USA and UK, but included seven other nations. A series of extensive interviews were also conducted with 15 expatriate managers and 15 local managers.

The questionnaire data indicated that respondents made no very sharp distinctions between the seven work events. All were seen as moderately well handled, and all were reported to be handled in relatively similar ways. The most strongly endorsed ways of handling events were compliance with the supervisor, following organisational policies and avoidance of conflict. There were few significant variations related to the nationality of the joint venture partner. However, employees within U.S. joint ventures were more likely to seek advice from other Belarus employees and to seek allies among Belarus colleagues in advancing their viewpoint. Thus the questionnaire data indicate that the hierarchical context that prevails within Belarus organisations exists also within Belarus joint ventures. Belarus faces adverse economic and political circumstances and these data provide sparse evidence that the arrival of joint ventures has had much effect on work place relations.

The interview data provided some rather more vivid illustrations of the challenges faced by these joint ventures. By conducting a series of interviews with each of the individual managers, a much more frank portrayal of prevailing circumstances was obtained. The first interview was relatively structured, while later ones elicited greater spontaneity. The comments quoted in Tables 4.1 and 4.2 indicate a situation of substantial mutual antipathy and stereotyping.

Table 4.1: Typical comments from expatriate managers

They avoid making decisions
They will not share thoughts openly
My partners are not honest
I feel hostility here
I pay good money, which they do not deserve
They should be thankful for such high pay
I do not delegate
Democracy is not demanded here
We use meetings to announce decisions that have already been made
The locals are working for themselves, not for me
The idea that all Russians are comrades is dead. They are only interested in money
Most of them are Soviet, with no desire for change

Table 4.2: Typical comments from Belarus local managers

When we try to explain local circumstances, we get a cold reception
They demand prompt performance without any allowance for our traditions
They deal with us as second rate aborigines
We get only one answer: Do it, we are paying you
A second rate expatriate is always preferred over a talented local
We do get information, but we do not trust it
Yes, there are meetings, but the decisions are already taken
There is pay discrimination against locals
If somebody wants my work to improve, he must respect me
I work poorly, to protest against discrimination

This data clearly indicates a set of circumstances in which joint venture organisations were falling well short of optimal effectiveness. Given greater resources than were available to these organisations, there is no doubt that much could be done to create improvements. However, from the point of view of the argument being advanced in this chapter, it is the data derived from the expatriate managers that is of greatest interest. The sample is tiny, so that definitive testing is out of the question. However, it is very unlikely that one could have predicted the perspective of these managers from a scrutiny of the Hofstede scores for their countries. They may of course have been specifically selected by their employers for work in Belarus on the basis of their preferred style of management. More likely they were selected on the basis of their relevant technical skills and/or ability to speak Russian. In any event, the quoted comments give some suggestion of attempting to implement preferred styles of management and then opting for a more coercive approach when it failed. For instance, they comment that employees do not share thoughts openly and do not desire democracy. In other words, these managers are speaking as though they have adapted their behaviour to prevailing local circumstances.

Conclusion

The two studies of joint venture employees have been discussed at rather greater length than those covered earlier, because they bear upon the central argument advanced in this chapter. If the context within which one works with a person from another culture elicits different types of behaviour, then cultural maps will be a poor guide to what happens in such circumstances. One could argue that the cultural map that was provided by Hofstede was itself drawn from a multinational organisation within which persons from many nations worked together. Consequently it might provide us with a relatively 'adapted' version of how managers behave within multicultural contexts. However, that line of argument would lead us toward a generalised model of how managers might behave in multicultural contexts in general. It is argued here that a sharper focus on more specific settings, events and contexts and indeed the passage of time is needed if we are to see clearly how managers contend with difference.

Large organizations in the US and elsewhere have struggled with the dilemmas of how to manage workforce diversity even within a single nation. Within the multinational context the same dilemmas are writ even larger. Acculturation researchers have noted how both immigrants and host nations are affected by one another over time. In a similar way, we can expect that within successful multinationals, joint ventures and especially mergers and acquisitions, there will occur over time a process of personal and organisational reconciliation of difference. To understand that process and to understand when and why it succeeds or fails will require much closer scrutiny.

Cross-cultural work relationships in the two settings that I have studied can both be considered as failures. In China, the Chinese hotel managers were aware that other ways of behaving would be more effective, but they had not found ways of changing their actual behaviours. Rather than apportion blame to them for this, we might enquire why their more senior non-Chinese partners had not initiated any form of training or other interventions to improve the situation. In Belarus, it appears that the expatriate managers had adapted their behaviour to local circumstances, but this had simply entailed a substantial lowering of their expectations as to the levels of effective performance that could be accomplished.

There are currently several perspectives on how to achieve more effective cross-cultural work relationships. Some favour improved selection and training for expatriate managers (e.g. Mendenhall, Kuhlmann and Stahl, 2001), while others assert that multinational organisations can make cultural differences irrelevant through effective knowledge management procedures (Holden, 2001). Undoubtedly, selecting managers who not only have relevant technical skills but also have skills in handling personal difference is helpful. Equally, a company that can diffuse the knowledge that drives everyday operating procedures will benefit from that. However, both these perspectives seem to me to involve subscribing to the idea that globalisation is going to involve increasing convergence toward a uniform set of business practices. I remain sceptical that cultural differences will prove so malleable.

In my view, effective management of difference will continue to require managers who can use their experience to think creatively about local circumstances. For instance, while undertaking the Chinese hotel study, I interviewed an expatriate manager working in another industry. His problem was that his subordinate managers wished to continue the traditional local practice of hiring relatives to work in their departments. He on the other hand was concerned to control mounting costs. This problem was addressed by creating devolved budgets for each department and permitting managers to hire whomever they wished. Since budgetary limits were rigidly enforced, the subordinate managers had a strong incentive to hire only relatives who were also effective workers. The expatriate manager had thus created a solution that integrated local and global priorities. Worm (1997) describes similar strategies adopted by Scandinavian managers working in China. Innovations were implemented in ways whereby local managers took ownership of them and loss of face was thereby minimised.

These instances are examples of the creation of what Earley and Mosakowski (2000) describe as hybrid cultures. The difficulties inherent in working across cultural boundaries are resolved not by the imposition of one pattern of cultural preference over another, but by the creation of a third pattern of preferences. Hybrid cultures may have elements of two or more cultures of origin. Indeed, a key element in the work of Earley and Mosakowski is a demonstration that teams with members drawn from numerous cultural backgrounds are better able to create hybrid cultures than teams whose members are drawn from just two differing cultures. Their teams were composed of peers. More typically, as in the two studies that have been reviewed here in more detail, some element of hierarchy is involved, and this places disproportionate emphasis on the cultural origins of the more senior manager, usually an expatriate.

A priority for the future is thus more extensive study of hybrid cultures and how effective managers set about creating them. In formulating hypotheses for such studies in any specific context, we can still draw on the culture-level maps provided by Hofstede and others. However, we need also to be more courageous in knowing when to fold up the maps and put them away. Some time ago Ratiu (1983) made a study of peer evaluations of managers in the French business school, INSEAD. Managers perceived as 'most international' were those who did hold stereotypic beliefs about how others from other nations behaved, but who were also especially observant of particular behaviours of individuals that did not fit the stereotype. These novel or surprising behaviours were then treated as the basis for learning. As researchers, we too need to venture more into settings where multicultural working is under way and learn from what we see.

References

Berry, J. W. & Sam, D. L. (1997), Acculturation and adaptation. In J. W. Berry, M. H. Segall & C. Kagitçibasi (Eds.) *Handbook of cross-cultural psychology*, Second edition, Volume 3. Needham Heights MA: Allyn & Bacon.

Bond, M. H. (1986), Mutual stereotypes and the facilitation of interaction across cultural lines. *International Journal of Intercultural Relations, 10*, 259-276.

Bond, M. H. (2002), Reclaiming the individual from Hofstede's ecological analysis: A 20 year odyssey. *Psychological Bulletin, 128*, 73-77.

Earley, P. C. (1993), East meets west meets mid-east: Further explorations of collectivistic versus individualistic work groups. *Academy of Management Journal, 36*, 319-348.

Earley, P. C. & Gibson, C. B. (2002), *Multinational work teams: A new perspective.* Mahwah, NJ: Erlbaum.

Earley, P. C. & Mosakowski, E. (2000), Creating hybrid team cultures: An empirical test of transnational team functioning. *Academy of Management Journal, 43*, 26-49.

Hofstede, G. (1980), *Culture's consequences: International differences in work-related values.* Beverly Hills, CA: Sage.

Hofstede, G. (2001), *Culture's consequences: Comparing values, behaviors, institutions and organizations across nations.* Thousand Oaks, CA: Sage.

Holden, N. J. (2001), *Cross-cultural management: A knowledge management perspective.* Harlow, UK: Financial Times/Prentice-Hall.

House, R. J., Hanges, P. J., Ruiz-Quintanilla, S. A. & 141 co-authors. (1999), Cultural influences on leadership and organizations: Project GLOBE. *Advances in Global Leadership, 1*, 171-233.

Kluckhohn, C. & Murray, H. A. (1948), *Personality in nature, culture and society.* New York: Knopf.

Leung, K. (1997), Negotiation and reward allocation across cultures. In P.C. Earley & M. Erez (Eds.) *New perspectives on international/organizational psychology.* San Francisco, CA: New Lexington.

Leung, K., Smith, P. B., Wang, Z. M. & Sun H. (1996), Job satisfaction in joint venture hotels in China: An organizational justice analysis. *Journal of International Business Studies, 27*, 947-962.

Leung, K., Smith, P. B., & Wang, Z. M. (in press), Job attitudes and organizational justice in joint-venture hotels in China: The role of expatriate managers. *International Journal of Human Resource Management.*

McCrae, R. R., & Costa, P.T. (1997), Personality trait structure as a human universal. *American Psychologist, 52*, 509-516.

Mendenhall, M., Kuhlmann, T. M. & Stahl, G. (2001), *Developing global business leaders: Policies, processes and innovations.* Westport, CT: Quorum.

Misumi, J. (1985), *The behavioral science of leadership*. Ann Arbor, MI: University of Michigan Press.

Piker, S. (1998), Contributions of psychological anthropology. *Journal of Cross-Cultural Psychology*, **29**, 9-31.

Rao, A. & Hashimoto, K. (1996), Intercultural influence: A study of Japanese expatriate managers in Canada. *Journal of International Business Studies*, **27**, 443-466.

Ratiu, I. (1983), Thinking internationally: A comparison of how international executives learn. *International Studies of Management and Organisation*, **13**, 139-150.

Schwartz, S. H. (1994), Beyond individualism-collectivism: New dimensions of values. In U. Kim, H. C. Triandis, C. Kagitçibasi, Choi, S. C. & Yoon, G. (Eds.) *Individualism-collectivism: Theory, method and applications*. Thousand Oaks, CA: Sage.

Smith, P. B. (2002), Culture's consequences: Something old and something new. *Human Relations*, **55**, 119-135.

Smith, P. B., Dugan, S. & Trompenaars, F. (1996), National culture and the values of organisational employees: A dimensional analysis across 43 nations. *Journal of Cross-Cultural Psychology*, **27**, 231-264.

Smith, P. B., Kruzela, P., Groblewska, B., et al. (2000), Effective ways of handling work events in central and Eastern Europe. *Social Science Information*, **39**, 317-333.

Smith, P. B., Misumi, J., Peterson, M. F., Tayeb, M. H. & Bond, M. H. (1989), On the generality of leadership styles across cultures. *Journal of Occupational Psychology*, **62**, 97-110.

Smith, P. B. & Peterson, M. F. (1988), *Leadership, organisations and culture: An event management model*. London: Sage.

Smith, P. B., Peterson, M. F., Misumi, J. & Bond, M.H. (1992), A cross-cultural test of the Japanese PM leadership theory. *Applied Psychology: An International Review*, 41, 5-19.

Smith, P. B., Peterson, M. F., Schwartz, S. H. & 36 co-authors (2002), Cultural values, sources of guidance and their relevance to managerial behaviour: A 47 nation study. *Journal of Cross-Cultural Psychology*, **33**, 188-208.

Smith, P. B., Wang, Z. M. & Leung, K. (1997), Leadership, decision-making and cultural context. *Leadership Quarterly*, **8**, 413-431.

Smith, P. B., Yanchuk, V. A., & Sekun, V. I. (2001), *Management behaviour in Belarus organizations*. Report to International Association for the promotion of co-operation with scientists from the newly independent states of the former Soviet Union (INTAS): Brussels.

Thomas, D. C., & Ravlin, E. C. (1995), Responses of employees to cultural adaptation by a foreign manager. *Journal of Applied Psychology*, **80**, 133-146.

Worm, V. (1997), *Vikings and mandarins: Sino-Scandinavian business cooperation in cross-cultural settings*. Copenhagen: Copenhagen Business School Press.

Chapter 5

Using Emics and Etics in Cross-Cultural Organizational Studies: Universal and Local, Tacit and Explicit

Mark F. Peterson

S. Antonio Ruiz Quintanilla

The terms "emic" and "etic" that were originally developed in linguistics have been used in cross-cultural psychology and organizational research for the past three decades. These terms have been adapted and modified from their original use in linguistics in a variety of ways in order to address the specific conceptual and methodological issues most pressing in other fields. This chapter describes the original derivation of emic and etic, reviews the ways they have been adapted and used in organizational research, discusses the implications of some omissions and departures from how the terms were originally coined, and suggests specific steps that can be taken to constructively use them in cross-cultural survey and ethnographic studies of organizations. We recommend that the field progress from using these ideas for promoting efforts to develop globally equivalent concepts and measures to using them to develop an etic science that includes some concepts and measures that are globally equivalent, some that are useful only within a few societies, and even some that are locally unique.

Universal and Local, Tacit and Explicit

Place yourself in the position of a linguist who is working during the middle decades of the 20th century on a field project to analyze and create a written form of what has previously been only a spoken language. How do you begin? What substantive conclusions or analytic frameworks can you take from what others have already learned about sound structures and grammars from analyzing other languages? What methods can you apply or adapt from methods that previously have been developed for analyzing other languages? How can you use your own personal experience and your nature as a human being to understand this new situation? How can you effectively collaborate with people who have spent their lives speaking the language you will be analyzing, but who have never been schooled by modern science? What can you take back home from your analysis of the new language to provide an even better starting point for analyzing other languages?

And what lessons does this sort of experience by field linguistics have for scholars working with other quite different kinds of social phenomena? The problems that cross-cultural organization scholars have chosen to study to this point in our field's development have been linked to our research designs. These designs typically require comparing averages of survey responses, relationships between predictors and criteria, or responses to experimental conditions in different societies. All of these methods share one thing in common. The nature of the comparisons we usually choose to make require that the phenomena we study and measures we use be equivalent in the societies we compare. More rarely, we use qualitative methods to document idiosyncrasies of a specific organization or nation.

Cross-cultural organization scholars sometimes evoke a perspective on cross-cultural analysis developed by Pike (1967) to support the approach taken to comparative research. During the 1950s and 1960s, Pike (1967) provided what was at the time an innovative perspective on what linguists do when they take their scientific knowledge and go into the field to explicate the sound structure and grammar of previously unanalyzed and often unwritten languages. He recognized that linguists were scientists who took with them the tools and capabilities of science, but he also recognized that they were people who took with them the interpretive and analytic capabilities that are part of being human. Pike's observations have subsequently influenced both theory and methods in many social sciences, including international organizational studies (e.g., Brett et al., 1997; Cheng, 1996; Morris et al., 1999; Peterson and Pike, 2002). The applications of Pike's research to our field until now have typically reflected a methodological interest in promoting global equivalence in the concepts and methods we use.

Peterson and Pike (2002) retrace the steps that Pike took to adapt his work from language to behavior in general. In the present paper, we briefly summarize this process and provide some further suggestions about how the very unique research situation faced by field linguists can inform the way cross-cultural organizational scholars do their research. We begin by describing the use of Pike's ideas of "emics" and "etics" in other fields besides linguistics. We then provide a formal analysis of a set of concepts related to emics and etics based on a two dimensional rather than bipolar view of these ideas. We continue by describing some purposes that can be achieved by using a more complete view of emics and etics than is typically provided and note some steps that can be taken to achieve these purposes. In particular, we consider the utility of using multicultural research teams. We then consider applications to effective survey research design and interpretive ethnography. Throughout, we affirm some constructive adaptations of his work that already appear and also draw attention to what remains to be learned.

Clarifying the Use of Emics and Etics Outside Linguistics

The elements from Pike's perspective that have caught the most scholarly attention are his ideas of etics and emics. Pike derived these from the terms "phon*etics*" and "phon*emics*" that are used to describe elements of speech. A phonetic analysis is one that develops, tests, or extends what a scholar or scholarly school intends to be a comprehensive taxonomy or framework for categorizing all the sounds that people everywhere use for language. A phonemic analysis is one that documents the way in which sounds are used in a particular language. On the theoretical side, Pike's (1943) doctoral dissertation provided a comprehensive catalogue of the speech sounds that people are able to make. On the applied side, much of his initial fieldwork was dedicated to analyzing sounds in previously unanalyzed languages.

Having satisfied himself with his analysis of sounds (Peterson and Pike, 2002), Pike sought to apply his insights to all of human behavior (Pike, 1967). In order to create terms suited for such broad use, phonetics became etics and phonemics became emics. In the process of generalizing his perspective on linguistic sounds, he became personally involved in the broader controversies of his day about the best way to move back and forth between comprehensive theory and local practice throughout the social sciences. Other scholars have described his work as moving back and forth between the comparative and interpretive approaches, switching between the outside and the inside perspective, or developing constructs that apply across cultures starting from terms that begin as being culturally and historically bound (Headland, Pike and Harris, 1990). Each of these distinctions captures some aspects of what Pike had in mind, but each one also leaves out other aspects (Peterson and Pike, 2002). As detailed below, most adaptations of the terms etic and emic in psychology and organizational studies, although useful for many purposes, miss some implications of Pike's original purposes.

Although the ideas of emic and etic have contributed to many fields, confusion about them has been so typical that some have called for abandoning the terms. Even Berry (1997) who introduced the terms to cross-cultural psychology sometimes now refrains from using them when reacting to their use and application by others. Given the idiosyncrasies of the field linguistics problems that Pike encountered, taking these ideas into other fields might be expected to run the same risk of being misconstrued and over applied that organizational scholars have experienced when moving the anthropological idea of culture from societies to organizations. However, transferring the emic-etic distinction to new fields reflects Pike's original intent and finds precedent in Pike's adaptation of the terms from speech to broader issues of human behavior.

Grammars and sounds are certainly important parts of some systems of meaning, but unique systems of meaning are found in many areas of behavior besides speech and in many kinds of communities other than those defined as groups sharing the same language. Unique systems of meaning are not only characteristic of what anthropologists have traditionally viewed as societies or communities defined as geographically bounded cultures consisting of family units that share a common language (Fiske, 2002). Pike's original published illustrations of emics were provided by a football game, a church service, and a family breakfast scene, all of which occur in the same larger culture (Pike, 1967; Peterson and Pike, 2002). In fact, all three involved some of the same people. To our knowledge, the idea that separate emic analyses can usefully be conducted for different life domains of the same people has never been discussed in psychological or organizational scholarship. Doing so would be consistent with the anthropological recognition that people engage in various domains of discourse associated with their different roles in life.

If the ideas of emic and etic are transferable to so many domains of life, why the confusion in their meaning and use (e.g., Headland, Pike and Harris, 1990)? Much of the difficulty is due to a nuance in the distinction between comprehensive theory and local practice noted above as a defining characteristic of the difference between etic and emic analysis. The nuance in this distinction is rooted in the specific kinds of problems that field linguistics face when taking what they know from prior research into a new application. Conceptually, the dynamic between etic and emic research purposes occurs because the distinction between them actually reflects two kinds of contrast that differ in principle, but that tend to correspond in practice.

One contrast is between those things that are common to all of human experience as compared to those that are unique to a particular set of people who live together or talk together about a common topic during a particular historical period; that is, comprehensive theory versus local practice. The comprehensive side of life is evident in that everyone everywhere thinks and everyone everywhere has experiences with a physical world. The local side of life appears in that people in different communities have patterns of thought that are shaped by their community and have physical experiences influenced by characteristics of their locale.

The second contrast is between those forms of thought that are theoretical (scientific) as compared to those that are experiential (concrete), or what Polanyi (1958/1962) calls the explicit and the tacit; that is, comprehensive theory versus local practice. The theory side of life includes systematic linguistic and symbolic representations of both thought and physical experience. The practice side of life includes the less systematic mental representations and the even less structured actions by which we deal with our physical experience.

Why do so many scholars so frequently understand these two aspects of etic and emic in ways that differ from their original meaning? Part of the reason in cross-cultural organizational studies is that Pike's ideas most often have been used to address problems of doing survey research. In the organizational survey research literature, scholars have been mainly concerned with two questions. One question is which theoretical concepts and associated measures can and which cannot be transferred with little change from one culture to another. The second question is which empirical relationships do and which do not generalize from one culture to another. Since these have never been the sorts of problem that Pike sought to address (Peterson and Pike, 2002), he has not made suggestions about how to transfer the ideas of emic and etic most usefully for this application. Instead, they trace to Berry's (1969) useful application to survey research that will be described below.

These two survey research problems are narrower and more abstract than those that Pike ordinarily faced. As someone interested in training linguists (and others) to use their science as well as other intuitive skills as human beings to fully adapt to life in the field, Pike's concerns were broader than representing the rather small number of constructs covered in any set of survey measures. Rather than understanding whether and how certain measures of something like work attitudes or leadership can be used in a particular setting, Pike's emic interests were to broadly understand human experience in a particular setting. Rather than understanding which measures could be transferred readily from one locale to another, Pike's etic interests were to develop comprehensive taxonomies and theories of relationships covering large areas of human experience, especially those related to texts (e.g., Pike and Pike, 1982, 1983).

Emic and Etic as Two Sets of Contrasts

If etic and emic are useful ideas outside linguistics, how can they be most effectively transferred? In this section, we offer a formal analysis of what Pike meant by emic and etic. We will then return to what they imply for cross-cultural organizational scholarship. Instead of arguing that Pike's purposes as a linguist should become ours, we seek to address the most pressing issues in organizational survey research and ethnography while also keeping attuned to what Pike learned from pursuing his original purposes.

In order to fully understand Pike's intent, what we described above as the distinction between comprehensive theory and local practice needs to be separated into two distinctions. One is between comprehensive and local, while the other is between theory and practice. The theory versus practice distinction transfers readily. Most cross-cultural psychology and organizational scholars are comfortable distinguishing between those aspects of experience that are explicated as theory and those that remain tacit as naïve experience or practice.

The distinction between comprehensive and local tends to be a bit more troublesome. Cross-cultural survey researchers in particular are more accustomed to thinking about those constructs and relationships that show similar psychometric properties and structural relationships in many settings than those constructs and relationships that are unique to relatively few settings. That is not the same, however, as the comprehensive-local part of Pike's etic-emic distinction.

An etic analysis, as an exercise to develop comprehensive theory analogous to the phonetic analysis of the full set of speech sounds that people are capable of making, is not restricted to that which is common to all people. In fact, as anyone who has struggled to reduce their native accent when speaking a new language has experienced, insisting that the comparison of sounds in different languages be based on only those sounds that are equivalent in all languages would be unreasonable. Hypothetically, linguists could restrict their comparative research to the relative use of a particular equivalent sound in different languages. However, given even a handful of languages having different origins, this sort of research would leave only a very small common base for comparison. For example, Japanese does not make the distinction between "l" and "r" that is made in most European languages, and does not have the long "a" sound, the short "i" sound, or the short "u" sound found in English. Also, there are no Japanese words ending in what would be equivalent to an English language consonant sound, except for the sound "n." Does this lack of equivalence mean that only a very small portion of the English and Japanese languages can be compared? Limiting comparison to such equivalent sound phenomena would be analogous to the practice of cross-cultural organizational researchers who argue that comparative research should only consider the frequency or extent to which equivalently measured values, practices, or attitudes are reported in different societies.

Instead, the etic analysis of sounds includes both the explicit theoretical analysis of what is relatively general and common (like sounds that most languages use), that which is characteristic of particular language groups, and even the explicit theoretical analysis of what is relatively local and unique. An important aspect of the etic theory of linguistic sounds for Pike was the analysis of tonal languages. These are languages like Chinese and Navajo in which the meaning of a sound depends on its pitch. These languages must be included in any complete etic theory of language (Pike, 1948), yet tonal languages are by no means universal. In cross-cultural organizational studies, by analogy, culturally idiosyncratic forms of status differentiation such as the "big man" of the Pacific islands (Stewart, 1990), for example, should be included in any etic theory of leadership or social hierarchy. Unlike ideas like leader or even boss in much of the world, the idea of "big man" includes a relative permanent status that pervades all areas of a tribal society. Even though this particular phenomenon is by no means universal, it needs to be included in any complete global theory of leadership. Similarly, quanxi should be part of any etic theory of relationships and networks even if it cannot be entirely reduced to phenomena known outside of Chinese cultures (Farh et al., 1998). The idea of quanxi linked as it is to the use of relationships when markets do not work is least useful for understanding networks where markets operate efficiently, yet it is an essential part of an etic theory of networks. More generally, in international organizational survey research, both psychometric structures that are equivalent across cultures and psychometric structures that are culturally variable would be, consistent with Pike's original use, part of the etics of a particular phenomenon. Where cross-cultural scholars are prone to separate theory into one part that is universally general and another part that is locally specific, Pike's use of etic is closer to the sum of those aspects of explicit theory that are universally general plus those aspects of theory that are locally specific.

The preceding is represented by the two kinds of contrasts depicted in Table 5.1. One contrast is between the universally general and the locally specific. The other contrast is between theoretically explicit and experientially tacit domains of knowledge, understanding, and behaving. Some ways of thinking associated with the four cells formed by these two contrasts are presented in Table 5.1. An etic analysis, one that is designed to be comprehensive and explicitly theoretical, combines the two lower cells. An emic analysis, one that thoroughly reflects a single setting in all its facets, is one that combines all four cells, but with the cells in the right hand column including only those aspects applicable to a single culture or system of meaning.

Table 5.1: Disentangling two elements of emic and etic

	Universally General	**Locally Specific**
	CELL 1	CELL 2
Experientially Tacit	Tacit or non-explicated aspects of individual and social experience common to all people	Individual and social experience unique to a particular group or domain of discourse. Experiential or tacit aspects of emic understanding.
	CELL 3	CELL 4
Theoretically Explicit	Broadly applicable theory or "Genotypic" theory. Aspects of etic theory equally applicable in all communities	Indigenous theory or "Phenotypic" theory. Aspects of etic theory emically meaningful for some, but not all, communities

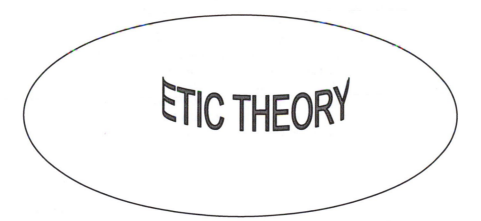

The universally general and the locally specific The contrast in Table 2.1 between the universally general and the locally specific applies to both theory (bottom row) and experience (top row). In the realm of theory, universally general means that some aspects of theory are designed to be equally applicable everywhere, while locally specific means that other aspects of theory are applicable in particular communities of people. For example, Peterson, Smith and colleagues (1995) indicate that one subset of role stress items show a factor structure that appears to be equivalent everywhere. Another subset of role stress items included in the original measures developed in the United States appears to be meaningful in that nation and perhaps a limited set of others. Those elements that are equivalent are roughly analogous to those sounds Pike identified that are used in most languages, while those elements that are unique to particular locales are analogous to sounds like those in tonal languages that are meaningful in only some languages. Together, the more common and the more unique make up the etic theory. This is the component of experience that has been explicated and that can be considered for possible use in any new setting subsequently analyzed.

The theoretically explicit and the experientially tacit The second contrast in Table 2.1, represented by the rows, is between the theoretically explicit and the experientially tacit. Organizational studies scholars sometimes distinguish that which is (or can be) fully explicated in theoretical abstractions and quantification from that which is (or can be) only partially explicated through stories or accounts. For example, explicit concepts related to power in any society are likely to be nuanced by historical associations with powerful people who are well known in that society. Cultural associations with names like Lincoln, Bolivar, or Hitler condition local ideas related to leadership, hierarchy and power in ways that can be only partially explicated. Furthest toward the tacit extreme are those experiences that may be reflected in behavior, but that the behaving party cannot represent at all in language. Some scholars take the position that these are the most important aspects of culture, albeit the least accessible (Kitayama, 2002). These sorts of contrasts are consistent with Polańyi's (1958/1962) distinction between that which is explicated in theory and that which is part of tacit experience. They are also reflected in recent cognitive psychological theories of the difference between more or less explicit or rationalized aspects of experience (e.g., Smith, 1998). Theories and stories are both explications, but the former are more fully rationalized while the latter can be arrayed on a continuum from relatively explicit fables with clear morals, to pointed stories, to relatively implicit descriptions of events. At the boundary of implicit, stories merge into the ineffably tacit.

Basic to Pike's view of theory building is that scholars, as human beings, are more than their explicit theories (Pike, 1993). Much of human experience, even experience general to all people and societies, remains experientially tacit. Over the past two decades, debates about the significance of a critical perspective on social theory and about the role of qualitative methods have made organizational scholars acutely aware of the nonrational in the sense of nonexplicit in organizational life and organizational studies. People have a basic ability to explicate.

The process of moving from experientially tacit to theoretically explicit is likely to occur when scholars working within a particular context become aware of anomalies in theories that are presented as general. For example, a Brazilian scholar senses that something about jeitinho, a Brazilian approach to getting work done despite a complex bureaucracy and set of social norms, appears not to be available in general organizational theory (Amado and Brasil, 1991). The dissonance created by the disparity between experience and theory stimulates theoretical analysis and the jeitinho construct is explicated and added to theories of leadership and social relationships. Graen and colleagues (1997) argue that becoming sensitized to this sort of learning opportunity and actively seeking such experiences to stimulate analysis is part of becoming an effective international scholar. Polanyi's (1958/1962) argument is that the ability to learn in this way is needed to be an effective scholar more generally.

Combinations of the two contrasts and the meaning of emic and etic Scholars often use the labels emic and etic to represent either the contrast between universal and local or that between tacit and explicit rather than to represent the combinations noted in Table 2.1. However, different aspects of the dynamic between emic and etic analysis are reflected in the relationship among the four cells that are created by crossing the two contrasts. In Table 2.1, the upper left hand cell (Cell 1) indicates that the nature of being human provides a common ground for all interactions, whether the interaction is between a linguist and a local non-linguist or between scholars. The upper right cell (Cell 2) reflects the cultural uniqueness of a particular group. This cell represents culturally unique experience as such rather than the theoretical representation of experience. One purpose of many emic analyses is to inductively explicate such unique experience in order to develop locally relevant theory. This kind of research attempts to move local knowledge from the experientially tacit to the theoretically explicit, from cell 2 to cell 4 for a single group.

The lower left cell (Cell 3) covers those aspects of a theory that can be used and applied with little modification for all people throughout all communities. As will be considered more fully below, theoretical ideas that are truly universal may be limited to either very basic physical things like temperature and hunger, very basic mental experiences like the ideas contrast and structure, or very broadly institutionalized things. Many scholars modify Pike's intent by restricting the word "etic" to phenomena of these sorts, however the idea of etic includes more. This cell taken alone includes only those aspects of etic theory that apply equally well everywhere, but not the parts of etic theory analogous to the theory of tonal languages in linguistics. These are the aspects that are explicit, yet that apply only to a subset of locales or situations.

Some international organizational scholars (e.g., Boyacigiller and Adler, 1991; Hofstede, 1980, 1993) note that most journal articles in psychology and organizational studies reflect theory that we would place in the lower right cell (Cell 4), even though authors may frame their work as showing cell 3 universals. cell 4 represents the aspects of theory that are applicable in some set of communities and not in others. This set might be quite extensive for some theoretical phenomena and quite limited for others. One very basic example is the idea of "work organization" has been relatively commonplace for the past 200 years, but was scarcely known before and still has little meaning in some contemporary non-industrial societies. Viewed from a broad perspective on societies (Fiske, 2002), the entirety of what cross-cultural organizational scholars study is unique to a particular historical period and not at all universal in time and place.

Some of the confusion that occurs when taking emic and etic from linguistics reflects a difference between how the dynamics between Cell 3 and Cell 4 play out in that field as compared to others. The etics with which a linguist as scientist starts includes the comprehensive set of theories and methods that the linguist takes into the field. It comprehensively includes not only Cell 3 universals, but also explicated Cell 4 specifics from other societies studied previously. It includes not only those aspects of sounds used everywhere, but also any theoretically explicated sets of sounds that may be used uniquely in only one previously studied locale. Typically, a linguist starts to work with an emic situation that mainly consists of Cell 2 aspects of previously unanalyzed (in an academic sense) experience. Increasingly as time passes, the linguist expands and develops the local emic theory represented by Cell 4 for the particular new situation being analyzed.

An agenda for new applications by cross-cultural organization scholars We have provided the preceding formal analysis of emic and etic in order to both support the use of these ideas for the earlier purpose of evaluating and promoting equivalence in concepts and measures, and to consider new uses. In particular, our position is that while we need to continue to seek universal concepts that provide a ready basis for comparing societies, we also need to avoid prematurely discounting research that shows that a measure designed in one society does *not* work well elsewhere. Such findings of non-equivalence may mean that the measures need to be better translated or refined, but they may also mean that an important new idea – like the idea a tonal language – underlies the nonequivalence. We will next consider applications to cross-cultural organizational scholarship that have been proposed for doing quantitative survey research as well as for cross-cultural ethnographic studies of organizations.

Purposes and Steps for Using the Emic - Etic Dynamic in International Organizational Survey Research

Multiple nation survey research remains the dominant method used in international organizational studies (Peng et al., 1991; Peterson, 2001; Van de Vijver and Leung, 1997), so the terms emic and etic have been applied most often in discussions of quantitative survey measures in this field. Although linguists, like survey researchers, use written word lists and ask informants to respond to them, organizational scholars ordinarily structure questions and response alternatives differently than do linguists. Likert-scaled, ranked, or semantic differential response alternatives are not customary tools in linguistics. Several useful approaches to cross-cultural questionnaire design, all of which are informed by the ideas of emics and etics, have been suggested that help bridge the divide between the tools used by linguists and survey researchers.

Berry's iterative approach and its legacy Berry (1969, 1989, 1990) began a major line of progress in cross-cultural psychology by applying emic and etic to questionnaire design in a way that appropriately highlights their complementarity when developing equivalent concepts and measures that approximate universal application. He suggests that scholars should start with what he calls an "imposed etic," a set of concepts and survey measures that have been designed previously in locations foreign to any new location where application is being considered. These could include measures that have been previously found to be very broadly useful (Cell 3) or measures that have been previously found useful in some limited set of communities (Cell 4). The measures are then applied in the new location. This application need not start with the ethnocentric conclusion that the measures will have the identical meaning or metric structure in their new application that they had been found to have elsewhere. Instead, the decision to expend effort and resources to use them need only assume that the measures have the potential to provide a useful starting point for contrast between prior research and a new application (Peterson and Pike, 2002). Subsequent psychometric comparisons of the structure of the measures and of their interrelationships provide part of the basis for evaluating whether or not the application has been successful, whether the measures are emically meaningful in the new application, and whether the measures should be further refined (Van de Vijver and Leung, 1997).

Roberts (1970) notes that success is quite informative when using methods designed to evaluate conceptual and metric equivalence, but the common situation of limited equivalence provides no direct guidance about what to do next. That is, where metric equivalence fails what is the conclusion? Does it mean that the concepts measured are meaningful in multiple locations but the measures are at fault, or does one conclude that the concepts do not transfer? The response from an emic-etic perspective is that this question arises because most applications of the emic-etic dynamic focus only on the equivalence issues suggested by the bottom row in Table 2.1. Instead, finding limitations in equivalence should become the finger that points to a need for qualitative analysis. In answer to Roberts (1970) question about what to do next, finding limited equivalence should initiate the sort of inductive work from tacit experience (top row of Table 1) that Pike, consistent with Polanyi, (1958/1962) suggests.

Several groups of scholars extend the cross-cultural psychology path that Berry (1969) began by suggesting a sequence of steps to take when moving back and forth between etic and emic analyses to develop a set of broadly applicable concepts and measures. They do so by identifying both steps for taking existing concepts into new settings and steps for identifying new concepts having potential for broad application.

Triandis (1978 Hui and Triandis, 1985) recommends beginning with a construct that prior research indicates to be applicable in many settings. Culturally appropriate ways to measure the construct in a specific new setting are locally developed by people trained as social scientists who also have an experientially tacit understanding of the setting. This emically represented etic construct can then be measured using questionnaire items developed by those scholars most familiar with the new setting. This approach and its dynamic relies heavily on a relationship between local experience and a combination of local and general theory. Scholars can begin taking advantage of this dynamic as they interact even before data are collected. Implicitly, this approach draws on all four cells in Table 2.1 in seeking to develop universally applicable measures by reinvigorating the field by importing ideas from new societies as they come to be studied. The result should be families of conceptually related measures, some refined over time by application in an increasing number of settings that show a high level of metric equivalence globally, some that show higher equivalence in some culturally similar part of the world than elsewhere, and some that are meaningful in only a particular nation or society. To date, we do not find a scholarly dedication to developing such families of concepts rather than a single universal concept. Nevertheless, families of concepts may be arising as different scholars are study the same research domain. For example, Oyserman et al. (2002) note that some research programs dealing with individualism and collectivism appear to be identifying some elements of the idea that may be of general use and others that are more idiosyncratic to particular studies. We would speculate that while some of the idiosyncrasies may be do to the predilections of particular scholars, others may be due to the nuances of individualism in different societies. Notably, the idea of valuing personal independence is appearing nearly universally in studies of individualism, while ideas like competition may be more important elements in individualism in some societies than in others.

Brett and colleagues (1997) recommend that international research teams progress through five steps. They should define a common research question, develop a model for each team member's culture, develop a joint model including both the common elements and the culturally unique elements, agree on a theory of culture to explain the common and idiosyncratic elements, and do follow up empirical research to test their theory. This group's advance in arguing for identifying the culturally unique elements takes a step forward. It argues for explicitly recognizing local idiosyncrasies rather than leaving them as error variance and for explicitly identifying locally specific concepts, some of which may later become integrated into a larger etic theory.

Morris and colleagues (1999) recommend that scholars start by conducting two parallel, independent research projects when studying any topic, justice judgments in their example. One project should be based on ethnographic methods and the other on translated surveys. At a second step, insights from both methods are incorporated into follow up research. That is, follow-up ethnographic research is conducted to emphasize themes that appear especially important based on both the initial ethnographic research and the survey research. Similarly, follow-up survey research includes additional and revised measures based on topics found important in the initial ethnographic research as well as providing possible ways to add or revise items to solve measurement problems identified in the initial survey research. One contribution of their approach is to answer Roberts's (1970) challenge described earlier by specifying ways to take advantage of the potential for complementarity between ethnographic and survey families of methods. Seeking this sort of complementarity is quite consistent with Pike's combination of established, very structured methods for formal language and grammar analysis with less structured relatively intuitive methods.

Seeking culturally limited forms of conceptual and metric equivalence in comparative research Given what scholars like Berry (1969) and his successors have already accomplished in applying the ideas of etics and emics to promote equivalence, what next steps should we now take to expand their use in international organizational studies? Cross-cultural scholars working with survey instruments have come to accept as axiomatic that comparison requires a high level of metric equivalence. How can one compare average levels on, say, values measures if the measures mean different things in different cultural settings? Or how can one compare the relationship between two measures, say organizational commitment and voluntary turnover, if the meaning of the measures of commitment and turnover are culturally contingent? The emphasis on demonstrating equivalence has been a necessary antidote to the earlier practice of comparing averages in different societies without first demonstrating their equivalence. Without wishing to detract from this important contribution, we encourage scholars to take a next step by attending to some underemphasized aspects of the etic-emic dynamic reflected in suggestions by scholars noted above. Our recommendations for the next steps to take are not to radically change others' recommendations about how to develop valid surveys. Instead, we recommend that two omissions that are likely to be screened out in the survey development process be retained.

One omission requiring remedy is inadequate attention to concepts and measures that apply in a substantial set of nations, albeit not the full set being studied in a given project. The problems in developing genuinely universal measures of collectivism provide a useful lesson (Miller, 2002; Oyserman et al., 2002). For example, group harmony appears to be less consequential to the idea of collectivism within the U.S. than elsewhere (Oyserman, 2002). Similarly, defining the self contextually (following Markus and Kitayama, 1991) appears to be an aspect of collectivism in some societies, but not others. Rather than developing a single global measure of collectivism, we might better include in our measures subsets of items that are relatively equivalent throughout the world and other sets that reflect collectivism regionally for sets of nations.

The etic-emic dynamic encourages scholars to expect such instances of non-equivalence within broadly similar families of concepts. Again, evidence for lack of equivalence in measures may mean that more effort is needed to refine the measures, but it may also mean that underlying concepts differ to some degree between cultures. Should we disregard concepts that are not universal to human experience in all societies? Doing so can place whole domains of social experience outside the realm of science as non-researchable. Of course, there may be so many local nuances and idiosyncrasies in frequently studied families of organizational concepts like work values, leadership, or social identity that documenting each and every one may be too big a next step for Cross-Cultural organization studies. As an intermediate step, we recommend that scholars should search for and increasingly publish research about the social equivalent of languages that distinguish between "l" and "r" as well as those that do not, and for languages where word meanings depend on tones as against those that do not. That is, we should look for such major exceptions as being phenomena that are important because they reflect social life in large, previously understudied populations, or that are important because they significantly augment some basic theory.

As large scale data sets representing many nations continue to be developed, we increasingly have reason to believe that there are cultural regions created by geographic proximity, colonization, immigration, and other mechanisms of culture spread (Diamond, 1997; Inglehart and Caballo, 1997; Ronen and Shenkar, 1985). Just as there are groups of related languages, so there are groups of related cultures. For example, perhaps the distinctly Chinese addition to leadership theory of leading without unethically exploiting followers would be a useful addition to leadership research (Peterson, 1988). At the time of writing, abuses by senior executives in major United States businesses make this sort of leadership freshly salient. The point of such research is that including aspects of leadership that may not be conceptually equivalent outside the context where they are identified may be quite important to an adequate etic theory of leadership. The same point applies throughout Cross-Cultural organization studies. This seems to be about the level of scope, broader than a single society yet not global, that Miller (2002) advocates as being needed in the study of individualism and collectivism, but there is a risk of taking societal specificity to the point where coherence in Cross-Cultural organizational studies could be lost.

Leaving room for minor non-equivalences and idiosyncrasies in cross-cultural research The second omission is to carefully document and publish concepts and measures that appear in a single society that is studied in an international project. This second omission is a little more difficult than the first, since an appearance of local uniqueness may be due to setting-specific measure limitations like translation inadequacies. Nevertheless, country-unique ideas, particularly those from infrequently studied parts of the world that are likely to be underrepresented in international research, provide the grist for identifying important new concepts that may have regional or global implications not previously identified.

Although the emphasis we consider most useful at the present stage of cross-cultural organization studies is not to develop unique theories for a tremendous number of small societies (e.g., Fiske, 2002), even this sort of research has some value. Such a highly fragmented approach would provide some grist for broader theory, but it seems to be best left to anthropology. Following Pike, knowing that each language has a uniqueness that limits comparability should awaken us to the likelihood that social behaviors of all sorts have cultural idiosyncrasies. The value of ethnopsychologies that fully and uniquely represent the psychology of people in particular societies is likely to remain. Hopefully, rather than being set against large etic theories, etic theories can be incorporated into ethnopsychologies. This can occur both by starting from etic theory to seek for areas of commonality with other cultures, and by using etic theory to provide a reference point to help locals explicate uniquenesses that they might remain unaware of without the opportunity for cultural contrast that an etic theory provides (Peterson and Pike, 2002).

The Multi-Country Team Approach to Managing the Emic-Etic Dynamic

No one person can possibly know or have experience with all that is important about any social phenomenon as it appears throughout the world. Consequently, collaboration among scholars from different nations has become an appropriate norm for doing international organizational research (Peterson, 2001). This means that the etic-emic dynamic is typically best carried out between social scientists rather than, as in Pike's typical case, between a linguist and a local informant who has not been scientifically trained.

How should scholars from different nations handle the practicalities of using emics and etics when doing research? Different scholars with experience working in multicultural teams have recommended that international research groups need to base their social process on a set of rules about the appropriate way to do science, a social contract drawn up by the participants, trusting relationships built over time, the personal collaborative skills and international experience of each researcher, or a strong leader and clear research administration structure (Peterson, 2001). The recommendations noted above from Berry's (1969) tradition emphasize a set of rule-like steps that should structure a team's research process. In practice, however even the steps to follow are negotiated by any international research team. Specifics of the purpose of a research project affect the appropriate way of conducting the research, while social relationships among team members are likely to affect the way a team actually operates. As an example, Drenth and Wilpert (1980) describe one way of operating multicultural research groups that can be adapted to include both the traditional etic-emic purpose of promoting equivalence as well as the purpose of developing etic theory that includes major cultural contingencies.

Rather than specify a complete set of steps, Drenth and Wilpert (1980) emphasize the first step of preparing the collaborative process by recommending how multicultural research teams should constitute themselves and manage their dynamics. A central purpose in their recommendation is to overcome from the outset the common limitation that international organizational research has typically included inadequate input from outside the culture in which an established set of measures or concepts were developed. They want to avoid the sort of "safari research" that is developed, implemented and controlled by one researcher or a research team from one country. A modest improvement, that they call "adaptation" research, encourages local collaborators to adapt a project by adding their own material, but they propose to improve on that as well. What they advocate as decentralized collective research is likely to have particular potential to constructively integrate universally general and locally specific, theoretically explicit and experientially tacit knowledge.

In the approach they recommend, collaborators from various countries jointly participate in the design, conceptualization, measure development, implementation, and analysis of a project. The collaboration assumes that every participant not only has experientially tacit understanding of some parts of the world, as is the case in linguistics field research, but that each also knows how to conduct theoretically explicit analysis. Every participant, as a scientist familiar with scientific theory from various parts of the world, is skilled in Cells 3 and 4 of Table 2.1. Local experience (Cell 2) and local theory (Cells 4) are contributed not just by a research project initiator and a collaborator who holds a clearly secondary role, but also by many scholars collaborating as colleagues. Drenth and Wilpert (1980) argue that success depends not so much on following a fixed sequence of steps, but on team qualities. Among these are the degree of consensus reached in the team, its flexibility and willingness to compromise, and its determination and goal orientation to stick together for extended periods of time. The process can be facilitated through starting the research process by drawing up an initial social contract in ways that Drenth and Wilpert detail.

Several international organizational research projects including half a dozen or more countries have relied on this sort of decentralized collective research model. Among these are the Industrial Democracy in Europe (IDE, 1981) project and the Meaning of Working (MOW, 1987) project. In some examples of which Drenth and Wilpert have been a part, the participation extends from a single project to a series of interrelated projects including partially overlapping participants. This continuity has the added value of taking unique lessons learned incidentally from any society studied at one stage of a research program and making those lessons more central to the design of a subsequent project.

What useful remedies to ethnocentrism in cross-cultural organizational research are being suggested and what is being left out in the Drenth and Wilpert approach? Their suggested approach helps take advantage of the scientific traditions and local experiences of colleagues from multiple countries throughout all phases of a project. What might be lost and what needs to be reaffirmed is the utility of including research instruments and theory from any given nation as part of the base for doing research elsewhere rather than taking the collaboration process to mean that all concepts and measures need to be developed anew.

The starting point that Drenth and Wilpert (1980) recommend is likely to be especially helpful, although contingencies of research purpose need to be considered as well (Peterson, 2001). Pike's view of the use of etic theory implies that beginning from a research and theory base in social science exporting nations, including the United States, provides a useful base for contrast with other nations. Some of the more influential cross-cultural projects have become influential by making just such contributions. They have either added a component to an earlier theory that is then used back in the country of origin as in Hofstede's use of Confucian dynamism (Hofstede, 2001), developed a focused new project by integrating a complex composite of prior projects developed in diverse locales as did the Meaning of Working project (MOW, 1987) when studying work centrality, or identified a particular phenomenon unique to a narrow range of societies as did Misumi when adding a pressure element to leadership theory (Misumi and Peterson, 1985). The research program spearheaded by Schwartz (1994) draws heavily in its measures and theory from the U.S. base in values research provided by Rokeach (1973). Nevertheless, this research group has augmented the original measures with new items derived from the experiences of scholars in many nations, restructured the concepts at both the individual and societal levels by analysis of global data, and improved the theory of generic theory of values both through these additions and by critiquing some of the original theory base (e.g., the difference between instrumental and terminal values). We see in these projects how beginning from a research base in one or a few nations and incorporating insights from elsewhere improves upon the original theory.

Incorporating the Emic-Etic Dynamic into Some Major Survey Research Tasks

What are some of the ways in which survey researchers can use prior research, biased as it is by the cultures of its original designers and of the locations in which the research was first conducted, and improve upon it by applying it in new settings? International research teams can incorporate an emic-etic dynamic into many facets of a survey research project.

Survey design The design of questionnaires for use in multiple countries includes identify or developing constructs and theories of their relationships, constructing a questionnaire, applying judgmental methods to evaluate and revise items, promoting and checking translation equivalence, and using psychometric information to aid in evaluating equivalence. In each of these tasks, one member's contribution draws from the general, explicit knowledge that the member has about the field (Cell 3 of Table 2.1). It also draws from the local, explicit knowledge each member has about both their own subspecialty and their own nation (Cell 4), from general, implicit knowledge each one has from working with and observing colleagues (Cell 1), and from the local implicit knowledge that each one has from doing research and from their life experience in their own country (Cell 2).

For example, in the process of designing constructs, the Meaning of Working (1987) project drew from a number of general literatures. This project was developed through equal collaboration by experienced organizational scholars in 8 nations to identify and consider the implications of cultural characteristics like entitlements and obligations, work goals, and work centrality. One particularly useful literature originating in the United States was that about central life interests (e.g., Dubin et al., 1975). This literature served as a source for constructing items about the importance of work. The judgmental method used to evaluate and refine the work importance measure drew heavily from issues salient to researchers in each of the participating countries. The issues each researcher found personally salient included both those made explicit in the country's academic literature and others of which each researcher was personally and less explicitly aware.

Translation Employing organizational scholars to translate and back translate the completed instruments is another way to stimulate discussions that combine general, theoretically explicit knowledge about the constructs to be measured with the experientially tacit understandings that the collaborators have about nuances of their own languages. In contrast, relying on an expert translator who does not understand the underlying theory gives more weight to experiential tacit understanding of the language and theoretically explicit knowledge about rules of translation. It gives less weight to the kind of combined explicit knowledge and tacit understanding that the researchers in a research team hold about the concepts that the instruments are designed to represent.

Interpreting result   Interpretation of psychometric analysis done jointly by a multinational research team follows as a complex intermediate step that includes sampling, survey administration, and preliminary data analysis. Through this intermediate step, locally specific meanings the constructs have to non-scholar populations of respondents are incorporated into the research by means of responses to items. In other words, the researchers construct the items, but the respondents provide the data. The analysis itself produces information reflecting respondents´ understandings of the items in the form of measures of psychometric properties as reliability coefficients, confirmatory factor analyses, and item response patterns (Van de Vijver and Leung, 1997). A multicultural team looking jointly at the results engages in a complex interpretive process that draws on all aspects of their knowledge – universally general and locally specific, theoretically explicit and experientially tacit – to reach conclusions about whether the measures mean what they were intended to mean. The process of conducting research as a multicultural team reduces the risk of major misunderstandings that can occur when a researcher or research team from a single culture goes abroad equipped only with theoretically explicit, universally general knowledge (Mezias et al., 1999).

Using the Emic-Etic Dynamic in Some Major Ethnographic Research Tasks

Pike notes that the first extension of emic and etic was into anthropology, a field that relies heavily on qualitative ethnography (Peterson and Pike, 2002). Among the major tasks of ethnography are finding an iterative method to identify what is most important to analyze in a given research setting as well as to know how to document those things that a researcher anticipates will be most important. Ethnography can be used to help accomplish the emic task of fully understanding a particular research setting, or the etic task of increasing the comprehensiveness of any theory about a particular phenomenon. Although structured quantitative methods have been part of the history of ethnography (e.g., Murdoch, 1949), what are now typically considered to be the most prototypically ethnographic methods are those that are the least pre-structured and rely most heavily on observation and intuition. Despite language to the contrary (Morey and Luthans, 1984; Morris, et al., 1999), ethnography is neither an inherently emic nor an etic set of methods, at least if one follows Pike's original use of emic and etic as described here.

Ethnography with a limited etic base   The first appearance of the terms etic and emic in organizational studies is in an article in which Morey and Luthans (1984) recommend that organizational scholars follow one of the applications of these terms in anthropology. They take Spradley's (1979) anthropological route that uses a deliberately constrained form of etic metatheory. The metatheory limits the etic starting point for analyzing a new culture to only six very basic, mainly methodological elements arranged as a set of step; description, domain, structure, taxonomy, contrast and components. The steps are designed to minimize the influence of more comprehensive and detailed prior etic theories when studying new situations. For example, the first step of asking descriptive questions attempts to use a native's language to gain information about cultural settings in terms of "the nine categories of space, object, act, activity, event, time, actor, goal and feeling" (pp. 30-31). In terms of Table 2.1, they advocate using a very skeletal form of Cell 3, universally general theory, in order to promote induction from Cell 2, locally specific tacit experience, in a way that minimizes the influence of either the more comprehensively detailed aspects of Cell 3 or of Cell 4, locally specific theories developed in *other* locales.

Morey and Luthan's (1984) discussion represents a particular position in an important debate that has recurred in many fields including organizational studies: how much prior etic theory should be used to inform the analysis of any new situation? Does using prior theory corrupt or inform subsequent analysis. In the analysis of new languages, Pike made moderate use of prior etic theory (see the description of his "monolingual demonstration, Peterson and Pike, 2002). Pike's view of the value of etic theory reflects considerable confidence in a researcher's intuition and in the potential for researcher and research participant to notice inconsistency between prior theory and the reality of a particular research setting (Pike, 1990). Analysts need to consider their research purpose when taking a position about the relatively utility of less structured ethnography and more structured survey research. To what extent does the analysis have the largely emic purpose of thoroughly representing an unfamiliar culture? Or, instead, to what extent does the project have the etic purpose to use the experience with the new culture to inform and improve some particular explicit theory?

Morey and Luthans's approach to limiting the etic starting point of a project may be particularly helpful for some research problems. Sometimes, a new situation being analyzed is so radically unique that any advantages of contrast with what has been learned elsewhere could be lost. This was the case, for example, in some of the early analyses by organizational scholars of organization forms emerging in the People's Republic of China as market-based reforms were introduced in the 1980s (Boisot and Child, 1988). Relying too heavily on prior categories to analyze such new situations could lead to a distraction from the original aspects of phenomenon and the effort to understand the new situation. For other purposes, though, avoiding prior theory could waste resources in rediscovering things already known and lead to lost continuity with prior research.

Ethnography with an extensive etic base   Ethnography can also complement a more extensive etic base than that which Morey and Luthans (1984) have in view. For example, Brannen (1996) has proposed a "bicultural alienation" construct. The main theme is that members of organizations in one country that have been acquired by a management group from another country can become alienated both from practices typical of those in their home country as well as practices typical of the country of the acquiring company. The etic theory with which she began her analysis was relatively limited, but included theories of alienation and various concepts related to organizational attachment and attitudes (e.g., commitment and satisfaction) together with the formal ethnomethodological techniques that she used in her analysis. Beginning with the very general etic base of broad social science knowledge, but with no specific intent to apply any particular part of it to her particular case, she recognized from her local interactions that alienation was indeed a locally important issue to consider.

She describes a complementary process of quantitative and qualitative research similar to that described by Morris et al. (1999), but with an emphasis on the qualitative side. She describes an ethnography based on participant observation with detailed field notes and in-depth interviews supplemented by historical and ongoing document analysis of press coverage and internal company documents. Having established some of the issues requiring careful analysis and seeing what aspects of etic theory might be usefully addressed in her research site, she designed Likert-scaled questionnaires. Some of the questionnaire measures, like items measuring job satisfaction, were selected from the existing literature. Other measures, like whether the outcome of meetings seemed to have been arranged in advance before the meetings were even held, reflected issues that were largely unprecedented in prior literature.

One result of her use of prior etic research was to improve her emic analysis of the particular site, in order both to assist the organization she was studying and also to contribute to improving etic alienation theory. A second outcome was the integration of the idea of "bicultural alienation" into a broader etic theory of alienation. Brannen's approach is consistent with that of organizational studies scholars who seek complementarity between ethnographic and quantitative methods (e.g., Sutton and Rafaeli, 1988; Barley, 1990). While informed by prior alienation theory, her inductive work suggested that alienation in her research setting had a "bicultural" quality that had not been previously documented. Hence, her emic analysis, an analysis limited in scope to bicultural settings, adds an element to the broader etic theory of alienation. In Brannen's case, nothing about the prior theories of alienation or attachment appear to have caused problems in developing the bicultural alienation idea.

Recommendations promoting an emic-etic dynamic when doing ethnographic research As in our discussion of survey research, our recommendations are not to radically modify what others have suggested about how to conduct ethnographies. They are rather to retain particular sorts of information at their conclusion. The original problem of etics and emics in linguistics was how to take explicit theory developed for many places and use it to support developing the understanding needed to function in a single place, then to explicate some of that information in a form that could be used to function in other places in the future. Careful analysis of this problem exposes the two quite different aspects noted in Table 2.1 – a contrast between theory versus experience, and another between local versus general. The four cells formed by these two contrasts help to identify ways to adapt emics and etics for other fields besides linguistics. Although adaptation is desirable and necessary, any application of these ideas must maintain one tenet that has been central to any constructive application – it is the going back and forth between perspectives that is critical to improving theory and to promoting application. Insiders talking to insiders, outsiders talking to outsiders, theorists talking to theorists, and conversations among people sharing stories and experiences all can be valuable. All, however, leave out a dynamic of contrast between different perspectives. Without that dynamic, they miss a significant learning opportunity. Although we have reviewed several recommendations about prescribed steps for doing cross-cultural research, the interdisciplinary transfer of these ideas from linguistics to international organizational studies requires the same creativity that is needed to transfer organizational theories between nations (Peterson, 2001).

Functional and Neo-Institutional Reasons for both Universal and Bounded Organizational Phenomena

We have used examples and analogies with language to this point rather than provided a theoretical base for arguing that methods need to be developed to promote attention to both relatively universal and relatively local phenomena. Two major alternative explanations, one functional and the other institutional, are ordinarily provided for the relatively universal components of any theory. Each explanation also provides a basis for expecting regional or local variability in basic concepts.

Functional necessity One explanation is based on the idea of functional necessity. For example, Malinowski proposes two axioms of functionalism in anthropology. "Functional" in his scheme means:

> "...first and foremost, that every culture must satisfy the biological system of needs, such as those dictated by metabolism, ...that every cultural achievement that implies the use of artifacts and symbolism is an instrumental enhancement of human anatomy, and refers directly or indirectly to the satisfaction of a bodily need" (Malinowski, 1939/1944, p. 171).

Kluckhohn and Strodtbeck's (1961) framework for analyzing universal cultural functions is among the most frequently encountered functional theories in international organizational studies. Most functional theories take the position that while basic functions are universal, ways of fulfilling functions are more localized and can change over time in any one locale. Hence, to varying degrees, functional theories tend to treat universal constructs and relationships as being at a higher level of abstraction than are locally unique constructs and relationships.

Some etic organizational theories designed for use throughout the world combine generally applicable functional components with components that are specific to particular locales or settings. Several examples appear in leadership theory. In Misumi's (1985; Misumi and Peterson, 1985) Performance-Maintenance leadership theory, two basic abstract functions of groups are universally general – the performance function and the maintenance function. The locally specific in his theory refers to the unique ways in which leaders fulfill these two functions in particular kinds of organizations (e.g., banking or government) or social settings (e.g., families), or even at particular hierarchical levels of organizations within a single industry. He does not expect functional equivalence between settings to be reflected in measure equivalence, although considerable measure equivalence would be expected within any one type of setting. In effect, he expects the performance and maintenance functions to be fulfilled in somewhat different ways in different settings. Not only would factor structures be expected to vary from setting to setting, but even the contextually appropriate questions to ask would vary. Later, Misumi's general-specific contrast was developed beyond industry type and type of social setting to include the specifics of leadership in different national cultures even within a single industry (Smith et al., 1989).

Other leadership scholars have made similar distinctions between the relatively universal and the relatively local aspects of their etic leadership theories. Graen and colleagues (1997) suggest that the basic nature of leader-member exchange has universal, functionally equivalent components, but that its specific expression is culturally contingent. The GLOBE leadership project (Den Hartog, et al., 1999; Dickson et al., 2000; House et al., 1999) makes a similar distinction between the universal basic idea of transformational leadership and the idiosyncratic expressions of transformational leadership as practiced in particular parts of the world.

Institutional spread A second major explanation for universals is neo-institutional. Traditional institutional explanations treat explicit agencies like governments, nation states, or organizations as real once explicitly created by devices like laws. Neo-institutional explanations reflect the position that practices (or values or assumptions) spread through a number of social mechanisms with coercive control by explicit devices like laws being only one example. Scott (1995) summarizes these social mechanisms that result in institutional spread as being rooted in coercion, norms, and imitation. For example, Krasner (1988) argues that the idea of nation state has become globally institutionalized. He argues that a set of people occupying a particular piece of geography needs to be identified with a nation state in order to be legitimate. Both the basic idea of a nation state and the structure of many component institutions like government agencies are nearly universals at this point in history. However, they are not universals if viewed over time. In cross-cultural research, theories akin to modernization (e.g., Harbison and Myers, 1959) and post-materialism (e.g., Inglehart, 1997) point to the broad, but not universal, institutional spread of many ideas and practices that organizational scholars take for granted. From a neo-institutional view, those concepts that are found to be most universal reflect success in the global spread of ideas. Not only the idea of nation state, but more taken for granted ideas like the 24 hour day and seven day week are examples of universal concepts that are more readily taken as due to institutional spread rather than functional necessity. While a functional view of universals leads to expecting somehow more functionally basic concepts (language as such) to be more universal from ones that allow for functional equivalence (languages plural), a neo-institutional view of relatively more universal and more local phenomena leads to expecting variability in the spread of ideas based on a variety of social influence mechanisms. Ideas that follow historically influential societies (e.g., Chinese, northern European) are more likely to have broader influence than those that follow societies that have had less global influence (e.g., Mayan).

Research implications   We believe that the priority often being placed on equivalence in organizational research, the expectation that survey measures or empirical relationships should be consistent across settings, in most cases reflects either an underlying functional equivalence or neo-institutional globalization view. In our view, to the extent that survey items are phrased at a more contextually specific level, non-equivalence can be expected unless the phenomena being studied are either functionally universal with the way of fulfilling the functions being universally invariant as well, or show global institutionalization. We expect these situations to be quite rare. In terms of Table 2.1, surveys that include both universally general and locally specific aspects of theory will include a strong local element that will reflect important elements of local meaningfulness, but not necessarily global equivalence. Following the leadership examples noted above, an etic leadership theory based on survey research should include not only concepts and measures that show equivalence across settings, but also concepts and measures that show local nuances. A scholar's task becomes to understand what are the universal, functionally equivalent, or broadly institutionalized parts of an etic theory, and which aspects of an etic theory are specific and culturally contingent.

Conclusion

The hypothetical linguist whose identity we asked the reader to assume at the outset is likely to approach a new setting with a combination of conceptual and methodological tools, including some that apply to language in general and others that apply to more local families of languages. If the linguist is going into the region including the southwestern United States and northern Mexico, these tools will include ways of representing tonal languages. The same sorts of tools may also be taken into China. The lesson that some conceptual tools will be relatively universal while others will be predictably constrained by some cultural region or regions is a good lesson for cross-cultural organizational studies at the present juncture. Our sense is that debates about the broad application of tools in cross-cultural organization studies become easily polarized between the extremes that all scientific constructs and measures should be universally equivalent as against the view that they need to be radically local.

We have suggested more constructive alternatives in the preceding. Pike's insight that emic and etic analysis can be intertwined was not an isolated one, but was part of a zeitgeist evident in many fields of social science and the humanities that stimulated scholars to reconsider the relationship between naïve experience and explicit social theory. Among its contemporaries, it is akin to Merleau-Ponty's (1964) analysis of the relationship between perception and rational thought, Polanyi's (1958/1962) analysis of the relationship between tacit experience and explicit knowledge, and Gestalt psychology's insights into the effect of context on perception (Markus and Zajonc, 1985). All of these perspectives struggled with the relationship between raw human experience structured only by what is there to be experienced and the patterns of thought used in everyday life as against explication structured by norms of systematic science.

Within this intellectual milieu, the ideas of emics and etics were first formulated for the particular kinds of problems faced by linguistics, then were taken into anthropology and cross-cultural psychology, and eventually into organization studies to address the specific research problems these fields were facing at the time the ideas were imported. Transferring these ideas has been challenged both when they are taken across disciplinary boundaries, but when they move across the boundaries of time. Research issues within any field of study evolve. We believe that it is time for the field of cross-cultural organization studies to progress by both retaining an interest in demonstrating rather than assuming equivalence when the same measures are being compared in different societies as well as adding on an interest in incorporating phenomena with more limited application into any given domain of organizational research. We have noted several examples – partially overlapping ideas like those of networks and quanxi, bureaucracy and jeitinho, and the families of concepts related to individualism/collectivism and leadership. We encourage scholars to development of more such examples of families of concepts that include both the relatively universal and the more constrained.

Overcoming two barriers to next steps　We see two barriers to taking this sort of next step. One barrier is the scholarly tradition of viewing etic research as being both universal and explicit, while viewing emic research as being both local and tacit. Explicit theory has come to be linked in many scholars' minds to the relatively universal aspects of human experience, and tacit understanding has come to be linked to the more locally unique aspects. How has the idea of comprehensive come to be so tightly bound to the idea of theory, while the idea of local has become just as tightly bound to the idea of practice?

For practical reasons, aspects of human experience that are common to all people have been more thoroughly studied by people who as social scientists are interested in making experience explicit. Aspects of experience that are unique to particular sets of people, especially to small or isolated groups, tend to be incorporated only slowly into more comprehensive social science theory simply because scholars encounter them less often. For example, the concept of alienation has been formalized more fully than has the concept of bicultural alienation (Brannen, 1996) because social scientists encounter the former more frequently. If some experiences are genuinely common to people everywhere, study of them in many places yields similar conclusions published in articles read and cited by many scholars in many places. For practical reasons, then, aspects of human experience that are universally general are often the ones that tend to be made theoretically explicit. Because of an empirical rather than conceptual correspondence, the idea of theoretically explicit is easily confused with the idea of universally general. As Pike (1993) indicates, this link is not conceptually necessary. For example, Brannen (1996) could begin with etic alienation theory and add the bicultural part to the etic theory only after an emic analysis of a particular, unique work situation.

A second barrier in transferring the ideas of etics and emics is the belief that structured and unstructured analyses somehow cannot communicate with one another – that they represent "incommensurable" paradigms. The experiences of linguists who have explicated the systems of sounds and grammars of real people speaking living languages helps avoid such an overly rationalized, narrowly theoretical view of scientific communication. Returning from theory to experience, from Cells 3 and 4 to Cells 1 and 2 in Table 2.1, can help scholars from different theoretical traditions overcome communication impasses between theories (Pike, 1993). A related lesson is that cultural differences need not preclude learning between cultures. One can certainly learn a second or third language and find points of contact between one's original language and the new language. In so doing, one may even learn to notice and understand aspects of one's first language better than before. Similarly, one can come to understand the theoretically explicit paradigm with which one begins even more adequately by learning a new one.

In the typical research of a cross-cultural organization studies scholar, any time a survey measure is translated and used in a new setting and found to have similar properties and correlates, a partial emic analysis of a new setting is being accomplished at the same time an etic analysis of the topic under study is being extended. When such an attempt to begin an emic analysis from an etic base is not successful, as Roberts (1970) suggests, the failure should not be taken as ultimate, but rather as indicating that some sort of qualitative, inductive form of emic analysis should take over. Nothing in Pike's extensive publications about the categories of sounds or the structure of grammars suggests that one should fear contaminating one's intuition by drawing from prior explicit theory. Neither does anything in his extensive analysis of the Mixtec language, an analysis lasting half a century that is being continued by his wife, suggest that the need for inductive work is ever likely to end.

Our challenge in organizational studies is to find means to conduct and report research that moves back and forth between fully using our skills at inducing from local experience as well as our skills at deducing from prior theory. In so doing, we need to develop both the means to effectively understand and work in many local settings and also to incorporate universals, near universals, and local idiosyncrasies into increasingly comprehensive theories of whatever phenomena we choose to study.

Note

This paper is based on a symposium presented at the meeting of the International Federation of Scholarly Associations of Management (IFSAM), August 1994. The authors would like to thank Mary Jo Hatch, Kenneth L. Pike, William T. Ryan, Peter B. Smith, and Marc Tyrell for comments. Preparation of this chapter was supported in part by a grant from the Starr Foundation.

References

Amado, G. & Brasil, H. V. (1991), Organizational behaviors and cultural context: The Brazilian "Jeitinho". *International Studies of Management and Organization*, **21**, 38-62.

Barley, S.R. (1990), The alignment of technology and structure through roles and networks. *Administrative Science Quarterly*, **35**, 61-103.

Berry, J.W. (1969), On cross-cultural comparability. *International Journal of Psychology*, **4**, 119-128.

Berry, J.W. (1989). Imposed etics-emics-derived etics: The operationalization of a compelling idea. *International Journal of Psychology*, **24**, 721-735.

Berry, J.W. (1990), Imposed etics, emics, derived etics: Their conceptual and operational status in cross-cultural psychology. In T.N. Headland, K.L. Pike & M. Harris (eds.). *Emics and etics: the insider/outsider debate*. Newbury Park, CA: Sage, pp. 28-47.

Berry, J.W. (1997), An ecocultural approach to the study of cross-cultural industrial/ organizational psychology. In P.C. Earley & M. Erez (eds.), *New perspectives in international industrial/organizational psychology*. San Francisco: New Lexington Press, pp. 130-147.

Boisot, M. & Child, J. (1988), The iron law of fiefs: Bureaucratic failure and the problem of governance in the Chinese economic reforms. *Administrative Science Quarterly*, **33(4)**, 507-527.

Boyacigiller, N. & Adler, N.J. (1991), The parochial dinosaur: Organizational science in a global context. *Academy of Management Review*, **16**, 262-290.

Brannen, M.Y. (1996), Ethnographic international management research. In B.J. Punnett & O. Shenkar (eds.), *Handbook of international management research*. Cambridge, MA: Blackwell, pp. 115-143.

Brett, J.M., Tinsley, C.H., Janssens, M. Barsness, Z.I. & Lytle, A.L. (1997). New approaches to the study of culture in industrial/organizational psychology. In P.C. Earley & M. Erez (eds.), *New perspectives in international industrial/organizational psychology*. San Francisco: New Lexington Press, pp. 75-129.

Cheng, J. (1996). Cross-national project teams: Toward a task-contingency model. In B. J. Punnett & O. Shenkar (eds.), *Handbook for international management research*. Cambridge, MA: Blackwell, pp. 507-520.

Chao, G.T. (2000). Multilevel issues and culture: An integrative view. In K.J. Klein & S.W.J. Kozlowski (eds.), *Multilevel theory, research, and methods in organizations*. San Francisco: Jossey-Bass, pp.308-346.

Den Hartog, D.N., House, R.J., Hanges, P.J., Ruiz-Quintanilla, S.A., Dorfman, P.W. and associates (1999), Culture specific and cross-culturally generalizable implicit leadership theories: Are the attributes of charismatic/transofmational leadership universally endorsed? *Leadership Quarterly*, **10**, 219-256.

Diamond, J. (1997), *Guns, germs and steel*. New York: W.W. Norton.

Dickson, M.W., Aditya, R.N. & Chhokar, J.S. (2000), Definition and interpretation in cross-cultural organizational culture research: Some pointers from the GLOBE research program. In N. Ashkenasy, C. Wilderom & M.F. Peterson (eds.), *Handbook of organizational culture and climate*. Thousand Oaks, CA: Sage, pp. 447-464.

Dorfman, P.W., Howell, J.P., Hibino, S., Lee, J.K., Tate, U. & Bautista, A. (1997), Leadership in Western and Asian countries: Commonalities and differences in effective leadership processes across cultures. *Leadership Quarterly*, **8**, 233-274.

Drenth, P. J.D. & Wilpert, B. (1980), The role of "social contracts" in cross-cultural research. *International Review of Applied Psychology*, **29**, 293-305.

Dubin, R., Champoux, J. & Porter, L. (1975), Central life interests and organizational commitment of blue-collar and clerical workers. *Administrative Science Quarterly*, **20**, 411-421.

Farh, J.L., Tsui, A.S., Xin, K., & Eheng, B.S. (1998),   The influence of relational demography and guanxi: The Chinese case. *Organization Science*, **9**, 471-488.

Fiske, A.P. (2002), Using individualism and collectivism to compare cultures – A critique of the validity and measurement of the constructs: Comment on Oyserman et al. (2002). *Psychological Bulletin*, **128**, 78-88.

Graen, G.B., Hui, C., Wakabayashi, M. & Wang, Z.M. (1997), Cross-cultural research alliances in organizational research: Cross-cultural partnership-making in action. In P.C. Earley & M. Erez (eds.), *New perspectives in international industrial/organizational psychology*. San Francisco: New Lexington Press, pp. 160-189.

Hofstede, G. (1980). Motivation, leadership, and organizations: Do American theories apply abroad? *Organizational Dynamics*, **9**, 42-63.

Hofstede, G. (1993). Cultural constraints in management theories. *Academy of Management Executive*, **7 (1)**, 81-94.

House, R.J., Hanges, P., Ruiz-Quintanilla,S.A., Dorfman, P.W., Javidan, M., Dickson, M., Gupta, V. & GLOBE (1999).   Cultural influences on leadership and organizations: Project GLOBE. In W. Mobley, J. Gessner & V. Arnold (eds.), *Advances in global leadership*, Vol. **1**. Greenwich, CT: JAI Press, pp. 171-233.

Harbison, F. & Myers, C.A. (1959). *Management in the industrial world*. New York: McGraw-Hill.

Headland, T.N., Pike, K.L., & Harris, M., eds. (1990), Emics and etics: The insider/outsider debate. Newbury Park, CA: Sage.

Hofstede, G. (2001). *Culture's consequences* (2nd ed.). Thousand Oaks, CA: Sage.

Hui, C.H. & Triandis, H.C. (1985), Measurement in cross-cultural psychology: A review and comparison of strategies. *Journal of Cross-Cultural Psychology*, **16**, 131-152.

Hussey, S.C. (1989), *An annotated bibilography of publications using the emic/etic concept*. Dallas: Summer Institute of Linguistics.

IDE International Research Group (1981), *Industrial democracy in Europe*.   Oxford, England: Clarendon Press.

Kluckhohn, F.R. & Strodtbeck, F.L. (1961), *Variations in value orientations*. Evanston, IL: Row, Peterson.

Krasner, S.D. (1988).   Sovereignty: An institutional perspective. *Comparative Political Studies*, **21**, 66-94.

Inglehart, R. (1997).   Modernization and postmodernization: Cultural, economic, and political change in 43 societies. Princeton, NJ: Princeton University Press.

Inglehart, R. & Carballo, M. (1997). Does Latin America exist? (And is there a Confucian culture?): A global analysis of cross-cultural differences. *Political Science and Politics*, **30**, 34-47.

Kitayama, S. (2002). Culture and basic psychological processes – Toward a system view of culture: Comment on Oyserman et al. (2002). *Psychological Bulletin*, **128**, 89-96.

Malinowski, B. (1939/1944). The functional theory. In *A scientific theory of culture and other essays*. Chapel Hill: University of North Carolina Press, pp. 146-176.

Markus, H. & Kitayama, S (1991). Culture and the self: Implicatoins for cognition, emotion and motivation. *Psychological Review*, **20**, 568-579.

Markus, H. & Zajonc, R.B. (1985). The cognitive perspective in social psychology. In G. Lindzey & E. Aronson (eds.), *Handbook of social psychology*, Vol. 1.   New York: Random House, pp.137-230.

MOW Meaning of Working International Research Team (1987), *The meaning of working*. London: Academic Press.

Merleau-Ponty, M. (1964), The primacy of perception and its philosophical consequences. In J.M. Edie, trans., ed., *The primacy of perception and other essays*, Part I, chap. 2,. Evanston, Il: Northwestern University Press, pp. 12-27.

Mezias, S.J., Chen, Y.R. & Murphy, P. (1999), Toto, I don't think we're in Kansas anymore: Some footnotes to cross-cultural research. *Journal of Management Inquiry*, **8**, 323-333.

Miller, J.G. (2002), Bringing culture to basic psychological theory – Beyond individualism and collectivism. *Psychological Bulletin*, **128**, 97-109.

Misumi, J. (1985), *The behavioral science of leadership*. Ann Arbor, MI: University of Michigan Press.

Misumi, J. & Peterson, M.F. (1985), The Performance-Maintenance Theory of Leadership: Review of a Japanese research program. *Administrative Science Quarterly*, **30**, 198-223.

Morey, N.C. & Luthans, F. (1984), An emic perspective and ethnoscience methods for organizational research. *Academy of Management Review*, **9**, 27-36.

Morris, M.W., Leung, K., Ames, D. & Lickel, B. (1999), Views from inside and outside: Integrating emic and etic insights about culture and justice judgment. *Academy of Management Review*, **24**, 781-796.

Murdock, G.P. (1949), *Social structure*. New York: Free Press.

Nonaka, I. (1994), A dynamic theory of organizational knowledge creation. *Organization Science*, **5**, 14-37.

Oyserman, D., Coon, H.M., & Kemmelmeier, M. (2002), Rethinking individualism and collectivism: Evaluation of theoretical assumptions and meta-analyses. *Psychological Bulletin*, **128**, 3-72.

Peng, T.K., Peterson, M.F. & Shyi, Y.P. (1991), Quantitative issues in cross-cultural management research: Trends and equivalence issues. *Journal of Organizational Behavior*, **12**, 87-108.

Peterson, M.F. (1988), PM Theory in Japan and China: What's in it for the U.S.? *Organizational Dynamics*, **16 (4)**, 22-39.

Peterson, M.F. (1998), Embedded organizational events: Units of process in organization science. *Organization Science*, **9**, 16-33.

Peterson, M.F. (2001), International collaboration in organizational behavior research. *Journal of Organizational Behavior*, 2001, **22(1)**, 59-81.

Peterson, M.F. & Pike, K.L. (2002), Emics and etics for organizational studies: A lesson in contrast from linguistics. *International Journal of Cross Cultural Management*, **2**, 5-19.

Peterson, M.F., Smith, P.B. with 22 co-authors (1995), Role conflict, ambiguity and overload by national culture: A 21 nation study. *Academy of Management Journal*, 1995, **38**, 429-452.

Pike, K.L. (1943), *Phonetics: A critical analysis of phonetic theory and a technic for the practical description of sounds*. Ann Arbor, MI: University of Michigan Press.

Pike, K.L. (1948), *Tone languages: A technique for determining the number and type of pitch contrasts in a language, with studies in tonemic substitution and fusion, University of Michigan publications in linguistics no. 4*. Ann Arbor, MI: University of Michigan Press.

Pike, K.L. (1967 [second edition; first edition, 1954, 1955, 1960]), *Language in relation to a unified theory of the structure of human behavior*. The Hague: Mouton.

Pike, K.L. (1990), *On the emics and etics of Pike and Harris*. Newbury Park, CA: Sage, pp. 28-47.

Pike, K.L. (1993), *Talk, thought, and thing: The emic road toward conscious knowledge*. Dallas, TX: Summer Institute of Linguistics.

Pike, K.L. & Pike, E.G. (1982), *Grammatical analysis* (2nd ed). Arlington, TX: The Summer Institute of Linguistics and the University of Texas at Arlington.

Pike, K.L. & Pike, E.G. (1983), *Text and tagmeme*. Norwood, NJ: Ablex.

Polanyi, M. (1958/1962), *Personal knowledge: Towards a post-critical philosophy.* Chicago: University of Chicago Press.

Roberts, K.H. (1970), On looking at an elephant: An evaluation of cross-cultural research related to organizations. *Psychological Bulletin*, **74**, 327-350.

Rokeach, M. (1973), *The nature of human values.* New York: Free Press.

Ronen, S. & Shenkar, O. (1985), Clustering countries on attitudinal dimensions: A review and synthesis. *Academy of Management Review*, **10**, 435-454.

Schwartz, S.H. (1994), Cultural dimensions of values: Towards an understanding of national differences. In U. Kim, H. C. Triandis, Ç. Kagitçibasi, S. C. Choi & G. Yoon (Eds.) *Individualism and collectivism: Theory, method and applications.* Thousand Oaks, CA: Sage.

Scott, W.R. (1995), *Institutions and organizations.* Thousand Oaks, CA.

Smith, E.R. (1998), Mental representations and memory. In D. Gilbert, S. Fiske, & G. Lindzay (eds.), *Handbook of social psychology.* New York: McGraw-Hill, pp. 391-445.

Smith, P.B., Misumi, J., Tayeb, M., Peterson, M.F. & Bond, M.H. (1989), On the generality of leadership style measures across cultures. *Journal of Occupational Psychology*, **62**, 97-110.

Spradley, J.P. (1979), *The ethnographic interview.* New York: Hot, Rinehart & Winston.

Sutton, R. I. & Rafaeli, A. (1988). Untangling the relationship between displayed emotions and organizational sales: The case of convenience stores. *Academy of Management Journal*, **31**, 461-487.

Stewart, A., (1990), The bigman metaphor for entrepreneurship: A "library tale" with morals on alternatives for further research. *Organization Science*, **1**, 143-159.

Triandis, H.C. (1978), Some universals in social behavior. *Personality and Social Psychology Bulletin*, 4, 1-16.

Van de Vijver, F. & Leung, K. (1997). *Methods and data analysis for cross-cultural research.* Thousand Oaks, CA: Sage.

Chapter 6

Human Resource Management in a Global World: The Contingency Framework Extended

Rosalie L. Tung

David C. Thomas

Much of the literature on International Human Resource Management (IHRM) has focused on comparative HRM practices across countries or on aspects of HRM in multinational firms. In particular, the selection and training of expatriate managers has been center stage in many discussions of IHRM activities. However, several developments in the global economic arena have affected the context of IHRM and hence require that we adjust our focus to more clearly define a systematic and holistic approach to International HRM. This chapter draws on the first author's prior work on managing overseas assignments (Tung 1981; Tung, 1998a) and extends these concepts to provide a global perspective on HRM with an emphasis on valuing cultural diversity, both cross-nationally and intra-nationally. Cross-national diversity refers to the differences across countries, while intra-national diversity arises from the growing ethno-cultural diversity within nation-states (Tung, 1998a). Both of these types of cultural diversity are critical considerations in framing international human resource management in a global context.

Changing Context of International Human Resource Management

Virtually all business conducted today is global in a sense. "Global business" is defined as transactions that involve input and output – be they innovations, concepts, products, services or personnel – that span international boundaries. Increasingly, it is difficult to identify a product or service that is not somehow influenced by one type of cross-border transaction or another. With growing intra-national diversity, during the course of a normal working day, a person often interacts with co-workers, customers and suppliers who come from a cultural background very dissimilar from one's own. To attain and sustain its competitive advantage, a global enterprise has to utilize effectively its strategic resources wherever they are located, the most important of which may be people (Tung, 1984). The context of IHRM has been shaped by dramatic developments in economics, politics, and technology in the past two decades or so. These include:

- Changes in global competition,
- The accompanying forces of global integration and local responsiveness,
- The formation of global strategic alliances and network organizations,
- The increase in cultural diversity in the workforce,
- The changes in career implications of overseas assignments.

(Tung, 1998a)

Each of these developments is reviewed briefly below.

Global competition Lee Taewon, president of the Hanjin Group, a Korean-based multinational and one of the largest transportation groups in the world, has defined globalization as "deregulation on a global scale" (Tung, 1998a). Under a deregulated environment, firms from around the world can compete on a more or less equal footing with each other. In other words, globalization has changed completely the calculus of global competition. As such, increasingly a firm has to face competition not only from the industrialized west, but also from developing regions of the world. Despite the recent setbacks in many of the Asian economies, the fact remains that both Singapore and South Korea have already joined the ranks of the OECD and are major players in the computer, electronic and automobile sectorsFor more than a decade now, China has experienced the fastest economic growth rate in the world. The advent of free trade areas has further enhanced economic permeability across nations. These regional integration agreements have become increasingly prominent in the 1990s. At the dawn of the 21st century the number of regional trade agreements has surpassed the one hundred-mark, up from about forty-five a decade earlier (WTO, 1999). The three largest trading blocs, the European Union (EU), the North American Free Trade Agreement (NAFTA), and the Asia-Pacific Economic Cooperation (APEC) together account for over 60 per cent of the world's trade (WTO, 1999). The result of these agreements is to create an unprecedented degree of interconnectedness among the world's economies. Therefore, local economic conditions are no longer the result of purely domestic influence, and economic barriers to competition have been reduced dramatically.

A significant force toward globalization and the one with perhaps the most potential to shape the IHRM landscape may be the dramatic advances being made in information technology (Naisbitt, 1994). Quantum advances in information technology have made access to information, resources, products, and markets possible with the click of a mouse. With a computer and internet access, it is now possible to establish a business that is almost entirely unconcerned with traditional boundaries and barriers, including those emanating from economies of scale and scope (Parker, 1998). The decreasing price and increased sophistication of computing systems have placed capabilities in the hands of business around the globe that only a few years ago were available only to a select group of large multinationals. Consider, for example, the case of a New Zealander who recently inherited a vintage watch from his/her grandparents and who sold it in the global marketplace through a competitive bidding process on ebay for a listing fee of only US$ 4.00. In the past, this same person would most probably have had to go through an intermediary, such as Christie's or Sotheby's to attract the attention of bidders from around the world.

Global integration and local responsiveness The emergence of global competitors and customers coupled with regional economic integration have meant that global firms often have to contend with the opposing forces of adaptation to the local environment (i.e., local responsiveness), on the one hand, and consistency within the organization (i.e., global integration), on the other (e.g., Bartlett, 1986; Porter 1986). According to Rosenzweig and Singh (1991), the pressures for global integration stem from two factors: 'organizational replication' and the 'imperative for control'. "Organizational replication" is the tendency of firms to duplicate in new environments existing structures and procedures that have been effective. The "imperative for control" suggests that standardisation of policies is used to reduce the complexity and uncertainty inherent in the control of international operations. Global corporations are confronted with additional complexity as a result of geographic and cultural differences among subsidiaries and between the subsidiary and headquarters. Conversely, in new environments the pressures for local adaptation derive from the social nature of organizations, and hence their tendency to reflect the values, norms, and accepted practices of the societies in which they operate (Westney, 1993). The balancing act that these dual pressures impart on the firm has been called the art of "being local worldwide" (Sullivan, 1996).

Strategic Alliances and Network Organizations In response to global competition, conventional organizational forms are giving way to networks characterized by less hierarchical relationships (Kogut, 1989) and cooperative strategic alliances with other firms (Jarillo, 1988). There is a growing recognition among international firms that to survive and flourish on a global scale they may have to collaborate even with their competitors. These alliances typically take one of three forms: informal cooperative alliances, formal cooperative alliances and international joint ventures (Lorange and Roos, 1992). The informal type of arrangement is usually limited in scope and has no contractual requirement. Formal arrangements typically require a contractual agreement and are often indicated by broader involvement. And, joint ventures are separate legal entities with joint ownership. The emergence of these new organizational forms implies that their will be a growing need to transfer personnel across countries to engage in such collaborative teamwork. Thus, domestic managers who are not transferred to work outside of their home country will have to contend with the types of challenges that were once limited to expatriate managers abroad (Tung, 1998a). An additional aspect of changing organizational boundaries is the emergence of virtual organizations where employees do not often meet face to face but are linked by computer technology (Erez and Earley, 1993). Geography has become less meaningful and a manager's physical location less consequential. What matters most under these new organizational forms is whether the manager can relate to his/her counterparts across functional, company, industry and geographic boundaries.

Increase in cultural diversity in the workforce   In the mid 1980s the Hudson Institute Report projected that by the year 2000 only about 15 per cent of the new entrants to the U.S. workforce would be white males (Johnston and Packer, 1987). Similar increases in cultural diversity, albeit on a more modest scale, are occurring throughout the world. Canada estimates that by the early 21st century, 20 per cent of its population will consist of ethnic minorities (Tung, 1998a), and Australia and New Zealand are home to some of the world's most culturally diverse national workforces. For example, the cultural composition of a typical New Zealand manufacturer might be 20 per cent Pakeha (New Zealand European), 15 per cent Maori (indigenous New Zealanders), 15 per cent Samoan, 10 per cent Cook Islanders, 10 per cent Tongans, 10 per cent Chinese, 10 per cent Malaysian, 5 per cent Korean and 5 per cent Indian. Industrial firms in major Australian cities, such as Sydney and Melbourne, often have more than 35 national cultures represented (Thomas, Ravlin, and Barry, 2000). Even homogeneous societies such as South Korea are anticipating greater diversity in organizations (Tung, 1998a). This intra-national diversity challenges policies and practices that were developed for a traditionally homogeneous workforce, white males in the case of the U.S. As a result, employers have to contend with a whole range of new workplace issues, such as discrimination/harassment based on ethnicity or gender, communications problems across cultures, and the relationship of families to the work situation. Also, traditional methods for resolving the conflicts that arise may not be effective and new processes that are perceived as legitimate by a diverse population must be devised (Kochan, 1995). This means that for many managers the global nature of their environment may consist largely of working with a multicultural workforce in their own country. One implication is that there will be a convergence of the core competencies required of domestic managers and international managers (Tung, 1993).

Changes in career implications of overseas assignments   The changing nature of the managerial environment suggests that tomorrow's successful managers will need to possess a very different skill set from that required in the past. In a survey of chief executives the successful manager of the 21st century was described as having multi-environment, multi-country, multifunctional, and even a multi-company, or multi-industry experience" (Bennett, 1989). Consistent with these ideas is the emergence of so-called "boundaryless career" where career progression is viewed more in the context of lateral moves across companies as opposed to vertical promotion within a given organization (Arthur and Rousseau, 1996; Schein, 1996). The new skills required of managers, coupled with this changed perspective on careers, have implications for the significance associated with overseas assignments. In the past, most expatriates were used for the specific technical skills that they possessed (Thomas, 1998). This trend appears to be changing, however, with firms such as Ford Motor Company vowing not to promote managers to senior positions without them having served overseas (Tung, 1998a). In the past, an overseas experience was often reported as having a negative effect on the returning expatriate's immediate job situation (Adler, 1981), but returning sojourners often reported considerable individual development along a wide range of knowledge and skill dimensions (Dunbar and Ehrlich, 1993). More recently, returning expatriates have expressed a belief that their international assignment has had a positive effect on their overall career development, albeit not always in the same company that sent them overseas (Tung, 1998b; Stahl, Miller and Tung, in press). Some evidence suggests that as many as one-half of repatriates are not guaranteed a position upon successful completion of an international assignment (Tung, 1998b). This failure to utilize the skills acquired abroad has contributed to the high turnover of U.S. expatriates within a year of their re-entry (Adler 1986). These findings, in combination with a view of careers that is centered on building skills to enhance a career within or across companies (Inkson, 1997) suggest that international assignments can be used to develop the skills and core competencies required for today's managers, but that firms are challenged to create environments where these skills are effectively utilized upon return or risk losing these talented employees.

As a result of the globalization of the international business environment just described, the management of human resources has to be reframed in a new and more comprehensive context. It is no longer adequate to just answer the question of what happens when we move HRM overseas. The global context of IHRM now forces a reconsideration of how different contextual elements influences IHRM policies and procedures. For example, while the influence of geography may be diminishing because of advances in information technology, globalization enhances the significance of culture because peoples from around the world are brought into daily contact at an unprecedented pace.

In order to specify the effect of these contextual changes, it is first necessary to define the domain of IHRM.

Mapping HRM in a Global Context

International Human Resource Management (IHRM) involves the worldwide management of people and its study initially focused on the selection, training, appraisal and rewards for international assignees (e.g., Tung, 1988). While the basic activities of human resource management may have remained relatively stable, the context in which the HRM system must function, as noted previously, has undergone significant change. The effect is to increase the complexity of HRM beyond a simple list of functions applicable to overseas employees. And, as intimated previously, because of growing intra-national diversity, the distinction between HRM and International HRM is becoming less clear (Tung, 1993; Tung, 1998a). Following Morgan (1986) and Murray, Jain and Adams (1976) we consider multiple facets in mapping the domain of IHRM. These facets are a) the types of employees involved, b) the human resource functions, c) the location of

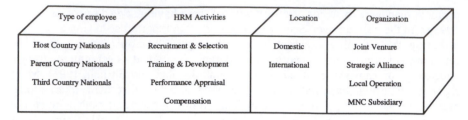

Type of employee	HRM Activities	Location	Organization
Host Country Nationals	Recruitment & Selection	Domestic	Joint Venture
Parent Country Nationals	Training & Development	International	Strategic Alliance
Third Country Nationals	Performance Appraisal		Local Operation
	Compensation		MNC Subsidiary

Figure 6.1: Domain map of HRM in a global context

activity (domestic or overseas), and d) the organizational context. These facets are shown above.

The first facet of the IHRM domain is the type of employee involved. In contrast to purely domestic HRM, the International context presents the opportunity for HRM practices and programs to affect more than one national group. These are host country nationals (HCNs), parent country nationals (PCNs), and third country nationals (TCNs). While the distinction between a parent country national and a host country national may become somewhat blurred in today's network organizations, we continue to view these distinctions as valuable from a mapping perspective. For example, it is still possible to distinguish between employees who work in the country in which they were born and educated, and perhaps where they began their careers, and those who have been transferred to another country. The special characteristics and needs of these different types of employees have been extensively documented (e.g., Thomas, 1998; Tung, 1988).

The second facet of the IHRM domain concerns the activities of HRM. These activities flow from a definition that characterizes Human Resource Management as involving "all management decisions that affect the nature of the relationship between the organization and employees – its human resources" (Beer, et al., 1984:1). While there is some debate as to the functions, and stakeholder interests that HRM serves, or should serve, in an international context (e.g., see Poole, 1990), there is perhaps less controversy concerning the idea that HRM activities include the following, at the very least: recruitment and selection, training and development, performance appraisal, and compensation.

The third facet of the IHRM domain defines the locus of HRM activities. Whether or not the HRM function is concerned with one or more overseas locations has numerous implications for the complexity of HRM policy and procedure. For example, Dowling (1988) has attributed the differences in complexity between domestic and international HRM to six factors. These are:

1. The requirement for more HR activities (e.g., international taxation, international relocation, language translation services, host government relations)
2. The need for a broader perspective because of different employee groups (HCNs, PCNs, TCNs have different concerns)
3. More involvement in employees lives because of the requirements of overseas employees for assistance with housing, health care, cost of living and tax issues, home visits, and repatriation

4. Changes in the emphasis of policies and procedures as the workforce mix varies among PCNs and HCNs
5. Higher risk exposure because of higher costs and political risk associated with assignments to certain locations
6. More external influence because of differences in economic and political factors in overseas locations. The inclusion of a domestic only alternative in the domain specification of Global HRM is recognition that HR activities might be conducted entirely within one country even though they are influenced by the global context of business discussed at the outset.

The final facet of the map of IHRM is the type of organization in which HRM activities take place. Joint ventures, strategic alliances, and subsidiaries of MNCs all place different requirements and constraints on HRM policies and procedures. In fact, HRM may become a more important factor in situations that require significant interactions among individuals from collaborating companies. As Cascio and Serapio (1991:63) suggest,

> "...in a global alliance, people with different cultures, career goals, compensation systems, and other HR baggage often have to hit the ground working together. Unless the ground has been smoothed this 'people factor' can halt an alliance's progress, sometimes permanently".

Even in the case of purely local operations, the growing ethno-cultural diversity in the domestic workforce has necessitated adjustments to HR policies and practices to accommodate to differences in values, attitudes and approaches to conflict resolution.

The use of the facet map as an analytical tool is straightforward. By choosing an item from each facet category (see Figure 6.1), a domain mapping statement is constructed that defines the specific HRM practice or policy under consideration. The utility of this facet mapping approach is that it captures the broad scope of IHRM (3 types of employees x 4 HRM activities x 2 location of activities x 4 organizational types = 96 domain statements) while still allowing a focus on relationships related to a specific HRM practice or policy. For example "recruitment and selection of host country nationals in an overseas joint venture" is an example of a domain statement that describes a specific HRM consideration. This approach is useful in defining the broad concept of IHRM. However, it is only the starting point for a comprehensive model of global HRM. That is, it tells us little about:

*   The priority ranking or relative importance of a particular domain
*   The feasibility of implementation of a given policy or practice
*   How the policy or practice might be organized   (Murray, Jain, and Adams, 1976)

To bridge the gap between these domain statements and these issues, we turn to the contingency paradigm for guidance.

Contingency Theory and International Human Resource Management

Contingency theories of organization (Burns and Stalker, 1961; Lawrence and Lorsch, 1967) were developed because of a recognition that deterministic theories, which suggested the one best way, failed to consider that organizations interact with and respond to their environment. One of the earliest applications of the contingency perspective to international human resource management (IHRM) was Tung's (1981) use of this framework to prescribe appropriate selection and training practices for overseas assignments. Her model identified contingency factors related to the task, the individual, and the environment, which influenced selection and training of people for international assignments. Specifically, different overseas assignments were categorized with regard to their requirement for intercultural interaction, the duration of the assignment abroad, and cultural distance between the host and home countries. Individual characteristics of technical competence versus relational ability were considered. An assessment of the extent to which the host country environment differed from the home country environment was called for. Contingent on these variables was the emphasis to be placed on particular selection criteria and the degree of training rigor required. For example, in assignments of longer duration that require extensive interaction with host country nationals in culturally-distant countries, such as that of chief executive officer, more weight should be placed on the candidate's human relational abilities and family situation in the selection criteria. In assignments of this nature, more rigorous cross-cultural training programs should also be provided to the candidate and family. In contrast, for short-duration assignments to that involve less contact with host country nationals, such as that of a trouble-shooter, or for assignments to culturally similar countries, greater emphasis should be placed on the individual's technical skills in the selection. Furthermore, in assignments of either kind, the candidate does not need to undergo intensive and extensive cross-cultural training. Further development of IHRM theory has adopted a contingency approach, by and large, with a sheer increase in the number and type of contingency variables to be considered.

Another stream of IHRM has deviated from explaining or predicting specific activities, functions, or processes to examining the fit between an aggregate of these HRM systems and the strategy of the firm (e.g., Schuler, Dowling, and DeCieri, 1993). While this strategic macro perspective may not be fully consistent with the perspective we have taken in this chapter, a number of these recent models inform our approach. Specifically, they help to identify factors, both endogenous and exogenous to the firm, that could moderate the relationship between the specification of a particular IHRM domain statement we proposed in Figure 6.1, on the one hand, and the important considerations of priority given to particular activities, the feasibility of these practices, and how these functions might be organized, on the other. We discuss these theoretical contributions below:

Organizational life cycle models　Some models (e.g, Adler and Ghadar, 1990; Milliman, Von Glinow, and Nathan, 1991) have suggested that the life cycle of the organization might be related to IHRM practices. The Milliman et al. (1991)

model, for example, suggested that the stage of development of an organization determine the ways in which it manages four types of fit: within IHRM functions, to the organizational life cycle, between the subsidiary and headquarters, and to the international environment. This, in turn, influenced organizational success. According to this approach, in new organizations, for example, which are characterized by a focus on entrepreneurship and short-term survival, IHRM will emphasize basic domestic recruitment and compensation programs. In later phases, the IHRM focus shifts, first to the development of more formal HRM practices, then to practices that facilitate control of large numbers of overseas units, and finally to a longer term perspective that includes the development of managers with the kind of global vision required to integrate business functions and adapt to a dynamic environment.

Adler and Ghadar (1990) presented a similar conception of the influence of stage of organization development with the additional notion that the importance of cultural diversity to IHRM will be influenced by developmental stage. Interestingly, this model suggested that it is not only the level of cultural diversity but also its source (external or internal) that varies in importance according to developmental stage. That is, in the earliest stage of development, cultural diversity is unimportant because the firm is unhampered by an ethnocentric perspective given its purely domestic focus. However, in the second phase, as the firm begins to compete for market and/or to produce overseas, in order to succeed it has to focus on the cultural diversity presented by its new external environment. In the third phase of development, firms are competing almost exclusively on price, which reduces the importance of cultural variability in the external environment. However, in order to gain competitive advantage these multinationals must be effective in managing the cultural diversity that exists within the firm. By phase four firms are engaged in geographically dispersed and culturally diverse networks of strategic partners, which requires attention to cultural diversity among these network partners as well as that that exists within the firm. These four phases remain important in identifying the dominant source of influence of culture. However, given the growing ethno-cultural diversity in the domestic workforce discussed previously, the need to contend with cultural diversity internal to the firm is now important at all stages of development.

Institutional models In another model, Rosenzweig and Nohria (1994) drew upon institutional theory (DiMaggio and Powell, 1983) to suggest that internal and external forces shape IHRM practices. The first are those processes internal to the firm that argue for consistency across the organization largely because of a desire for control or internal equity. The second consists of the effect of the environmental agents (e.g., regulatory agencies, professional societies, consulting firms) in adapting organization to isomorphic with local practices. DiMaggio and Powell (1983) defined three categories of environmental pressures toward isomorphism. These are:

- *Coercive* isomorphism - patterns of organization imposed on the firm by an outside authority, such as government.

- *Normative* isomorphism - professional bodies promote 'proper' organizational structure.
- *Mimetic* isomorphism - organizations copy the structure of firms that have been successful in dealing with a particular environment.

In addition to identifying both internal (e.g., control orientation, international experience, cultural distance from headquarters) and external (e.g., local dependence, unionisation, regulatory pressure) sources of influence and mechanisms through which both organizational and environmental factors influence IHRM, their study found that, as anticipated, these factors had differential effect across HRM practices. That is, HRM practices with precise or mandated local norms were more influenced by the local environment, whereas those HRM practices that had to do with executives or related to international decision making were more susceptible to the influence toward internal consistency. The difference in the susceptibility of different HRM practices to different environmental pressures is an important consideration in assessing contingency effects.

Strategic IHRM models In an integration of various prior models of IHRM, Schuler, Dowling and De Cieri (1993) reinforced the need to consider the influence of both endogenous and exogenous factors on IHRM. Their model emphasized the recognition that in international operations the quality of human resources is even more critical than in domestic operations (Tung, 1984) and stressed the link between firm strategy and human resource management. They identify two major strategic components – inter-unit linkages and internal operations – that can influence IHRM. Inter-unit linkages refer to the choices that firms make with regard to differentiating or integrating their various subunits; while internal operations encompass other strategic issues such as environmental and strategic fit. The implication of the model is that IHRM is not simply a tool for the implementation of strategy but a key component of organizational strategy formulation.

The staffing strategy of the firm is also a key endogenous variable in the model underlying Welch's (1994) examination of the IHRM activities of four Australian companies. Additionally, she identified both stage of internationalisation and industry type as influential in the determination of the staffing practices of these firms. Interestingly, she also emphasized the linkage between organizational culture and HRM practices. Organizational culture may in part be managed through HRM practices (Evans, 1986). However, it may also provide a vehicle for control (Schneider, 1988).

The role of strategy is also central to a model of IHRM presented by Taylor, Beechler, and Napier (1996). However, they also identified the developmental aspects of IHRM and emphasized both the centrality of home country HRM systems to this development, and the need to consider IHRM differences among different types of affiliates and different types of employees. Key contingencies are the role of the affiliate, the nature of establishment of the affiliate, the cultural distance between home country and the affiliate, and the criticality of particular groups of employees to the firm.

The models described previously have advanced our understanding of IHRM in several ways. One, they have identified variables that can have important influences on IHRM, including firm strategy, organizational life cycle, industry type, and culture. Two, these models have suggested mechanisms through which both internal and environmental factors influence IHRM. Three, they have highlighted that optimal IHRM systems at the aggregate level require an appropriate balance between forces toward internal consistency and local adaptation. In other words, there is no one best way. Rather the best approach is contingent upon circumstances specific to the organization. Treating IHRM as an aggregate of systems has been important in developing a strategic perspective on IHRM. However, the types of predictions that this level of theorizing produces are quite general (e.g., Schuler et al. 1993).

In order to provide a more middle range perspective while building on these previous developments, we extend the facet map of IHRM (Figure 6.1) by considering the contingencies identified in the previous models reviewed. In so doing we present a model that identifies the influence of both exogenous and endogenous factors on specific IHRM domains (Figure 6.2). That is, the model presented in Figure 6.2 begins with the domains statements derived from Figure 6.1, and proceeds to show how the organizational and environmental contingencies just described act to influence important considerations in global HRM.

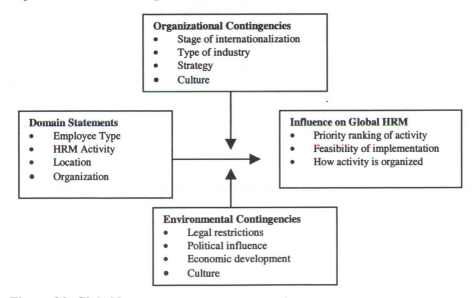

Figure 6.2: Global human resource management

The model posited in Figure 6.2 provides a broad platform for understanding HRM in a global context. As opposed to a prescriptive approach advocated in more recent work on SIHRM, our model offers a framework for the analysis of HRM in a global context. Therefore, it serves as a vehicle to explain and predict the influence of various contingencies on the IHRM domain. By presenting IHRM as a discrete set of domain statements the moderating effect of both organizational and environmental contingencies can be examined in terms of a) the prioritisation of an particular domain, b) the feasibility of implementing a particular practice, and c) in the organization of that activity.

Each of the contingency variables presented in Figure 6.2 has one or more mechanisms that directly or indirectly influence the specific HRM domain statement under consideration or through an interaction with one or more of the other contingencies. While the list of contingencies identified may not be comprehensive, neither are they arbitrary. Previous research has suggested that each of these factors can have a major influence on HRM in a global context. Additionally, for each of these organizational factors the process through which it influences HRM has been articulated to some degree in prior literature.

Organizational Contingencies

The degree or stage of internationalisation has been suggested as a major factor in IHRM in several models (e.g., Adler and Ghadar, 1990; Milliman et al., 1991). As firms move through different stages of internationalisation, the location of their production, nature of international activity, and the importance of international activity change (Adler and Ghadar, 1990). In order to accommodate these shifts in focus of international activities the priority ranking of a particular activity and how it is organized will be affected. Likewise, the relationship of strategy to HRM is well defined (Schuler, Dowling, and DeCieri, 1993). For example, different strategies require different role behaviours of employees, which indicate different priorities and methods of organizing HRM activities (Schuler and Jackson, 1987). Rosenzweig and Nohria (1994) proposed that firms in global or multi-domestic industries would have different propensities to be internally consistent with regard to HRM. While their direct test of this relationship was inconclusive, results from other studies (e.g., Boyacigiller, 1990; Welch, 1994) lend support to the logic of the argument that industry type affects the priority and organization of IHRM.

Environmental Contingencies

A long-standing classification of the international environment includes legal, political, economic and cultural forces. All of these factors have a clear influence on HRM. For example, a firm operating in a particular society often has little choice but to adjust its HRM practices to comply with the laws of the land. This coercive isomorphism is one reason for inconsistent HRM practices across local subsidiaries of MNCs. However, in addition to the inconsistencies of laws around the world, the gray areas of international law present the International HRM with significant challenges (Sundaram and Black, 1995). Societies place other limits on HRM through the level of resources (e.g., skilled labor, capital) made available to firms, and the regulations (laws or customs) that influence acceptable behavior by both employees and employers (Rousseau and Schalk, 2000). For example, laws influence employees with regard to what is allowed in a relationship with a firm and also directly influence the ability of workers to bargain. Additionally, societies vary in the extent to which they support a free market economy, and the economic environment in a country affects issues such as workforce demographics, quality of the labor force, hours of work, working conditions, and compensation levels (Parker, 1998). Moreover, government is a major employer in many countries and therefore exerts a powerful influence on the establishment of normative standards of HRM practice (Rousseau and Schalk, 2000). Finally, the socio-cultural environment, such as educational and family systems influence both the characteristics of the labor force as a whole and the characteristics of individuals (educational level, skills, social status). While these legal, political, and economic factors of society all have significant influence on the prioritization and organization of HRM activities, we have chosen to expand our discussion of the cultural contingency factor for three reasons.

First, to a great extent the economic, legal, and political characteristics of a country are a manifestation of a nation's culture. That is, these systems are derived from a country's culture and history. Cross-national culture stems from the fundamental ways in which a society learns to interact with its environment. Therefore, the economic, legal, and political systems that have developed over time are the visible elements of a more fundamental set of shared meanings. Culture affects the institutions of society in their goals, the way they operate, and in the attribution their members make for policies and behavior (Schwartz, 1992). Second, unlike economic, legal and political aspects of a country, which are observable, culture is largely invisible. That is, the influence of culture is difficult to detect and managers therefore often overlook it. While culture may or may not be the most important influence on HRM, it is the aspect of the IHRM context that is most often neglected. Finally, HRM is influenced by the cultural diversity that exists within the firm as well as in the broader external environment.

Culture: The Key Contingency Variable

Building upon Kluckholn's (1951) and Hofstede's (1980) perspectives, we define culture as an,

> "evolving set of shared beliefs, values, attitudes, and logical processes which provides cognitive maps for people within a given societal group to perceive, think, reason, act, react, and interact" (Tung, 1995: 491).

This definition recognizes the fact that culture is not static, but evolves over time. Based on this definition of culture and the perspectives on contingency relationships presented previously, two mechanisms by which national culture influences IHRM emerge.

Cultural norms In the first case, the priorities and organization of HRM practices can be seen as a manifestation or 'symptom' of the manager's cultural values. Thus, HRM decisions that managers make are guided, by and large, by their culturally-based value orientations even though they may not necessarily be aware of these subconscious influences. For example, in a high power distance culture the organization of HRM activities would be more hierarchical and centralized. In highly collectivistic cultures, teamwork is emphasized and singling out an employee for praise may be inappropriate (Hofstede, 1980).

Environmental pressure The second avenue for cultural influence relies on environmental pressure to shape HRM. That is, HRM systems are less the product of conscious design than a reflection of the structures that members of society will accept. In other words, pressures from the organizational environment, which includes the cultural context, dictate the type of HRM policies and organization that is seen as appropriate and/or legitimate. Many of the pressures that society brings to bear on organizations can be seen to emanate from the institutions (e.g., legal, political) of a society. However, the culture and the institutions of society are inevitably linked as they have evolved together over time. For example, because of the general belief in equality of humankind in the U.S., discrimination in employment decisions on the bases of race or gender is prohibited.

These two mechanisms underscore our assertion that culture exerts a strong influence on IHRM. Three additional aspects of culture also merit attention. These are the number of cultures represented in an organization or its environment (i.e., cultural diversity); the degree of cultural distance among these cultures; and Tung's (1995) definition of culture as evolving, albeit slowly.

Cultural Diversity Cultural diversity can have both positive and negative effects in organizations. On the negative side, a culturally-diverse workforce can add to the complexity of decision making in an organization because of problems of communication, both verbal and non-verbal, and may increase the incidence of conflict stemming from differences in values and norms. On the positive side, however, cultural diversity can result in more creative and higher quality HRM decisions. Also, having specific knowledge of another culture may increase the ability for some organizations to make effective IHRM decisions (Cox and Tung, 1997). Research on minority influence has shown that the expression of alternate views by culturally different organization members may raise the quality of decision making and problem solving by increasing the attention of that the organization pays to the decision making process (Nemeth, 1992). Some empirical evidence even suggests that cultural diversity is positively related to the financial performance of an organization (Ng and Tung, 1998).

Relative Cultural Difference A second way in which the cultural composition of the organization influences IHRM is the extent to which some individuals in the organization are culturally different from the other members. Culturally different organization members are aware that they are different, and this awareness causes them to compare themselves to others (Bochner and Ohsako, 1977; Bochner and Perks, 1971). Based on this comparison they evaluate the appropriateness of their behavior and their status in the organization. If organization members perceive their status in the organization favorably, they are likely to participate more fully and to perceive the organization positively (Mullen, 1987; Mullen and Baumeister, 1987; Tajfel and Turner, 1986). Greater cultural difference may result in a lower expectation of a successful interaction with the other organizational members and a higher estimate of the effort required to achieve success. Individuals may be reluctant to invest high amounts of effort in interacting with others who are very different because these interactions may be viewed as costing more in time and effort than the potential benefit (Thibaut and Kelley, 1959).

The implications for IHRM of this influence of culture are two-fold. First, in decision-making groups the degree of cultural distance among group members can influence the extent to which individuals participate and have influence over IHRM decisions. For example, individuals from cultures that have higher status in the organization will have more influence. Second, the acceptance on the priority ranking, method of implementation and organization of IHRM activities will likely be less uniform when the organization is composed of individuals who are from highly dissimilar cultures. For example, individuals who are culturally very different from the organizational mainstream may see policies and procedures as less applicable to them.

Culture as evolving Culture is not static, but evolves over time, albeit slowly (see Tung, 1995). The dynamic nature of culture has important implications for HRM policies and practices, particularly in work places characterized by a high degree of ethno-cultural diversity. When individuals live for long periods in a new country they gradually acculturate to it. As individuals go through this process of acculturation they develop attitudes and beliefs that embrace many of the concepts in their new environment (Berry, 1990). Additionally, the presence of people who have different culturally based attitudes, values and beliefs gradually changes the shape of organizations and society as whole. Thus, the sophisticated stereotypes that characterize countries and firms from those countries along a small number of cultural dimensions may be less useful. For example, it may no longer be prudent to characterize the U.S. and U.S. firms as individualistic and low power distance because in some organizations employees may come from a wide variety of different ethnic and cultural backgrounds. Thus, HRM practices must be adjusted to accommodate different patterns of communication, conflict resolution, and so on.

Conclusion

The global nature of today's business environment is axiomatic. The effective management of organizations in this global environment requires effective management of their most important resource – people. In the face of global competition, forces for global integration versus local responsiveness, the formation of global strategic alliances and network organizations, and the increase in cultural diversity internal human resource management must adopt a global perspective. In this chapter we argue that this global perspective can best be achieved by extending the contingency approach, which has served so well as a core paradigm for organization theory (Donaldson, 2001) and for the management of overseas assignments (Tung, 1981; 1998a). This extension requires the consideration of both internal and external contingencies that have been influenced by the changing context of international business. Furthermore, we argue that the key contingency variable for a global perspective on HRM is culture, which has a moderating effect, both internal and external to the organization.

Our approach builds on the contingency paradigm that has been fruitfully used by others, but unlike popular treatments of HRM as an aggregated bundle of activities, we advocate analyzing the domain of international HRM through the use of a framework known as facet mapping. In this way predictions of the influence of specific contingencies on the IHRM domain can be articulated at a level that is closer to HRM practice. Also, we outlined specific outcomes with regard to the domains of IHRM as opposed to a vague notion of fit either between HRM and other management practice or with the environment. This middle range approach is meant to provide an explanatory framework unlike the currently popular prescriptive approaches. In this way it is hoped that prescriptions for IHRM practice will be founded on the rigorous testing of relationships among the key variables we have identified here. For example, numerous interesting research questions can be derived from the model, including the following:

- How does the emphasis on particular HRM activities vary as the mix of the workforce (HCN, PCN, TCN) changes over time?
- How do cultural diversity inside the organization and the cultural context in which the organization exists interact to influence the priority of particular IHRM activities?
- How does the form of the organization (joint venture, strategic alliance, and so on) influence the design and implementation of a particular HRM policy?
- How does the emerging concept of "boundaryless careers" affect HRM policies and practices with regard to selection, training, development, appraisal and compensation?

These questions are derived from an extension of the contingency paradigm, which has been updated to include the global context of HRM, and which are specified at a level that their answers will have relevance for HRM policies and practices.

References

Adler, N. J. (1981), Re-entry: Managing cross-cultural transitions. *Group and Organization Studies*, **6**, 341-356.

Adler, N. J. (1986), Do MBAs want international careers? *International Journal of Intercultural Relations*, **10**, 277-300.

Adler, N. J., & Ghadar, F. (1990), International strategy from the perspective of people and culture: The North American context. In A.M. Rugman (Ed.), Research in global strategic management: *International business research for the twenty-first century* (pp.179-205). Greenwich, CT: JAI Press.

Arthur, M. B. & Rousseau, D. M., Eds. (1996), *The boundaryless career: A new employment principle for a new organizational era*. Boston, MA: Cambridge University Press.

Bartlett, C. (1986), Building and managing the transnational: The new organizational challenge. In M. Porter (Ed.), *Competition in global industries* (pp.367-401). Boston: Harvard Business School Press.

Beer, M., Spector, P. R., Lawrence, D., Mills, D. Q., & Walton, R. E. (1984), *Managing Human Assets*. New York: Free Press.

Bennett, A. (1989), The chief executives in year 200 will be experienced abroad. *Wall Street Journal* (February 27), 1.

Berry, J. W. (1990), The psychology of acculturation: Understanding individuals moving between cultures. In R. Brislin (Ed.), Cross-cultural research and methodology series: Vol. 14. *Applied cross-cultural psychology* (pp.232-252). Newbury Park, CA: Sage.

Bochner, S., & Ohsako, T. (1977), Ethnic role salience in racially homogeneous and heterogeneous societies. *Journal of Cross Cultural Psychology*, 8, 477-492.

Bochner, S., & Perks, R.W. (1971), National role evocation as a function of cross-national interaction. *Journal of Cross Cultural Psychology*, 2, 157-164.

Boyacigiller, N. (1990), Staffing in a foreign land: A multi-level study of Japanese multinationals with operations in the United States. Paper presented at the *annual meeting of the Academy of Management*, San Francisco.

Burns, T., & Stalker, C. M. (1961), The management of innovation. London: Tavistock.

Cascio, W. F., & Serapio, M. G. (1991), Human resources systems in an international alliance: the undoing of a done deal. *Organizational Dynamics*, 19(3), 63-74.

Cox Jr., T. and Tung (1997), R.L. The multicultural organization revisited. In C.L. Cooper and S.E. Jackson (Eds.), *The handbook of organizational behavior*. John Wiley & Sons, 1-28.

DiMaggio, P. J., & Powell, W. W. (1983), The iron cage revisited: Institutional isomorphism and collective rationality in organizational fields. *American Sociological Review*, 48, 147-160.

Donaldson, L. (2001), The contingency theory of organizations. *Thousand Oaks*, CA: Sage.

Dowling, P. J. (1988). International HRM. In L. Dyer (Ed.) *Human resource management: Evolving roles and responsibilities* (Vol. 1, pp. 228-258). Washington, DC: BNA.

Dunbar, E., & Ehrlich, M. (1993), Preparation of the international employee: Career and consultation needs. *Consulting Psychology Journal*, 45, 18-24.

Erez, M., & Earley, P. C. (1993), *Culture, self-identity and work*. New York: Oxford University Press.

Evans, P. A. L. (1986), The strategic outcomes of human resource management. *Human Resource Management*, 25(1), 149-167.

Hofstede, G. (1980) *Culture's consequences: International differences in work related values*. Beverly Hills, CA: Sage.

Inkson, K. (1997), Organizational forms and the restructuring of careers. In T. Clark (Ed.), *Advances in organizational behavior*. Louth: UK: Ashgate Press.

Jarillo, J. (1988), On strategic networks. *Strategic Management Journal*, 9, 31-41.

Johnston, W. B. & Packer, A. H. (1987), *Workforce 2000: Work and workers for the twenty-first century*. Washington, DC: Hudson Institute.

Kluckholn, C. (1951), "The study of culture". In D. Lerner and H.D. Lasswell (Eds.). *The policy sciences*. Stanford, Ca.: Stanford University Press.

Kochan, T. A. (1995, May), Launching a renaissance in international industrial relations. *Presidential address to the annual meeting of the International Industrial Relations association*. Washington, D.C.

Kogut, B. (1989), A note on global strategy. *Strategic Management Journal*, 10, 383-389.

Lawrence, P., & Lorsch, J. (1967), Differentiation and integration in complex organizations. *Administrative Science Quarterly*, **12**, 1-47.

Lorange, P., & Roos, J. (1992), *Strategic alliances. Cambridge*, MA: Blackwell.

Milliman, J., Von Glinow, M. A., & Nathan, M. (1991), Organizational life cycles and strategic international human resource management in multinational companies: Implications for congruence theory. *Academy of Management Review*, **16**(2), 318-329.

Morgan, P. V. (1986), International HRM: Fact or fiction? *Personnel Administrator*, **31**(9), 43-47.

Mullen, B. (1987), Self-attention theory: The effects of group composition on the individual. In B. Mullen & G. R. Goethals (Eds.), *Theories of group behaviour* (pp. 125-46). New York: Springer-Verlag.

Mullen, B., & Baumeister R. F. (1987), Groups effects on self-attention and performance: Social loafing, social facilitation, and social impairment. In C. Hendrick (Ed.), *Review of personality and social psychology* (pp. 189-206). Newbury Park, CA: Sage.

Murray, V. V., Jain, H. C., & Adams, R. J. (1976), A framework for the comparative analysis of personnel administration. *Academy of Management Review*, **19**, 47-57.

Naisbitt, J. (1994), Global paradox. NY: William Morrow.

Nemeth, C. J. (1992), Minority dissent as a stimulant to group performance. In S. Worchel, W. Wood, & J.A. Simpson (Eds.), *Group process and productivity* (pp. 95-111). Newbury Park, CA: Sage.

Ng, E.S.W. and Tung, R.L. (1998), Ethno-cultural diversity and organizational effectiveness: A field study. *International Journal of Human Resource Management*, **9**(6), 980-995.

Parker, B. (1998), *Globalization: Managing across boundaries*. London: Sage.

Poole, M. (1990), Editorial: Human resource management in international perspective. *International Journal of Human Resource Management*, **1**(1), 1-15.

Porter, M. E. (1986), Changing patterns of international competition. *California Management Review*, **28**(2), 9-40.

Rosenzweig, P. M., & Nohria, N. (1994), Influences on human resource management practices in multinational corporations. *Journal of International Business Studies*, **25**(2), 229-251.

Rosenzweig, P. M., & Singh, J. V. (1991), Organizational environments and the multinational enterprise. *Academy of Management Review*, **16**(2), 340-361.

Rousseau, D. M., & Schalk, R.,Eds.(2000), Psychological contracts in employment: Cross-national perspectives. *Thousand Oaks*, CA: Sage.

Schein, E. (1996), Career anchors revisited: Implications for career development in the 21st century. *Academy of Management Executive*, **10**(4), 80-88.

Schuler, R. S., Dowling, P. J., & De Cieri, H. (1993), An integrative framework of strategic international human resource management. *Journal of Management*, **19**(2), 419-459.

Schuler, R. S., & Jackson, S. E. (1987), Linking competitive strategies with human resource management practices. *Academy of Management Executive*, **1**(3), 207-219.

Schneider, S. C. (1988), National versus corporate culture: Implications for human resource management. *Human Resource Management*, **27**(2), 231-246.

Schwartz, S. H. (1992), Universals in the content and structure of values: Theoretical advances and empirical tests in 20 countries. In M. P. Zanna (Ed). *Advances in Experimental Social Psychology* (pp. 1-65). San Diego: Academic Press.

Stahl, G.K., Miller, E.L. and Tung, R.L. Toward the boundaryless career: A closer look at the expatriate career concept and the perceived implications of an international assignment. *Journal of World Business* (in press).

Sullivan, D. (1996), Organization structure in multinational corporations. In M. Warner (Ed.). *International encyclopaedia of business and management* (pp. 3573-3597). London: Routledge.

Sundaram, A. K. & Black, J. S. (1995), The international business environment. *Englewood Cliffs*, NJ: Ptentice-Hall.

Tajfel, H., & Turner, J.C. (1986), The social identity theory of intergroup behaviour. In S. Worchel & W.G. Wood (Eds.), *Psychology of intergroup relations* (pp. 7-24). Chicago: Nelson-Hall.

Taylor, S., Beechler, S., & Napier, N. (1996), Toward an integrative model of strategic human resource management. *Academy of Management Review*, 21(4), 959-985.

Thibaut, J. W., & Kelley, H. H. (1959), *The social psychology of groups.* New York: Wiley.

Thomas, D. C. (1998), The expatriate experience: A critical review and synthesis. *Advances in International Comparative Management*, 12, 237-273.

Thomas, D. C., Ravlin, E.C., & Barry, D. (2000), Managing multicultural teams. *University of Auckland Business Review*, 2(1), 10-25.

Tung, R. L. (1981), Selection and training of personnel for overseas assignments. *Columbia Journal of World Business*, 16(1), 68-78.

Tung, R. L. (1984), Strategic management of human resources in the multinational enterprise. *Human Resource management*, 23(2), 129-143.

Tung, R. L. (1988), The new expatriates: Managing human resources abroad. Cambridge, Mass.: Ballinger.

Tung, R. L. (1993), Managing cross-national and intra-national diversity. *Human Resources Management*, 32, 461-477.

Tung, R. L. (1995), International organizational behavior. In F. Luthans (Ed.). *Virtual OB.* New York: McGraw-Hill, Inc.,487-518.

Tung, R. L. (1998a), A contingency framework of selection and training of expatriates revisited. *Human Resource Management Review*, 8(1), 23-37.

Tung, R. L. (1998b), American expatriates abroad: From neophytes to cosmopolitans. *Journal of World Business* 33(2), 125-144.

Welch, D. (1994), Determinants of international human resource management approaches sand activities: A suggested framework. Journal of Management Studies, 31(2), 139-164.

Westney, D. E. (1993), Institutionalization theory and the multinational corporation. In S. Ghoshal & E. Westney (Eds.), *Organization theory and the multinational corporation.* New York: St. Martin's Press.

WTO (1999). *WTO annual report.* Geneva: World Trade Organization.

Chapter 7

Cultural Diversity in Cross-Border Alliances

Susan E. Jackson

Randall S. Schuler

Introduction

Increasingly, firms are using cross-border alliances to strengthen and maintain their position in the market place. Although often seen as a relatively fast and efficient way to expand into new markets and incorporate new technologies, the success of cross-border alliances is by no means assured. To the contrary, such alliances often fall short of their stated goals and objectives. While some failures can be explained by financial and market factors, the failure of others can be traced to neglected human resource issues and activities associated with managing the cultural diversity present in these organizations. This chapter describes the special challenges that cultural diversity creates for effectively managing human resources within cross-border alliances. Drawing upon the extensive literature regarding the management of domestic alliances and domestic diversity, we offer suggestions for how human resource management practices might be used to improve the success of cross-border alliances.

Regardless of industry, it appears that it has become all but impossible in our global environment for firms to successfully compete without growing and expanding through deals that result in cross-border alliances (CBAs) (Lucenko, 2000). In some industries, e.g., insurance, cross-border alliances provide a means for moving into new markets. In other industries, e.g., pharmaceuticals and software technology, small enterprises that are developing new products may enter into alliances with larger firms that can more efficiently manufacture and distribute those products. Other reasons for cross-border alliances include gaining access to the talents of another country's labor market, acquiring access to new technologies, controlling distribution channels, exploiting new opportunities created by government deregulation and privatization, and to facilitate rapid inter-organizational learning.

These drivers of cross-border alliances are expected to intensify in the future, as globalization continues – even in the face of difficult economic conditions (Charman, 2000; Cyr, 1995; Doz and Hamel, 1998; Hitt, Harrison, and Ireland, 2001; Inkpen and Beamish, 1997; Lane, Salk and Lyles, 2001; The Economist, 2000). For example, the U.S. biotechnology industry is characterized by networks of relationships between new biotechnology firms dedicated to research and new product development and established firms in industries that can use these new products, such as pharmaceuticals. In return for sharing technical information with the larger firms, the smaller firms gain access to their partners' resources for product testing, marketing, and distribution (Liebeskind, Oliver, Zucker, and Brewer, 1996). Big pharmaceutical firms such as Merck or Eli Lily gain from such partnerships because the smaller firms typically develop new drugs in as little as five years, versus an eight-year average development cycle in the larger firms (Robertson and Jett, 1999; Schonfield, 1997; Sager, 1996).

Types of Cross-Border Alliances

When using cross-border alliances to implement their business strategies, firms have many options. Representing the least intense and complex form of cross-border alliances are licensing agreements and various forms of limited partnerships. These are governed primarily through legal agreements and they often require very little adjustment or change in the normal operations of the firms involved. More complex forms of cross-border alliances include international joint ventures (IJVs), international acquisitions, and international mergers. Typically, these forms of cross-border alliances involve interdependencies that cannot be managed merely through legal agreements; the firms involved must learn to manage their operations in ways that take into account similarities and differences between the partners. In this chapter, we focus on international joint ventures and international mergers or acquisitions to illustrate the issues associated with cultural diversity in cross border alliances. (For a more detailed discussion of these topics, see Schuler, Luo and Jackson 2003). Note, however, that issues of cultural diversity may become even more complex in other forms of cross-border alliances, such as those that involve a large network of organizations linked together through various forms of interdependencies (e.g., see Doz and Hamel, 1998). Despite several differences among these forms of cross-border alliances, the success of each requires effectively managing issues that arise due to the many types of cultural diversity present in the organizations created by such alliances.

International Joint Ventures (IJVs) In an international joint venture, two (or more) parent firms from different countries establish a new legal entity that is subject to the joint control of the parent firms. This new entity is located outside the country of at least one of the parent firms (Shenkar and Zeira, 1987). In an international merger, two firms headquartered in different countries agree to integrate their operations and share control of a newly established firm. Typically, in both international joint ventures and international mergers, a new identity is established for the new legal entity.

Davidson-Marley BV is an example of an international joint venture created as a 50-50 partnership. This IJV was formed in order to supply instrument panels to Ford Motor Company, which was developing its world car concept. The joint venture allowed Marley Automotive Components, in the United Kingdom, to meet Ford's requirements for its suppliers, and it met the desire of Davidson-Textron, in the United States, to expand into Europe. Prior to the IJV, Marley was a licensee of Davidson. Based on their past experiences with each other, managers at the two firms felt confident that they could succeed in establishing an IJV, which they chose to locate in The Netherlands. Throughout this chapter, we use the Marley-Davison case to illustrate how cultural diversity can affect the management of an international joint venture. More details about the evolution of this IJV can be found in Schuler and van Sluijs (1992), Schuler, Dowling and DeCieri (1992), and van Sluijs and Schuler (1994).

International Mergers and Acquisitions (IM&As) In an international acquisition, a firm headquartered in one country acquires and fully controls a firm headquartered in another country. In the case of an acquisition, the acquired firm ceases to exist as a legal entity and the acquired firm takes on the identity of the acquiring firm. The majority of acquisitions are friendly – that is, the acquired firm solicits bids and enters into an acquisition voluntarily. Sometimes, however, a firm becomes a takeover target. A takeover acquisition usually occurs when an unsolicited bid is made for a poorly performing firm. Although mergers, acquisitions, and takeovers are technically different, it's common to refer to all three means for combining the operations of two firms as mergers and acquisitions, or just M&As (Deogun and Scannell, 2001;Charman, 1999).

Four Prototypical Approaches to Managing Cross-Border Alliances

Many specific conditions present in a particular cross-border alliance determine the challenges of managing cultural diversity that will be faced by members of the alliance. For example, the number of organizations involved and the number of countries involved can be only two, as would be true if two domestic organizations from two countries enter into a merger or acquisition. However, the diversity may be greater if either company involved in the merger or acquisition has international operations, or if either company has recently engaged in other mergers or acquisitions.

For an international joint venture, at least three organizations are involved – two parents and the venture itself – and by definition the companies are located in at least two countries. But this is just the simplest scenario. When the joint venture is located in a third country and/or when more than two parent firms collaborate to form the joint venture, then challenges of managing cultural diversity increase accordingly. In the Marley-Davidson example, three countries and three organizations were involved: Davidson-Textron was located in the United States,

Marley was located in the United Kingdom, and the Marley-Davidson venture was located in The Netherlands.

Regardless of the number of companies and countries involved, however, the general management approach used in cross-border alliances can be characterized as fitting one of four approaches. These approaches reflect substantially different ways to deal with the cultural diversity that is present in any cross-border alliance. As illustrated in Figure 7.1, these approaches can be labeled portfolio, blending, new creation, and absorption.

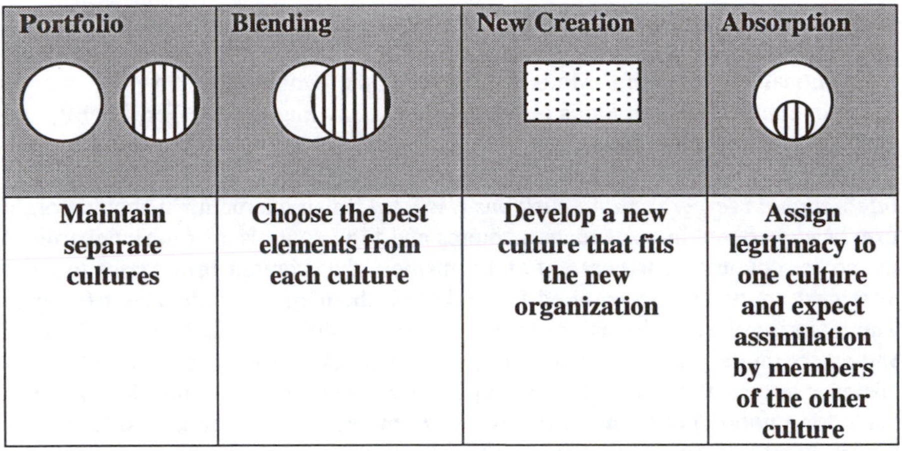

Portfolio	Blending	New Creation	Absorption
Maintain separate cultures	Choose the best elements from each culture	Develop a new culture that fits the new organization	Assign legitimacy to one culture and expect assimilation by members of the other culture

Figure 7.1: Four approaches to managing cultural diversity in cross-border alliances

© S. E Jackson and R.S Schuler

Portfolio In the portfolio approach, managers in the organizations involved in the alliance retain a great deal of autonomy. Although the alliance creates legal and economic interdependencies, the top management team assumes that the organizations involved in the alliance will continue to operate more or less as they had operated prior to the formation of the alliance. Presumably, the strategic value of the alliance does not require integrating the separate organizational systems, so cultural diversity is "managed" by maintaining segregated organizations. This scenario often occurs when one firm acquires another firm in order to diversify into another business or region and then allows the acquired firm to operate as a relatively autonomous subsidiary. For example, when Nestle purchased Purina, in expanded into pet foods and did not attempt to merge the Purina operations with other Nestle units.

Blending The blending scenario arises when top managers expect the two (or more) organizations involved in the alliance to come together or merge into a new organization that retains the best aspects of the alliance partners. In this scenario, the intent is to manage cultural diversity through integration, with members of each culture adapting to the other culture. The blending approach may be used in a joint venture or a merger or an acquisition, but it is perhaps most common in M&As that occur within an industry between firms that are believed to complement each other's strengths and offset each other's weaknesses.

Presumably, Daimler and Chrysler executives intended to use blending to make that deal a success. During the initial stages of the merger, Chrysler President Thomas Stallkamp indicated that Daimler intended to adopt Chrysler's product development methods, which emphasized teamwork rather than individual-oriented work procedures. Chrysler in turn would adopt Daimler practices such as rigid adherence to timetables and their methodological approach to problem solving.

New Creation A third scenario arises when the partners agree to create a new firm that is truly different from either of the original partners. This is most likely to occur for joint ventures, especially if the joint venture is located in a country other than the countries of the parent firms. The Davidson-Marley IJV is one example of this arrangement. The parent companies established a greenfield plant in a third country. During the formation and development stages of the IJV, managers from the parent firms agreed that they wanted to hire Dutch managers for the IJV and give them great autonomy in making decisions about the plant's design and operation. In reality, managers from the parent firms developed fairly detailed plans before hiring the IJV managers, so the diversity management approach for the new plant actually fell somewhere between "new creation" and "blending" (Schuler and van Sluijs, 1992).

Mergers may also be initiated for the purpose of creating a new organization, although it seems to be less common. One indication that a merger is intended to form a new creation is that the resulting firm takes on a completely new name. Novartis, which was created through a merger of Sandoz and Ciba-Geigy, is one example. Novartis also is an example of a merger that might seem to not involve differences in national culture, because Sandoz and Ciba-Geigy were both headquartered in Switzerland. In actuality, however, a large portion of Ciba-Geigy's pharmaceutical business was based in the United States, while Sandoz's pharmaceutical base was in Switzerland. Thus, what may appear to be a domestic merger in fact required managing a create deal of diversity created by differences in national cultures.

Absorption Finally, in some acquisitions, the buyer clearly intends to take over and control the target. The target firm may be an attractive candidate for an acquisition because it has some valuable assets, yet for various reasons it is clear that the target firm cannot continue to survive on its own. In this scenario, the expectation is that the target firm will lose its identity and adopt the management practices of the acquiring firm. In other words, the target firm is expected to assimilate into the acquirer. This is what happened in Pfizer's hostile take-over of Warner-Lambert. When Pfizer acquired Warner-Lambert, they adopted a few of Warner-Lambert's practices, but observers say that little of the Warner-Lambert culture remains today. Not surprisingly, most of Warner-Lambert's top-level managers have left the firm, leaving a top management team that is not much more diverse today than it was before the acquisition.

We assume that each of the four approaches described above can be an effective way to manage cultural diversity in a cross-border alliance. These approaches are more likely to be successful if they have been intentionally adopted by top managers and communicated to employees in the relevant organizations. By making explicit the guiding philosophy that underlies subsequent planning and decision making, managers can more easily align their own actions to be consistent with the philosophy, and employees should be able to more accurately interpret managerial actions. The consequences of these philosophies can affect cross-border alliances differently at each stage in their evolution.

Stages in the Evolution of Cross-Border Alliances

Each of the four alternative approaches to managing cultural diversity in cross-border alliances has associated with it different challenges that must be overcome in order for a cross-border alliance to eventually succeed. Furthermore, these different challenges arise at different stages in the evolution of an alliance, so we briefly describe these evolutionary stages next.

IJVs and IM&As are distinct types of cross-border alliances, and the management literatures that have developed to address these different types of alliances have evolved with little reference to each other. One consequence of this history is that different terms have been used to describe the stages through which IJVs and IM&As evolve. To simplify our discussion, Figure 7.2 describes the general stages that occur during the formation and life of both types of alliances (cf., Schuler, 2001; Schuler and Jackson, 2001).

Stage 1—Precombination and Initial Planning
<ul><li>Identifying reasons for the alliance and setting objectives</li><li>Identifying and evaluating potential alliance partners</li><li>Negotiating the arrangement</li></ul>
Stage 2—Development
<ul><li>Choosing locations for the operations</li><li>Establishing the structure</li><li>Recruiting and retaining key talent</li></ul>
Stage 3—Implementation
<ul><li>Establishing the vision, mission, values, strategy</li><li>Developing management policies</li><li>Translating policies into managerial practices and behavior</li><li>Staffing and managing the employees</li></ul>

Stage 4—Advancement and Beyond
• Monitoring the organizational culture • Learning from the alliance partner • Transferring new knowledge throughout the organization (and back to the parent, for IJVs)

Figure 7.2: Evolutionary stages of cross-border alliances

Initial planning All types of cross-border alliances involve an initial planning stage. For IM&As, this stage is somewhat more regulated than for IJVs. Nevertheless, for both types of alliances, the common activities include identifying reasons for the alliance and setting objectives, identifying and evaluating potential alliance partners, and negotiating the arrangement. In many cases, formal assessments of cultural issues that might influence the success of the alliance are conducted at this stage, but sometimes this assessment occurs later or perhaps not at all.

Formation and development During formation and development of the alliance, the their implications of cultural diversity usually become more apparent although they may not be fully understood. As the new entity is formed, recruiting and selecting of key executives to staff the new organization often is viewed as a key task, so cultural differences in how to recruit and evaluate candidates are likely to become salient. As employment contracts are negotiated, cultural differences related to monitoring and compensation key executives also usually become apparent.

Implementation During implementation, a key management task is aligning employees' skills and motivations with the business objectives. Cultural issues that arise during the implementation stage may be many or few, depending on the partners' general approach to managing the alliance. If one or more of the partners feels the new organization must be managed in a way that is consistent with their culture (i.e., the blending approach), then managing country, industry and corporate cultural diversity may all be salient issues at this stage. However, if the partners agree to adopt a portfolio approach, then challenges associated with managing domestic cultural diversity may be salient for the venture managers.

Advancement During the advancement stage, knowledge transfer is a key issue. At this stage, the salience of cultural diversity may again be relatively great or small. If the new organization has been managed using a hands-off approach, then little attention will have been devoted to dealing with the cultural differences between the partners. In order for knowledge sharing to occur, however, issues of cultural diversity will now have to be addressed. If, on the other hand, a blending approach was used, the cultural differences will be smaller at this stage, so transferring knowledge now may be easier.

In the Davidson-Marley example, several expatriate managers were assigned to work in the IJV for limited periods of time. Originally, the expatriates carried knowledge from the parents to the IJV. Later, when they returned to the parent firms, the repatriated managers transferred knowledge learned in the IJV back to the parents. The use of a few expatriates early in the life of the IJV was an example of the parent firms deciding to compromise their approach to managing cultural diversity. Their long-term plan called for the IJV to operate as an independent organization, but the parent firms also wanted to continue to learn from the IJV and transfer new knowledge back into the parents. Apparently, they believed that their own managers could more easily transfer the new knowledge being created back to the parents. Also, the presence of these expatriates in the early days of the IJV ensured that the IJV did not develop an organizational culture that clashed sharply with the organizational cultures of the parent firms.

The general approach to managing diversity taken by the organizations involved cross-border alliances has important implications for the issues faced at each stage of the development. If an acquiring firm expects to use the portfolio approach and allow an acquired firm to operate more or less autonomously, then there may be little need to invest resources in assessing the fit between the corporate cultures of the two firms during the initial planning stage. Assessing cultural fit at this stage may also seem relatively unimportant if the acquired firm expects to impose its own culture on the acquired firm. In contrast, assessing cultural fit and understanding the implications of cultural differences is more likely to be a high priority during the planning stage if the blending or new organization approach is adopted.

Failure and Success in Cross-Border Alliances

With the importance of and need for cross-border alliances' growth, and the base of experience expanding, it may seem reasonable to also assume that success is more likely to occur than failure in these types of combinations. In fact, the opposite is true.

Failure Rates Statistics show that fewer than 20 per cent of all mergers and acquisitions in the United States achieve their financial objectives. In Europe, where international mergers and acquisitions (IM&As) are more common, success rates are very similar (Charman, 2000). Estimating the success rates of IJVs is more difficult, due in part to the different objectives that partners often have for such alliances. Learning and other nonfinancial goals may be met even when an IJV looks unsuccessful in terms of profits or other bottom-line indicators (Schaan, 1988).

Reasons for Failure Cross-border alliances between businesses fail for a variety of reasons, and often several reasons operate simultaneously. Typical reasons for failure include:

- Unrealistic expectations
- Hastily constructed strategy, poor planning, unskilled execution
- Inability to unify behind a single macro message
- Talent is lost or mismanaged
- Culture clashes between the partners go unchecked
- Lack of trust between managers from the previously separate firms
- Unexpectedly high costs associated with the transition and co-ordination

Of these, clashing cultures is among the most cited reason, and often this reason is intertwined with other reasons (Bianco, 2000; Weber 2000). In cross-border alliances, culture clashes are common, e.g., clashes due to differences in corporate cultures and clashes due to differences in country cultures. Of course, the two types may be related, and in any event they are difficult to disentangle from each other. The situation that DaimlerChrysler faced is not uncommon. Despite proclamations indicating that executives were hoping to blend together the best aspects of each company, the lack of true sharing and co-operation was soon evident – for example, Daimler executives refused to use Chrysler parts in Mercedes vehicles. Although DaimlerChrysler was "one" company in name, two separate operational headquarters were maintained; one in Michigan and one in Germany. Two years after this merger was legally completed, Daimler's Chief of Passenger Car's, Juergën Hubbert, was quoted as saying, "We have a clear understanding: one company, one vision, one chairman, two cultures" (The Economist, 2000).

The Nature of Cultural Diversity in Cross-Border Alliances

In this chapter, we use the term culture to refer the unique pattern of shared assumptions, values, and norms that shape the socialization, symbols, language, narratives and practices of a group of people. Thus, culture provides a context for interpreting events and assigning meaning (Rafaeli and Worline, 2000; Trice and Beyer,, 1993; Denison, 1996). Cultures develop in both large and small groups of people, so cultural differences occur at many levels. Some cultural differences become most evident when comparing large geographic regions, while others can be found at the level of countries, regions within countries, industries, organizations, occupational groups, demographic groups within a country, and so on. For any particular international joint venture, merger or acquisition, cultural differences at many or all of these different levels are likely to be relevant. The specific nature and location of a cross-border alliance determines which elements of culture become most salient and require the most attention.

National Cultures

Depending on the cultural distance between the national cultures involved in a cross-border alliance, managing differences in country cultures or regional cultures may be of relatively great or only minor significance. In some cross-border alliances, such as those between U.S. and Canadian business, differences in country cultures are relatively small. In others, however, cultural differences is such key areas as leadership styles and decision making procedures can be substantial (Brodbeck et al., 2000). Even when an alliance occurs between companies within a single country, cultural differences may be significant due to regional differences. A study of more than 700 managers in large cities in China suggests that there are at least three distinct regional subcultures in that country. Thus, cultural diversity may create just as great a challenge for an alliance between companies from different regions in China as it would for other cross-border alliances (Ralston, Kai-Cheng, Wang, Terpstra, and Wei, 1996).

Variations (or similarities) in the institutional environments of the alliance partners may further complicate (or help to alleviate) the challenge of managing differences due to national cultures. For example, the European Union, the Asia-Pacific Economic Cooperation, and the North American Free Trade Agreement all represent institutional arrangements that seek to provide a common framework or perspective that can be used to guide some relationships between companies in the member countries (see Luo, 2000). As these institutional arrangements become more well established, it is likely that cross-border alliances within an economic trade region will become easier even in the face of significant differences in national cultures. Nevertheless, even within economic trade zones, differences in institutional arrangements among countries result in differences in the functioning of corporate boards and top management teams as well as approaches to managing an organization's human resources (Brewster, 1995; Glunk, Heijltjes, and Olie, 2001; Mayer and Whittington, 1999).

Industry Culture Similarly, differences in industry cultures may be important in some cross-border alliances and nearly irrelevant in others. Industry boundaries are both fuzzy and unstable, so the question "What industry are we in?" isn't always easy to answer. Furthermore, some companies compete by constantly pushing at the boundaries of the industry and, eventually, redefining the industries in which they compete (Hamel, 2001;Hamel and Prahalad, 1994). Nevertheless, companies within an industry experience similar patterns of growth and eventually a common industry culture may develop. Unfortunately, there is very little empirical research evidence available to use in understanding industry-based cultural differences. An exception is the work of Hofstede (1997), who suggested that industry cultures can be described using four dimensions: employee-oriented vs. job-oriented; parochial vs. professional; open vs. closed system; and loose vs. tight control. Although Hofstede's dimensions for describing industry differences have not been widely used in empirical research, his work supports the assumption that cultural clashes are more likely to be disruptive in alliances that are formed by firms that formerly had competed in different industries.

Organizational Cultures

As is true for industry cultures, describing differences in organizational cultures can be difficult because there has been little empirical work directed at understanding the nature of these differences and how they are manifested across different countries (Adler and Jelinek, 1986; Aquinis and Henle, in press). One popular typology for describing organizational cultures uses two dimensions to create a typology of four cultures, with each culture characterized by different underlying values. In this typology, one dimension reflects the formal control orientation, ranging from stable to flexible. The other dimension reflects the focus of attention, ranging from internal functioning to external functioning (Quinn and Rohrbaugh, 1983; Hooijberg and Petrock, 1993).

Based on research in ten companies located in three European countries, Hofstede proposed using six dimensions to conceptualize organizational cultures (Hofstede, Neuijen, Ohayv, and Sanders, 1990): process versus results orientation; employee versus job orientation; parochial versus professional; open versus closed system; loose versus tight control; and normative versus pragmatic. Rather than reflecting different values, these dimensions reflect differences in management practices (see also Peterson and Hofstede, 2000).

Using yet a third approach to conceptualizing organizational culture, the GLOBE project (Dickson, Aditya, and Chhokar, 2000; House and colleagues, 1999) has made the assumption differences in organizational cultures can be understood using the same dimensions that differentiate among national cultures.

Domestic Sub-Cultures

In any organization, differences in personality and behavioral styles contribute to workforce diversity. Other forms of domestic diversity are associated with membership in various demographic groups. Within the United States, research on domestic cultural diversity is based on the assumption that membership in some demographic groups results in socialization experiences that effectively create identifiable subcultures within a national population. Gender, ethnicity and age are the characteristics most often associated with demographic cultural influences. Of course, differences found among demographic groups within a country are shaped by and also contribute to the country's national culture. For example, gender differences appear to be more pronounced in some countries than others as do the relationships between men and women (Best and Williams, 2001; Williams and Best, 1990). Furthermore, in other countries, it is likely that meaningful cultural variations are associated with other demographic subgroups – for example, cultural differences due to religion may be more salient while those due to race or ethnicity may be less salient. Regardless of which other forms of diversity must be managed in cross-border alliances, domestic diversity is always an issue.

In the Davidson-Marley IJV, the Dutch workforce hired to staff the manufacturing plant shared a societal culture, but other forms of domestic diversity proved challenging nevertheless. Recruitment and selection practices intentionally sought to represent the demographic diversity (gender, age, and so on) of the Dutch labor market within the plant. Additional diversity was introduced unintentionally, however, because employees were hired in two distinct waves. All employees who were hired had to meet the same technical skill requirements, but different personalities were sought during these two hiring waves. In selecting the first 100 employees, the IJV sought people who were willing to contribute to building up the firm in its pioneering phase. Good problem-identification and problem-solving abilities were needed. In addition, the IJV looked for employees with an international orientation because these employees would be traveling to the U.S. or the U.K. to receive training.

A Dynamic, Multi-Level Model of Cultural Diversity

Scholars who study culture at different levels of analysis disagree about how to describe cultures, the social levels of analysis at which it is appropriate to apply the concept of culture, and many other issues that are beyond the scope of this chapter. [An overview of these issues can be found in Ashkanasy and Jackson (2001). For more detailed discussions, see Ashkanasy, Wilderom and Peterson (2000)]. Without attempting to either summarize or resolve these debates, in this chapter we make some simplifying assumptions about the nature of "culture".

One assumption is that our understanding of the consequences of cultural diversity in cross-border alliances can move ahead without resolving questions about how best to assess the "content" of culture. We do not intend to suggest that empirical work of a comparative nature is unimportant. However, a complete understanding of the ways that the cultures of various subgroups are similar or different from each other is not needed in order to begin to understand how the presence of cultural differences shapes behavior in organizations. That is, we assume that the structure of cultural diversity represented in the four prototypical approaches to managing cross-border alliances, described above, has some predictable consequences, and that these arise regardless of the content of the cultural diversity present in a specific cross-border alliance.

We also assume that the behavior of an individual is influenced by multiple cultures, which are associated with the person's multiple memberships in and identification with a variety of overlapping and intersecting social entities (societies, organizations, professions, ethnic populations, and so on). These multiple cultures provide the individual with a variety of value systems (which need not be consistent with each other) for interpreting and responding to events in the environment. Depending on the social setting, some of the value systems available to an individual become more salient and important in guiding behavior. This perspective of how cultures impact behavior is consistent with social identity theory, which views social identification processes as situationally determined.

Jackson, May and Whitney (1995) developed a model to illustrate how domestic diversity influences behavior in organizations. Here we have adapted their model to illustrate how many aspects of cultural diversity can combine to influence the behavior of employees in cross-border alliances. First, we describe the model and then we illustrate its implications for understanding the challenge of managing cultural diversity in cross-border alliances.

Levels and Dynamics of Cultural Diversity

Shown in Figure 2.3, the model recognizes that the cultural context includes several layers or levels. To some extent, these layers of culture are nested, with the more inclusive levels of culture operating as constraints around the "lower" levels of culture. For example, the organizational cultures of single-business domestic firms tend to be constrained by and reflect their country and industry cultures. We do not intend to imply that the more inclusive levels of culture determine the cultures of more delimited social systems, however. Nor do we intend to suggest that a lower-level social system is fully nested within only one higher-level social system. Indeed, for cross-border alliances, this is definitely not the case – instead, at least some individuals (e.g., the top management team) within any organization formed by a cross-border alliance are embedded in multiple organizational and country cultures, and perhaps also multiple industry cultures.

Recognizing that cultural diversity can be created in many ways, the model shown in Figure 2.1 organizes constructs into four general categories that are linked as follows: cultural diversity → mediating states and processes → short-term behavioral manifestations → longer-term consequences. The model can be used to analyze the behavior of individuals, dyads, and larger social units, such as work teams, departments, business units, and so on.

Cultural Diversity

Beginning on the left, the content and structure of cultural diversity are viewed as (partial) determinants of the way people feel and think about themselves and each other. The content of cultural diversity simply refers to the specific values, norms, language and other elements of a culture. The structure of cultural diversity refers to how cultural differences are distributed within the team or organization.

The specific circumstances of a particular cross-border alliance mean that both the structure and content of cultural diversity may be somewhat unique to each alliance. For example, in the development stage of IM&As, the structure of organizational-level diversity within the integration teams is likely to be balanced (or, some might describe it as polarized), especially if the partners adopt a blending approach for managing diversity. If each of the partners is a domestic firm with little societal-level diversity represented, then the integration team also will be balanced in terms of societal cultural diversity. In this situation, the alignment of societal and organizational membership reinforces the cultural divide between the subgroups within the team, creating a cultural fault-line (Lau and Murnighan, 1998).

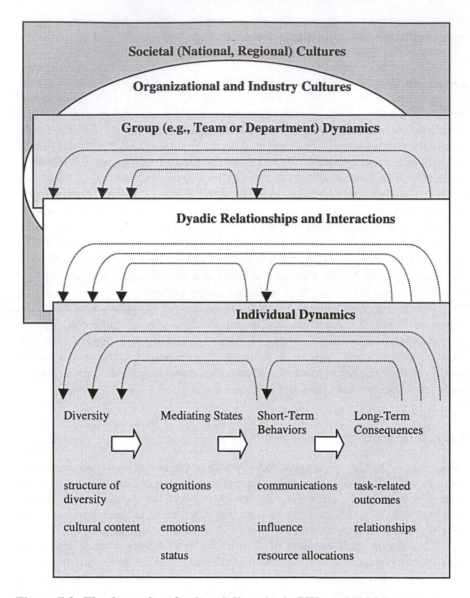

Figure 7.3: The dynamics of cultural diversity in IJVs and IM&As
© Susan E. Jackson and Randall S. Schuler

Next, consider the example of an IJV that is located outside the countries of the two parents and staffed completely with local talent. In that case, there may be little societal diversity within the IJV. Nevertheless, if employees were hired from the local external labor market, a great deal of organizational and industry-based diversity may be present. If the local labor market for jobs is demographically diverse, and if employment practices encourage hiring across the full range of the labor force, then demographic diversity will also be present in the workforce. Under this scenario, the expectation might be that the structure of diversity should not create a strong fault-line or polarization between any two groups. Nevertheless, cultural faultlines and polarization may arise even under this type of scenario.

In the Davidson-Marley IJV, a cultural fault-line was inadvertently created among employees in the Dutch manufacturing plant. The fault-line developed because employees were hired in two distinct waves. The first group of 100 employees who were hired worked in a start-up operation and were deeply involved in working out the details of how the operation was run. After the new plant was established and growing, the IJV hired 200 more employees. For this wave of hiring, they sought people who were willing to accept and adjust to the management practices of the now-thriving operation, and who could work well in teams. Thus, differences in the job tenure of employees were aligned with differences in personality. Furthermore, due to the timing of the hires, these two waves of employees found themselves working under different employment contracts. And, due to the seniority differences in the two groups, those who were hired first were always assigned to more advanced job categories and received higher pay. This divide within the workforce created unexpected conflicts, and in retrospect, the HR manager realized that it would have been better to hire on a continuous basis rather than in two distinct waves (van Sluijs and Schuler, 1994).

The content of cultural differences has received the most attention in past research. However, research on group dynamics clearly shows that the structure of cultural diversity has important consequences. For example, inter-group conflict is almost inevitable when cultural fault-lines are present, regardless of the cultural values or norms that separate the groups. In contrast, when differences are more broadly distributed and diffuse, problems of co-ordination may be more problematic than overt conflict, especially in the early stages of a group's development. However, given enough time, very diverse multinational teams in which there is no opportunity for nationality-based cliques to form can overcome these problems and outperform more homogeneous teams in the long run (Earley and Mosakowski, 2000).

Mediating States and Processes

Mediating states and processes refer to the individual thoughts and feelings through which the effects of cultural diversity are translated into observable behaviors. These mediators include emotional reactions (e.g., attraction, discomfort, and admiration) and cognitive structures (e.g., mental models and stereotypes) as well as perceptions of status and power.

Emotional Reactions Regardless of the basis for identifying people as similar or dissimilar, people tend to feel more comfortable with and positive about others who they perceive to be similar. Loyalty and favoritism characterize interactions with similar others while distrust and rivalry characterize interactions with those who are dissimilar. The tendency to be attracted to and biased in favor of similar others is so pervasive that it operates even when people judge their similarity based on meaningless information (such as randomly determined group membership).

At the level of teams and larger organizational units, feelings of attraction or liking among members translate into group cohesiveness. Although there has been little research on the effects of shared societal, industry or organizational cultures on group cohesiveness, there is a great deal of evidence showing this effect of similarity for other background characteristics, including age, gender, race, education, prestige, social class, attitudes and beliefs (Jackson et al., 1995). As will soon become apparent, this similarity-attraction-cohesiveness dynamic can have important consequences for the emotional landscape within which members of cross-border alliances conduct their work.

Cognition Cultural diversity also shapes the cognitive landscape of cross-border alliances. In order to simplify and make manageable a world of infinite variety, people naturally rely on stereotypes to inform their evaluations of others, guide their behavior towards others, and predict the behavior of others. Mental models are another cognitive short-cut for making sense of a complex world and deciding how to act. In work organizations, the mental models of employees may include beliefs about the priority assigned to various performance objectives (e.g., speed versus friendliness in customer interactions) and well as beliefs about cause-and-effect relationships (e.g., what a group should do if it wants to increase speed). The content of stereotypes and mental models reflect past experiences, and are almost inextricably bound up with the content of a culture (e.g., see Beyer, 1981; Leung, 1997; Leung, Au, Fernandiz-Dols, and Iwawaki, 1992). Furthermore, stereotypes and mental models influence what aspects of the environment people attend to and they guide the actions people take. Thus, they can either contribute to or interfere with co-ordinated action. When cultural diversity results in greater diversity of stereotypes and mental models, misunderstandings among employees are more likely, so more time and effort will be needed to avoid or correct the harm that such misunderstandings may cause.

Status Even in the flattest and most egalitarian social systems, some groups enjoy more status than others. Although cultures differ in the role that status plays in shaping interactions, status differences are recognized in all cultures.

In cross-border alliances, status hierarchies may reflect differences in the sizes and reputations of the organizations involved, as well as the specific circumstances of the alliance. Although we know of no research that has investigated status dynamics within joint ventures or M&As, anecdotal evidence suggests that employees of acquired firms experience feelings of lost or lower status. Status relationships may also be shaped by an acquiring firm's use of the absorption approach to managing cultural diversity, which implies that the culture is to be subsumed or obliterated.

The dysfunctional effects of status characteristics are likely to be greatest when low status individuals have resources or expertise that the work group needs to perform their task, and high status people do not. Compared to those with lower status, higher status persons display more assertive non-verbal behaviors during communication; speak more often, criticize more, state more commands, and interrupt others more often; have more opportunity to exert influence, attempt to exert influence more, and actually are more influential (Levine and Moreland, 1990). Consequently, lower status members participate less. Because the expertise of lower-status members is not fully used, status differences inhibit creativity, contribute to process losses, and interfere with effective decision making.

In newly formed cross-border alliances, observed conflicts often are attributed to disagreements that reflect an ongoing contest over the establishment of a status hierarchy among the members of the organization. In the case of acquisitions, the status hierarchy is perhaps most quickly established, with higher status going to members in the acquiring firm. In deals described as mergers, power-sharing structures may be set up to communicate the message that employees from the two firms are to be accorded equal status. Such structures seldom endure however, and a clear status hierarchy eventually emerges. Similarly, joint ventures often are structured to communicate a message of equality among the partner firms. Inevitably, however, status hierarchies emerge and become established within the joint venture firm (e.g., see Salk and Shenkar, 2001; Yan and Luo, 2001).

Short-Term Behavioral Manifestations

Short-term behavioral manifestations of cultural diversity refer to the observable interpersonal behaviors that are affected by the content of structure of diversity within a group or organization. Among the most important behaviors for understanding how diversity affects organizations are; communication, resource sharing and influence attempts.

Communication Because different cultures use different languages and communication styles, misunderstandings are common when people from different cultures attempt to communicate. Despite careful planning for the Davidson-Marley IJV, the American engineers who designed the Dutch manufacturing plant sent measurements calculated in feet, inches and U.S. gallons, which meant that local Dutch engineers had to convert all of the measurements before letting contracts and gaining approval from government officials. However, low fidelity communication and misunderstandings are not the only short-term manifestations of cultural diversity – and they may not be the most important. Cultural diversity also shapes who speaks with whom, how often and what they speak about. That is, cultural diversity shapes the structure of communication as well as its content (for examples of this in cross-border alliances, see Luo, 2001; Salk and Shekar, 2001).

In general, the structure of an organization's communication network is likely to reflect the structure its cultural diversity because, just as people are attracted to similar others they spend more time in communication with similar others (Brass, 1984; Lincoln and Miller, 1979). Although they are not well-documented, these same dynamics are likely to shape communication networks in cross-border alliances. That is, the more diversity that is present in a cross-border alliance, the more fragmented communication networks are likely to be.

Resource Allocation Through their communications, members of an organization seek, offer, and negotiate for work-related information and resources. Each person's access to information and resources, in turn, has important consequences for the individual's performance as well as the group's performance. Access to resources also determines other important outcomes, such as whether a person can take advantage of personal and career enhancing opportunities within the organization. Research conducted in laboratory settings shows that people who are similar share resources more readily (Brewer; 1979; Kramer and Brewer, 1984; Tajfel,1978). Presumably, the same is true in organizational settings (Ilgen, LePine and Hollenbeck, 1999; Armstrong and Cole, 1996).

Social Influence The basic dynamics of social influence include attempts aimed at changing the attitudes and behaviors of others as well as the responses made to such attempts. Social influence processes appear to be a universal aspect of group behavior that is found in most cultures (Mann, 1980). Nevertheless, the specific influence tactics used and the means through which conformity is expressed are somewhat culture bound. Comparative studies of social influence reveal a variety of differences among national cultures (Smith, 2001). For example, in collectivist cultures, people are relatively more responsive to influence attempts; that is, they conform more to social pressure from others (Bond and Smith, 1996). Comparative studies also show that managers from different cultural backgrounds use different influence tactics in their attempts to influence subordinates (Sun and Bond, 1999).

   Unfortunately, there have been few investigations into how influence processes are affected by cultural diversity. However, findings such as these suggest that the contours of cultural diversity in an organization are likely to shape how, and how effectively influence is wielded.

Long-Term Consequences of Cultural Diversity

So far, we have argued that the cultural diversity present in cross-border alliances has important implications for employees' emotions, cognitions, and interpersonal behaviors. In this section, we describe the longer-term consequences that are the reasons why cultural diversity is important for organizations to understand and learn to manage. Several published reviews of the extensive literature addressing this topic suggest that cultural diversity can affect organizations and individuals in a variety of ways – some effects are potentially beneficial and others may be detrimental; some are directly relevant to the organization's performance and others are personally relevant to individual employees. (For more details, see Jackson, 1992; Williams and O'Reilly, 1998; Milliken and Martins, 1996).

Potential Benefits of Cultural Diversity In alliances that adopt either a blending approach or a new organization approach, it is likely that the executives who promoted the alliance believed that (a) the creation of an alliance would enable the partners to learn from their differences, and/or (b) the new organization would approach issues in new and innovative ways that were less likely to be found in either of the partner organizations. The establishment of NUMMI by Toyota and General Motors is a well-known example of a U.S. auto maker's attempt to learn about the lean manufacturing methods that were being used so successfully in Japan. Conversely, Toyota was able to gain access that enabled them to learn about the competitive strategies of their partner and to more easily monitor developments within the U.S. auto industry (Doz and Hamel, 1998).

When learning is cited as an objective for alliances, the learning process often is depicted as one partner learning something that the other partner already knows. In other words, learning is viewed as knowledge transfer. For knowledge transfer opportunities to be valuable, the two partners must have different knowledge bases – or example, one partner may hope to acquire knowledge that the other partner has about a national market and its culture, a different industry, or a different technology or management system, etc. This view of learning through knowledge *transfer* may understate the value of knowledge diversity in alliances where learning is a key objective, however, because it ignores the potential value of diversity as a catalyst for knowledge creation.

Knowledge creation occurs when new problems are identified or new solutions are developed to address well-known problems. For teams working on tasks that require developing new and creative solutions to problems, diverse perspectives seem to be beneficial on several counts. During the environmental scanning that occurs in the earliest phase of problem-solving, people with diverse perspectives can provide a more comprehensive view of the possible issues that might be placed on the group's agenda. Subsequently, discussion among members with diverse perspectives can improve the group's ability to consider alternative interpretations and generate creative solutions that integrate their diverse perspectives. As alternative courses of action and solutions are considered, diverse perspectives can increase the group's ability to foresee a wide range of possible costs, benefits, and side-effects. Finally, diversity can enhance the group's credibility with external constituencies, which should improve their ability to implement their creative solutions (for a detailed review, see Jackson, 1992).

It seems reasonable to assume that the presence of diversity creates opportunities for learning – including learning that occurs through knowledge transfer and learning that is associated with creativity and innovation. Unfortunately, however, there has been very little research on how cross-border alliances can take advantage of such learning opportunities. In fact, there are many reasons to believe that the partners in cross-border alliances often are not able to take advantage of the learning opportunities that their diversity presents because cultural diversity also generates conflict and turnover.

Detrimental Effects of Cultural Diversity Cultural diversity seems to interfere with the development of cohesiveness among members of an organization. An important caveat to note here, is that this conclusion is based almost exclusively on research investigating the cultural diversity associated with demographic differences. Nevertheless, the pattern of greater diversity resulting in lower levels of cohesiveness has been found for diversity in age, gender, race, education, prestige, social class, attitudes and beliefs.

Low levels of cohesiveness can be detrimental to both organizations and individual employees. The positive feelings of attraction to coworkers which is present in a cohesive organization promote helping behavior and generosity, cooperation and a problem – solving orientation during negotiations (for a review, see Isen and Baron, 1991). Cohesiveness may also translate into greater motivation to contribute fully and perform well as a means of gaining approval and recognition (Chattopadhyay, 1999). If cultural diversity reduces these positive social behaviors, the performance of individuals as well as the organization as a whole is likely to suffer.

In addition to lowering feelings of attraction and cohesiveness among co-workers, dissimilarity often promotes conflict, which may influence one's decision to maintain membership in a group or organization. This was illustrated in a study of 199 top management teams in U. S. banks. During a four-year period, managers in more diverse teams were more likely to leave the team compared to managers in homogeneous teams. This was true regardless of the characteristics of the individual managers, and regardless of how similar a manager was to other members of the team. Simply being a member of a diverse management team increased the likelihood that a manager would leave (Jackson, Brett, Sessa, Cooper, and Julin, and Peyronnin, 1991). Presumably, more diverse teams experienced greater conflict and were less cohesive, creating feelings of dissatisfaction and perhaps increasing the perceived desirability of other job offers. Some evidence indicates that the relationship between diversity and turnover holds in cultures as different from each other as the United States, Japan (Wiersema and Bird, 1993), and Mexico (Pelled and Xin, 1997). As Hambrick and his colleagues have described, when diversity in the top management group of an IJV creates interpersonal conflict, the results is likely to be a downward spiral in the IJV's effectiveness (Hambrick, Li, Xin, and Tsui, 2001).

Implications for Managing Cultural Diversity in Cross-Border Alliances

Organizations that engage in cross-border alliances do so for a variety of reasons. Regardless of those reasons, however, they must effectively manage cultural diversity of many forms in order to achieve their objectives. Ideally, the employees who participate in cross-border alliances will be able to leverage their differences for the benefit of the organization while at the same time enriching their own experiences. But how can this ideal be achieved, given all of the interpersonal challenges that diversity creates?

Soft due diligence processes are perhaps the most widely used tools for managing cultural diversity in cross-border alliances. Through soft due diligence, alliance partners seek to identify the cultural differences that must be addressed in order for an IJV or IM&A to succeed. If cultural differences between partners are judged to be too great given the preferred approach for managing diversity (portfolio, blending, new creation, or absorption), a deal may be halted (e.g., see Coff, 2002). More typically, the soft due diligence process is used to develop a plan for changing current HR practices or instating new ones. We cannot provide a complete discussion of human resource management in cross-border alliances here (for an excellent and more extensive discussion, see Evans, Pucik, and Barsoux, 2002). Instead, we simply provide examples of how HR practices might possibly be used in cross-border alliances to improve the ability of the organization to effectively leverage its diversity. We do not intend for these examples to serve as prescriptions for managing the many aspects of diversity present in cross-border alliances. Rather, we offer these as proposals that require verification through further research. Our proposals are grounded in the work of Allport (1954), who addressed the question of how to reduce prejudice and its negative consequences. Allport hypothesized that the following conditions were necessary in order for intergroup contact to lead to reduced prejudice: active striving toward a common goal that requires interdependent co-operation, equal status shared by members of each group, and explicit social sanctions supporting the development of intergroup relationships. After reviewing research designed to test Allport's theory, Pettigrew (1998) concluded that creating these conditions requires learning about the other group, creating positive emotions, gaining new insights, and creating behavioral change. Thus, Allport's original theory and subsequent research designed to test his theory suggests six conditions that must be created in order to effectively manage cultural diversity in cross border alliances:

1. A shared understanding of the objectives for the alliance
2. A belief that each partner contributes to the success of the alliance, and thus is deserving of equal esteem and respect
3. An organizational culture that rewards cooperation between members of different cultural groups, and penalizes behavior that appears to be biased or prejudicial
4. Opportunities for members of different cultural groups to learn about and from each other
5. Opportunities for members of different cultural groups to develop personal friendships
6. Activities that encourage everyone to reflect on their own values and gain insights into how their values influences both their own behaviors and the ways that they interpret the behaviors of others.

To maximize the probabilities of success, participants in cross-border alliances should attend to creating these conditions at each evolutionary stage of the alliance. Following these principles is likely to improve the chances of success of all types of cross-border alliances, but the criticality of each principle at each evolutionary stage may depend on the general diversity management approach being followed (portfolio, blending, new creation, absorption), as well as the total amount of diversity within the alliance.

As described next, a variety of human resource management practices may be helpful for organizations that wish to create the conditions needed for success in the presence of considerable amounts of cultural diversity. Together, the entire set of practices should communicate a single message to employees (e.g., see Jackson and Schuler, 2003).

Work and Organization Design

Throughout all evolutionary stages of IJVs and IM&As, teams are a basic form of organization. During pre-combination and formation, teams typically serve to ensure that the perspectives of all alliance partners are represented when key decisions are made. During the early stages of evolution, teams may be used to assess cultural similarities and differences between the partners and plan for their integration. As an alliance evolves, teams may continue to be used to facilitate co-ordination on daily activities and ensure transfer of learning. In the DaimlerChrylser merger, for example, over 100 integration teams were used to handle co-ordination between the various functional areas and the different management levels in the organization (Charman, 1999). Most of the practices described below apply to the management of all the various teams and task forces likely to be present in IJVs and IM&As, as well as to the organization's workforce as a whole.

Staffing

Throughout the lives of IJVs and IM&As, numerous staffing decisions must be made, including decisions regarding who to hire, who to promote, and perhaps who to let go. In addition to ensuring that an alliance is staffed with people who have the technical proficiencies required, staffing practices can improve the organization's effectiveness by identifying individuals who are more likely to be effective working amidst cultural diversity. Staffing practices also should be sensitive to the composition of teams (i.e., the content and structure of cultural diversity).

Staffing for cross-cultural competency Based on their experiences and a review of the literature, Schneider and Barsoux (1997) proposed a set of behavioral competencies needed for effective intercultural performance. These included: linguistic ability; interpersonal (relationship) skills; cultural curiosity; ability to tolerate uncertainty and ambiguity; flexibility; patience; cultural empathy; ego strength (strong sense of self); and a sense of humor. When evaluating employees for staffing decisions, competency models such as this one provide useful guidance that can increase an organization's ability to staff its alliances with employees who easily adjust to and enjoy cultural diversity. However, it should be noted that competency models for cross-cultural adjustment often are developed based on the experiences of expatriates (e.g., Tung, 1981; Black, Gregersen and Mendenhall, 1992). While expatriate assignments may share some similarities with IJV or IM&A assignments, there also are many differences. Much more research is needed to identify the personal characteristics most likely to contribute to success in these settings. When an organization's strategy requires that it participate in a large number of IJVs and IM&As, it has the opportunity to conduct such research. Doing so can help it further refine its understanding of how various personal characteristics relate to the performance of employees in culturally diverse organizations.

Staffing for composition Cross-cultural alliance partners often establish teams to ensure the airing of multiple perspectives prior to decision making. Especially during the early stages of the alliance's evolution, these teams often are staffed with equal numbers of representatives from each partner involved in the alliance. For example, following a merger, this tactic might be used ensure that the two companies have equal representation in the new top management team (Schwieger, Ridley and Marini, 1992). This tactic also is likely to be used when forming the board that oversees an IJV, when staffing IM&A integration and transition teams, and so on.

While representational staffing has many benefits, it may inadvertently lead to unnecessary conflict, divisiveness and turnover if it creates teams characterized by strong faultlines. Faultlines can be avoided if staffing decisions take into consideration the structure and content of diversity created by a combination of people selected to staff a team. In other words, selecting the "best" people for a team assignment involves more than evaluating the performance potential of individuals – it requires evaluating the performance potential of the team as a whole.

In addition to avoiding the creation of teams or departments with clear faultlines, staffing decisions also need to consider the status dynamics that are likely to arise within a team or organizational unit. When members of a group perceive a clear status hierarchy, lower participation and involvement can be expected from those at the lower rungs of the hierarchy, regardless of their actual expertise and knowledge.

Training and Development

Training and development activities can address a number of challenges created by the cultural diversity present in IJVs and IM&As. Training to improve cultural awareness and competencies may seem the most relevant form of training for improving inter-cultural relations, but appropriate business training should also be helpful.

Cultural awareness and competency training Perhaps most obviously, cultural awareness and competency training can quickly teach employees about cultural similarities and differences, and perhaps diminish their reliance on inaccurate stereotypes. Although stereotypes can be resistant to change, they can be modified with sufficient disconfirming evidence (Triandis, 1994).

As implied by our earlier discussion of the many types of cultural diversity present in some IJVs and IM&As, awareness training should not be limited to learning about national cultures – employees may also benefit from information about differences (and similarities) due to regional locations, industries, organizations and membership in various demographic groups. Besides imparting knowledge, effective training provides employees with opportunities to practice and hone their interpersonal skills. Nor should awareness training be viewed as a one-time event. Educational briefings may be helpful initially, but as the alliance evolves, more intensive team-building workshops and joint problem-solving sessions will likely be needed as employees experience the many implications that cultural diversity has for their daily interactions.

Business training The potential benefits of cultural awareness training seem obvious, but business training also can improve the alliance's ability to manage its cultural diversity. Business training can help to establish two of the conditions that enable diverse groups to reap the benefits of their diversity: an understanding of shared goals and mutual respect. Unless participants in an alliance believe they share the same interests, they may assume a competitive relationship exists between the alliance partners. Furthermore, unless they understand why the capabilities and resources of each partner are needed to succeed in achieving their shared goal, they may perceive that the contributions of one partner are more important, more valuable, and thus more deserving of respect. Through business training, employees in an alliance can develop an appreciation for how the capabilities and resources of each partner can contribute to success. For example, if IJV partners enter a relationship that is not based on a 50-50 equity relationship, employees in the venture may assume that higher equity partner will ultimately have more influence and control, placing the lower equity partner in a position of lower status. Yet, in such a venture, it is likely that the intangible resources of the lower equity partner are essential to the venture's success (Yan and Gray, 1994). Thus, teaching employees about the complementary value of capital and intangible resources provides employees with a solid foundation for developing mutual respect.

Performance Management

For any organization, performance management is an important and very complex aspect of human resource management. For IM&As, creating a unified performance management system is perhaps the greatest challenge faced by organizations that seek to blend two disparate cultures (Fealy, Kompare, and Howes, 2001). For IJVs, a major challenge is creating a performance management system that aligns the interests of managers in the venture with those of the parents (Evans et al., 2002). In addition to contributing to employee's performance in the technical aspects of their jobs, performance management systems can improve cross-cultural relations by ensuring that employees' efforts are directed toward shared goals, providing them with feedback that provides insights about how people from other cultures interpret their behaviors, and rewarding them for developing the competencies required to be effective in a culturally diverse organization.

Shared goals and objectives Training programs can inform employees about the shared goals of alliance partners, but performance management systems must convince employees that the rhetoric is also the reality. Ideally, at each evolutionary stage, all employees involved will understand how their performance is assessed and how performance assessments relate to the goals for the alliance. Rewards and recognition for performance that contributes to achieving the alliance goals serve to reinforce the message.

Feedback that promotes insight The norms that govern giving and receiving feedback in various cultures differ greatly, yet in any culture giving and attending to feedback is necessary for maintaining effective relationships. Cultural differences mean that feedback communications are particularly prone to misunderstandings and misinterpretations. One response to such problems is to avoid giving feedback to people from other cultures. Well-designed performance management practices can ensure that employees receive the feedback they need in a culturally appropriate way.

Rewards for developing cultural competencies Often organizations provide training but do not mandate full participation nor do they reward employees who apply the training lessons in their work. According to a study involving several hundred U.S. organizations, the success of domestic diversity interventions was enhanced when supporting sanctions were in place. Requiring everyone to attend cultural awareness and competency training communicates their importance, as does providing rewards to employees who provide evidence of improvement (Rynes and Rosen, 1995).

Organizational Development and Change

Organizational development and change activities can serve many purposes during the formation and subsequent management of cross-border alliances. Here we focus on organization development aimed at developing the informal organization. Research and anecdotal evidence alike point to the important role of personal friendships in the success of cross-cultural alliances. For example, in explaining the factors that resulted in a successful joint venture between an Italian and U.S. firm, managers pointed to the strong friendship between the two chairmen of the parent companies. Conversely, the lack of personal friendships between employees at FESA – a joint venture between Japanese Fujitsu and Spanish Banesto – made it difficult for them to develop the level of trust that was required in order for learning and knowledge transfer to occur (Yan and Luo, 2001).

Due to the many forms of cultural diversity that often are present in cross-border alliances, employees may find it more difficult than usual to develop close personal relationships with their colleagues from other cultural backgrounds. Yet, the positive feelings associated with one close friendship with someone from an "outgroup" culture (e.g., the joint venture partner) are likely to generalize to the entire group (Pettigrew, 1997). Thus, organizational development activities that help employees develop even a few friendships may be quite beneficial to an alliance. As is true for all HR practices, however, a major challenge is designing activities that have the intended effects across all segments of the organization. OD interventions are most effective when the assumptions that guide the OD activities fit the assumptions of the culture (Aguinis and Henle, in press Hui and Luk, 1997; Jaeger, 1986). Within culturally diverse organizations, meeting this condition is particularly challenging. The assumptions underlying an OD effort may be congruent with the cultural background of some employees, but unless there is little cultural diversity, the same assumptions will not be shared by all employees.

Conclusion

As businesses globalize, they will continue to use cross-border alliances as a means to expand and grow both their operations and knowledge base. To succeed, such businesses must effectively manage the many forms of cultural diversity inherent in such organizations. Although IJVs and IM&As represent only two types of cross-border alliances, our discussion here illustrates how cultural diversity can affect alliances of other types. The challenge of managing cultural diversity involves much more than assessing the degree of cultural fit between alliance partners and creating plans to close (or otherwise manage) the cultural gap, for example, by designing a new HR system. Creating alignment among the formal systems is a necessary first step, but additional efforts are needed to ensure that organizational structures do not create additional barriers to cross-cultural collaboration and to develop a workforce with the competencies needed to work effectively amidst cultural diversity. Additional research that examines how organizations achieve these objectives promises to improve our understanding of both how to manage cultural diversity and how to improve the effectiveness of cross-border alliances.

References

Adler, N. J., & Jelinek, M. (1986), *Is "organization culture" culture bound?* Human Resource Management, *25, 73-90.*

Aguinis, H., and Henle, C. A. (in press), The search for universals in cross-cultural organizational behavior. In J. Greenberg (Ed.), *Organizational behavior: The state of the science (2nd ed.)*. Mahwah, NJ: Lawrence Erlbaum Associates.

Allport, G. W. (1954), *The nature of prejudice.* Reading, Mass.: Addison-Wesley.

Armstrong, D., and Cole, P. (1996), Managing distances and differences in geographically distributed work groups. In S. E. Jackson and M. N. Ruderman (eds.), *Diversity in Work Teams: Research Paradigms for a Changing Workplace,* pp. 187-215. Washington DC: American Psychological Association.

Ashkanasy, N. M., and Jackson, C. R. A. (2001), Organizational culture and climate. In Anderson, N., Ones, D. S., Sinangil, H. K., and Viswesvaran, C. (Eds.), *Handbook of industrial, work and organizational psychology, Vol.* 2, pp. 399-415. London: Sage.

Ashkanasy, N. M., Wilderom, C. P. M., and Peterson, M. F. (Eds.) (2000), *Handbook of organizational culture and climate*. Thousand Oaks, CA: Sage.

Best, D. L., and Williams, J. E. (2001). Gender and culture. In D. Matsumoto (Ed.), *The handbook of culture and psychology* (pp. 195-219). Oxford: Oxford University Press.

Beyer, J. M. (1981), Ideologies, values, and decision making in organizations. In P.C. Nystrom, & W. H. Starbuck (Eds.), *Handbook of organizational design* (Vol. 2, pp. 166 – 202). New York: Oxford University Press

Bianco, A. (2000, July 17), When a merger turns messy. *Business Week,* pp. 90-93.

Black, J. S., Gregersen, H. D., and Mendenhall, M. E. (1992). *Global assignments: Successfully expatriating and repatriating international managers*. San Francisco: Jossey-Bass.

Bond, M. H., and Smith, P. B. (1996), Culture and conformity: A meta-analysis of studies using Asch's line judgment task. *Psychological Bulletin,* **199**, 111-137.

Brass, D.J. (1984), Being in the right place: A structural analysis of individual influence in organization. *Administrative Science Quarterly,* **29**: 518-539.

Brewer, M. B. (1979), In-group bias in the minimal intergroup situation: a cognitive-motivational analysis. *Psychological Bulletin,* **86**, 307-324.

Brewster, C. (1995), Towards a European model of human resource management. *Journal of International Business Studies,* **26**, 1-21.

Brodbeck, F. C., et al. (2000), Cultural variation of leadership prototypes across 22 European countries. *Journal of Occupational and Organizational Psychology,* **73**, 1-29.

Charman, A. (1999), Global mergers and acquisitions: the human resource challenge. *International Focus*. Alexandria, VA: Society for Human Resource Management.

Charman. C. D. (2000), A CEO Roundtable on making mergers succeed. *Harvard Business Review,* May-June, 145-154.

Chattopadhyay, P. (1999), *Beyond direct and symmetrical effects: The influence of demographic dissimilarity on organizational citizenship behavior*. Academy of Management Journal, *42*: 273-287.

Coff, R. W. (2002), *Human capital, shared expertise, and the likelihood of impasse in corporate acquisitions*. Journal of Management, *28, 107-128.*

Cyr, D. J. (1995), The human resource challenge of international joint ventures. *Quorum Books: Westport.*

Denison, D. R. (1996), What is the difference between organizational culture and organizational climate? A native's point of view on a decade of paradigm wars. *Academy of Management Review,* **21**, 619–654.

Deogun, N. and Scannell, K. (January 2, 2001), Market swoon stifles M & A's red-hot start, but old economy supplies a surprise bounty. *The Wall Street Journal,* p. R4.

Dickson, M. W., Aditya, R. M., and Chhokar, J. S. (2000), Definition and interpretation in cross-cultural organizational culture research: Some pointers from the GLOBE research program. In N.M. Ashkanasy, C. P. M. Wilderom and M.F. Peterson (Eds.), *Handbook of organizational culture and climate* (pp. 447 – 464). Thousand Oaks, CA: Sage.

Doz, Y.L., and Hamel, G. (1998), Alliance advantage: The art of creating value through partnering. *Boston: Harvard Business School Press.*

Earley, P. C., and Mosakowski, E. M., (2000), Creating hybrid team cultures: An empirical test of international team functioning. *Academy of Management Journal,* **43**: 26-49.

Evans, P., Pucik, V., and Barsoux, J.-L. (2002), *The global challenge: Frameworks for international human resource management*. Boston, MA: McGraw-Hill.

Fealy, E., Kompare, D., and Howes, P. (2001), Compensation and benefits in global mergers and acquisitions. In C. Reynolds (Ed.), *Guide to global compensation and benefits, (2nd ed)* (pp. 25-54). San Diego, CA: Harcourt.

Glunk, U., Heijltjes, M. C., and Olie, R. (2001), Design characteristics and functioning of top management teams in Europe. *European Management Journal, 19,* 291-300.

Hambrick, D. C., Li, J., Xin, K., and Tsui, A. S. (2001), Compositional gaps and downward spirals in international joint venture management groups. *Strategic Management Journal,* **22,** 1033-1053.

Hamel, G. (2001, April 2), Avoiding the guillotine. *Fortune*, pp.139-144.

Hamel, G., and Prahalad, C. K. (1994), *Competing for the future: Breakthrough strategies for seizing control of your industry and creating the markets of tomorrow.* Boston: Harvard Business School Press.

Hitt, M. A., Harrison, J. S., and Ireland, R. D. (2001), *Mergers & acquisitions: A guide to creating value for shareholders.* Oxford University Press: New York.

Hofstede, G. (1997), *Culture and organizations: Software of the mind (Rev. Ed.).* New York: McGraw-Hill.

Hofstede, G., Neuijen, B., Ohayav, D. D., and Sanders, G. (1990), Measuring organizational culture: A qualitative and quantitative study across twenty cases. *Administrative Science Quarterly,* **25,** 286-316.

Hooijberg, R., and Petrock, F. (1993), On cultural change: Using the competing values framework to help leaders execute a transformational strategy. *Human Resource Management,* **32,** 29-50.

House, R. J., Hanges, P. J., Ruiz-Quintanilla, S. A. , Dorfman, P. W., Javidan, M., Dickson, M., Gupta, V., and 170 country investigators (1999), Cultural influences on leadership and organizations: Project GLOBE. In W. Mobley, J. Gessner, and V. Arnold (Eds.), *Advances in global leadership, Vol.* 1 (pp. 171-234). Stamford, CT: JAI Press.

Hui, C. H., & Luk, C. L. (1997), Industrial/organizational psychology. In J. W. Berry, M. H. Segall, & C. Kagitçibaşi (Eds.) *Handbook of cross-cultural psychology* (Vol. 3, pp. 371-411). Boston: Allyn and Bacon.

Ilgen, D., LePine, J., and Hollenbeck, J. (1999), Effective decision making in multinational teams. In P. Christopher Earley and Miriam Erez (eds,), *New Approaches to Intercultural and International; Industrial/Organizational Psychology,* pp. 377-409. The New Lexington Press: San Fransisco.

Inkpen, A. C., and Beamish, P. W. (1997), Knowledge, bargaining power, and the instability of international joint ventures. *Academy of Management Review,* **22,** 177-202.

Isen, A. M. and Baron, R. A. (1991), Positive affect as a factor in organizational behavior. In L.L. Cummings and B. M. Staw (eds.), *Research in organizational behavior.* Greenwich, CT: JAI Press.

Jackson, S. E. (1992), Team composition on organizational settings: issues in managing an increasingly diverse work force. In Worchel, S., Wood, W. and Simpson, J. A. (Eds.), Group process and productivity *(pp. 204-261). Newbury Park: Sage Publications.*

Jackson, S. E., and Schuler, R. S. (2003), *Managing human resources through strategic partnerships.* (Cincinnati, Ohio: South-Western).

Jackson, S. E, May K. E., and Whitney, K. (1995), Under the dynamics of diversity in decision-making teams. In R. A. Guzzo and E. Salas (Eds.) *Team effectiveness and decision making in* organizations (pp. 204-261). San Francisco: Jossey-Bass.

Jackson, S. E. Brett, J. F., Sessa, V. I., Cooper, D. M., Julin, J. A., and Peyronnin, K. (1991), Some differences make a difference: Individual dissimilarity and group heterogeneity as correlates of recruitment, promotions, and turnover. *Journal of Applied Psychology,* **76,** 675-689.

Jaeger, A. M. (1986), Organization development and national culture: Where's the fit? *Academy of Management Review,* **11**, 1787-190.

Kramer, R.M. and Brewer, M.B. (1984), *Effects on group identity on resource use in a simulated common dilemma.* Journal of Personality and Social Psychology, *46, 1044-1057.*

Lane, P. J., Salk, J. E., and Lyles, M. A. (2001), *Absorptive capacity, learning, and performance in international joint ventures.* Strategic Management Journal, *22, 1139-1161.*

Lau, D. C. and Murnighan, J. K. (1998), *Demographic diversity and faultlines: The compositional dynamics of organizational groups.* Academy of Management Review, *23, 325-340.*

Levine, J. M., and Moreland, R. L. (1990), Progress in small group research. *Annual Review of Psychology,* **41**, 585-634.

Leung, K. (1997), Negotiation and reward allocation across cultures. In P. C. Earley and M. Erez (Eds.), *New perspectives on international industrial/organizational psychology* (pp. 640-675). San Francisco: New Lexington.

Leung, K., Au, Y. F., Fernandez-Dols, J. M., and Iwawaki, S. (1992), Preferences for methods of conflict processing in two collectivist cultures. *International Journal of Psychology,* **27**, 195 – 209.

Liebeskind, J. P., Oliver, A. L., Zucker, L. and Brewer, M. (1996), Social networks, learning, and flexibility: Sourcing scientific knowledge in new biotechnology firms. *Organization Science,* **7**, 428–443.

Lincoln, J. R., and Miller, J. (1979), Work and friendship ties in organizations: A comparative analysis of relational networks. *Administrative Science Quarterly,* **24**, 181-199.

Lucenko, K. (2000, September), *Strategies for growth.* Across the Board, *p.63.*

Luo, Y. (2000), *Toward a conceptual framework of international joint venture negotiations.* Journal of International Management, *5, 141-165.*

Luo, Y. (2001), *Antecedents and consequences of personal attachment in cross-cultural cooperative ventures.* Administrative Science Quarterly, *46, 177-201.*

Mann, L. (1980), *Cross-cultural studies of small groups. In H. C. Triandis & R. W. Brislin (Eds.),* Handbook of cross-cultural psychology, *Vol. 5. (pp. 155-209). Boston: Allyn & Bacon.*

Mayer, M. C. J., and Whittington, R. (1999), Strategy, structure, and "systemness": National institutions and corporate change in France, Germany, and the UK, 1950-1993. *Organization Studies,* **20**, 933-959.

Millikin, F. J. and Martins, L. L. (1996), Searching form common threads: Understanding the multiple effects of diversity in organizational groups. *Academy of Management Review,* **21**, 402-433.

Pelled, L.H. and Xin, K.R. (1997), Birds of a feather: Leader-member demographic similarity and organizational attachment in Mexico. *Leadership Quarterly,* **8**: 433-450.

Peterson, M. F., & Hofstede, G. (2000), Culture: National values and organizational practices. In N.M. Ashkanasy, C.P.M. Wilderon, & M.F. Peterson (Eds.), *Handbook of organizational culture and climate* (pp. 401-416). Thousand Oaks, CA: Sage.

Pettigrew, T. F. (1998), Intergroup contact theory. *Annual Review of Psychology,* **49**, 65-85.

Pettigrew, T.F. (1997), *Generalized intergroup contact effects on prejudice.* Personality and Social Psychology Bulletin, *23,173-85.*

Quinn, R. E., & Rohrbaugh, J. (1983), A spatial model of effectiveness criteria: Toward a competing values approach to organizational analysis. *Management Science,* **29**, 363 – 377.

Rafeli, A., & Worline, M. (2000), Symbols in organizational culture. In N. M. Ashkanasy, C. P. M. Wilderom, & M. F. Peterson (Eds.), *Handbook of organizational culture and climate* (pp. 71 - 84). Thousand Oaks, CA: Sage.

Ralston, D. A., Kai-Cheng, Y., Wang, X., Terpstra, R. H., and Wei, H (1996), The cosmopolitan Chinese manager: Findings of a study on managerial values across the six regions of China. *Journal of International Management*, 2, 79–109.

Robertson, C. and Jett, T. (1999), Pro-environmental support: the environmental and industrial benefits of project XL at Merck & Co., Inc., *Organizational Dynamics*, 81-88.

Rynes, S. and Rosen, B. (1995), A field survey of factors affecting the adoption and perceived success of diversity training. *Personnel Psychology*, **48**, 247-270.

Sager, I. (1996, April 15). The new biology of big business, *Business Week*, p. 19.

Salk, J. E., and Shenkar, O. (2001), Social identities in an international joint venture: An exploratory case study. *Organizational Science*, **12**, 161-178.

Schaan, J.L. (1988). *How to control a joint venture even as a minority partner.* Journal of General Management, *14 (1), 4-16.*

Schneider, S. C., and Barsoux, J.-L. (1997), *Managing across cultures* (London: Prentice-Hall).

Schonfeld, E. (1997, March 31), Merck vs. the biotech industry: Which one is more potent? *Fortune*, pp. 161–162.

Schuler, R. S. (2001, February), *HR issues in international joint ventures.* International Journal of Human Resource Management, *pp. 1-50.*

Schuler, R.S. and Jackson, S.E. (2001, June), *HR issues and activities in mergers and acquisitions.* European Management Journal, *pp. 59-75.*

Schuler, R. S., and van Sluijs, E. (1992), *Davidson-Marley BV: Establishing and operating an international joint venture.* European Management Journal, *10 (4), 428-437.*

Schuler, R. S., Dowling, P. J., and DeCieri, H., (1992, September). *The Formation of an international joint venture: Marley Automotive Components Ltd.* European Management Journal, *pp. 304-309.*

Schuler, R. S., Luo, Y., and Jackson, S. E. (2003), Managing human resources in cross-border alliances. *London: Routledge.*

Schweiger, D.M., Ridley, J. R. Jr., and Marini, D. M. (1992), Creating one from two: The merger between Harris Semiconductor and General Electric Solid State. In S. E. Jackson (ed.), *Diversity in the workplace: Human resources initiatives*, pp. 167 -201. New York: Guilford Press.

Shenkar, O. and Zeira, Y. (1987), *Human resource management in international joint ventures: Directions for research.* Academy of Management Review, *12 (3), 546-557.*

Smith, P. B. (2001), Cross-cultural studies of social influence. In D. Matsumoto (Ed.), *The handbook of culture and psychology* (pp. 361-374). Oxford: Oxford University Press.

Sun, H., & Bond, M. H. (1999), The structure of upward and downward tactics of influence in Chinese organizations. In J.C. Lasry, J. G. Adair, & K.L. Dion (eds.), *Latest contribution to cross-cultural psychology* (pp. 286 – 299). Lisse, The Netherlands: Swets & Zeitlinger.

Tajfel, H. (1978), *Differentiation between social groups: Studies in the social psychology of inter-group relations.* San Diego, CA: Academic Press.

The Economist. (2000, July 29-August 4), The DaimlerChrysler emulsion. http://members.tripodasia.com.sg/batsmile/article05.htm.

Triandis, H. C. (1994), *Culture and social behavior.* New York: McGraw-Hill.

Trice, H. M., and Beyer, J. M. (1993), *The culture of work organizations.* Englewood Cliffs, N.J.: Prentice-Hall.

Tung, R. L. (1981), Selection and training of personnel for overseas assignments. *Columbia Journal of World Business*, **16(1)**, 57-71.

Van Sluijs, E., and Schuler, R. S. (1994). *As the IJV grows: Lessons and progress at Davidson-Marley BV.* European Management Journal, *12 (3), 315-321.*

Weber, Y. (2000), Measuring cultural fit in mergers and acquisitions. In N. M. Ashkanasy, C. P. M. Wilderom, & M. F. Peterson (Eds.), *Handbook of organizational culture and climate* (pp. 309 – 320). Thousand Oaks, CA: Sage.

Wiersema, M.F. and Bird, A. (1993), Organizational demography in Japanese firms: Group heterogeneity, industry dissimilarity, and top management team turnover. *Academy of Management Journal,* 36, 996-1025.

Williams, J. E., and Best, D. L. (1990), *Measuring sex stereotypes: A multinational study.* Newbury Park: Sage.

Williams, K., and O'Reilly, C.A. (1998), Demography and diversity in organizations: A review of 40 years of research. In B. Staw and L. Cummings (Eds.) *Research in organizational behavior,* (Vol.20, pp. 77-140). Greenwich, CT: JAI Press.

Yan, A. and Luo, Y. (2001), International joint ventures. *New York/London: M.E. Sharpe.*

Yan, A., and Gray, B. (1994), Bargaining power, management control, and performance in United States-China joint ventures: A comparative case study. *Academy of Management Journal* 37, 1478-1517.

Yan, A., and Luo, Y. (2001), *International joint ventures: Theory and Practice* (Armonk, NY: Sharpe).

Chapter 8

Knowledge in Cross-Cultural Management in the Era of Globalization: Where do we go from here?

Rabi S. Bhagat

B. Ram Baliga

Karen South Moustafa

Balaji Krishnan

Introduction

The purpose of this paper is to assess the significance and rigor of cross-cultural knowledge in the era of globalization. After reviewing the major paradigm developments since the 1960s, we propose a schematic framework for understanding behavior in and of organizations in dissimilar cultural contexts. A major thesis of this paper is that future researchers should be concerned with issues such as globalization, computer-mediated communication, and organizational and societal culture syndromes. In the final analysis, we present a socially contextualized model of cultural influences on behavior of individuals and groups in organizational contexts. Implications for theory and research are discussed.

Knowledge in Cross-Cultural Management: Where do we go from here?

From time to time, researchers pause from their data collection and theory generation efforts to pursue a systematic evaluation of the intellectual performance of their scientific discipline. Existing conceptual models, empirical research methods, and applicability of the discipline to dissimilar contexts are typically among various subjects that are reviewed under the general rubric of intellectual performance. As a measure of the intrinsic intellectual performance of a discipline, the significance and utility of its discoveries and effectiveness of pre-eminent paradigms are also of concern.

To enable research in cross-cultural management to evolve in harmony with the trend towards creating a global marketplace, scholars must reexamine the process of examining behavior in organizations as a function of relevant antecedents. Hui and Luk (1997) noted that there is a need for developing appropriate frameworks as organizations enter the global marketplace and are confronted with the applicability of Western psychological and management theories in dissimilar parts of the world. In this paper, we review the intellectual history of the field of cross-cultural management and examine the effectiveness of knowledge that has been generated. Before describing the significance of cross-cultural knowledge, as it is evolving in the era of globalization, we need to distinguish between the concepts of data, information, and knowledge.

Data, Information and Knowledge

Data reflects discrete, objective facts about events or about a given context. In organizational contexts, data is reflected in structured records of current or past transactions that have been important in the organization's history. Data reflecting socio-economic conditions of a society where a global organization might choose to locate (such as the level of literacy or degree of political stability) are important in cross cultural research, but they do not aid in the development of knowledge unless one develops it into meaningful information.

Information is data that makes a significant difference in our understanding and interpretation about certain objective events. Unlike data, information has meaning only in terms of what the receiver interprets. This is particularly true for cross-cultural research, where the frame of reference adopted by the researcher frames a given body of data into information.

Knowledge however, may assume many forms, but its quality is revealed in the range of capabilities that the cross-cultural researcher can accumulate as a result of a given body of information. Davenport and Prusak (1998) defined knowledge as:

> "... a fluid mix of framed experiences, values, contextual information, and expert insight that provides a framework for evaluating and incorporating new experiences and information. It originates and is applied in the minds of knowers. In organizations, it often becomes embedded not only in documents or repositories but also in organizational routines, processes, practices, and norms" (p. 5).

The basic tenet of this definition is also appropriate for understanding the significance of what knowledge is and what knowledge can do to transform social and organizational life in the cross-cultural context. There has been a tendency in some past empirical studies to confuse unrelated bodies of data and information as construing knowledge. We hope that the above section is helpful in moving away from this tendency and be more effective in creating frameworks that reflect distinct and related bodies of knowledge in this important area of human inquiry. It is important to rely on appropriate bodies of data and information to create knowledge that will be crucial as globalization proceeds in parts of the world that may have different cultural orientations and might not be adequately prepared to embrace the various consequences of globalization.

Cross-Cultural Research in a Historical Perspective

Our purpose in this section is not to provide a detailed account or review of cross-cultural and cross-national research that has characterized the development of the field since the landmark study of Haire, Ghiselli, and Porter (1967) and the publication of *Industrialism and the Industrial Man* by Kerr, Dunlop, Harbison, and Myers (1960). Broad reviews of the field are found in Roberts (1970), Barrett and Bass (1976), Child (1981), Bhagat and McQuaid (1982), Drenth (1985), Ronan and Kuman (1986), Bhagat, Kedia, Crawford, and Kaplan (1990), Arvey, Bhagat, and Salas (1991), Triandis (1994), Hui and Luk (1997), Bhagat (1997), and recently in Bhagat, Kedia, Perez, and Moustafa (2003, in press). Schneider and Barsoux (1997) have written a comprehensive text with excellent commentary on the development of the global manager and the global mindset. A number of special journal issues (Adler, 1982; Negandhi, 1983) have examined several aspects of the topic. A noteworthy book by Joynt and Warner (1985) deals with the diversity of conceptions in management from a cross-cultural point of view, and discusses the significance of country specific management styles in various parts of the world, not just the West.

The definition of culture has been broad, but in general, it has included differing patterns of customs, roles, values, and attitudinal predisposition that a given group in a specific location shares, along with a common language. Hofstede (1980) described culture as collective mental programming among a group of people, and later, as the "software of the mind" (Hofstede, 1991). Triandis (1994) noted that culture is to a society what memory is to an individual. Scientific study of the construct of culture should be accomplished by using a broad set of valued inputs: history of the location, systematic observations, selected interviewing techniques, and questionnaires.

Research in the area of cross-cultural management, until the publication of Hofstede's (1980) landmark study of the IBM Corporation, was characterized by the following:

* Cultural patterns of one or two societies were briefly described in the research
* Static group based designs characterized the distributions of a variable of interest (such as emphasis on paternalistic practices, adherence to work group norms) in two contrasting cultures (such as the US and Mexico) which differ on the dimension of individualism-collectivism without a detailed examination

of other proximal variables which are embedded in the social and organizational context

- Static group designs which involved contrasting attributes of variable X (such as emphasis on task oriented leadership versus nurturant leadership) in cultures that might differ on a given dimension (such as individualism-collectivism or power distance or associativeness-abstractiveness)

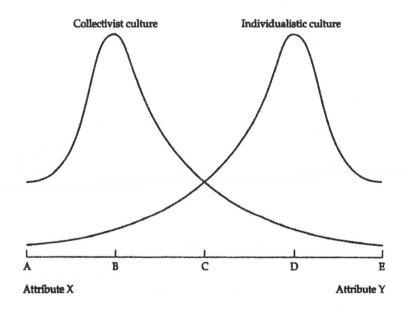

Figure 8.1: Contrasting distributions of attributes X and Y in collectivistic and individualistic cultures

In Figure 8.1, we provide a diagram that shows theoretical distribution of contrasting attributes, X versus Y, in individualist and collectivistic cultures. Extreme levels of trait X are exhibited by several collectivistic individuals at point A, but the individualistic culture has few members that display this trait. At point B, there are many individuals in the collectivistic culture that demonstrate this trait, but still few in the individualist culture. At point C, neither culture has a marked number of individuals displaying either X or Y. Individualistic cultures have a large number of individuals exhibiting trait Y at point D, but few individuals in the collectivistic culture. Extreme levels of trait Y are demonstrated by several individualistic individuals at point E, while the collectivistic culture has few members that exhibit this trait.

A typology of research in cross-cultural management as embedded in three distinctive contexts is shown in Figure 8.2. There has been an emphasis on research involving Areas X, which deal with studies describing interactions between the organization and its local institutional, socio-political, and cultural environment and their effects on organizational functions at both macro and micro level. Some level of emphasis has been found in Area Y, which deal with studies describing interactions between local and international environments and their effects on organizational functions at both macro and micro level, but studies concerned with Areas Z and W are not as frequent as we would expect to see at this point of theoretical and empirical development. Although there has been some work in Area Z, which describes interactions between the organization and the various facets of international, multinational, and global environments and their effects on organizational functioning, these have been primarily in the area of strategic management and not in the behavior of individuals in global organizations. There have been few studies in Area W, describing interactions among the organization, local institutional/cultural environments, and various facets of international, multinational, and global environments and their effects on organizational functions at both macro and micro level.

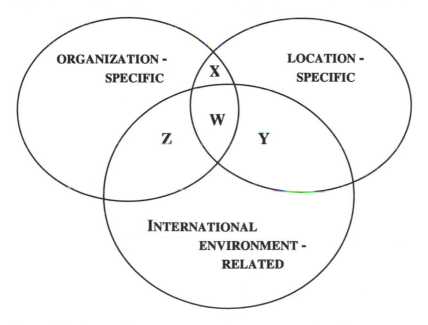

Figure 8.2: A typology of research in cross-cultural management as embedded in three distinctive contexts

Organization-Specific: Research focusing on characteristics, organizational processes, and performance of an organization and/or its members

Location-Specific:

Research focusing on the nature of institutional and cultural environments in a given location and its influence on organizational functioning, at both the macro and micro levels

International-Environment
Related:

Research focusing on the nature of international and global environments which affect functioning of the organization in more than one national context at a given point in time, or over time

Area X:

Studies describing interactions between the organization and its local institutional, socio-political, and cultural environment their effects on organizational functions at both macro and micro level

Area Y:

Studies describing interactions between local and international environments and their effects on organizational functions at both macro and micro level

Area Z:

Studies describing interactions between the organization and the various facets of international, multinational, and global environments and their effects on organizational functioning

Area W:

Studies describing interactions among the organization, local institutional/cultural environments, and various facets of international, multinational, and global environments and their effects on organizational functions at both macro and micro level

In order for the field of cross-cultural management to advance the status of knowledge in the era of globalization, we need more studies in Area W, which is concerned with complex interactions. Strict adherence to static group designs, which were criticized for their ineffectiveness in creating a sound body of knowledge in Malpass (1977), Bhagat and McQuaid (1982), and Bhagat, et. al. (2003, in press), should be replaced by sophisticated theoretical frameworks which deal with both positive as well as adverse affects of globalization and information technology.

In reviewing the literature that characterized the field in the 1970s and 1980s, it became clear that the majority of the researchers were primarily interested in demonstrating the significance of cultural influences without examining simultaneous covariates of the phenomenon. A tendency to quickly jump into the cultural explanation of significant statistical differences on a variable of interest by comparing its distribution in two contrasting cultures does not aid in the development of knowledge. In order to embrace the complexities of interactions among the various determinants of behavior in and of organizations, one should be concerned with the following facets as depicted in Figure 8.3. The figure shows that behavior in and of organizations in any given location is a function of (1) the extent of globalization that exists in that location, (2) the role of computer-mediated information and information technology, (3) the role of organizational culture, and (4) last, but not least, the role of the unique cultural syndrome that characterize the society. There are other determinants, but we see these four as the major determinants involved in both behavior and, therefore, knowledge management in multinational and global corporations. We discuss the relevance of these important determinants, starting with the role of globalization.

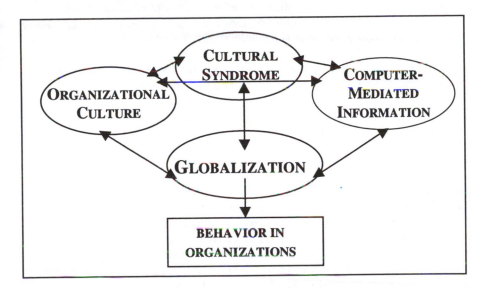

Figure 8.3: A conceptual framework representing determinants of behavior in and of organizations in the international context globalization

Globalization refers to those *processes* that, operating on a global scale, cut across national boundaries, integrating and connecting communities and organizations in new space-time combinations, making the world more interconnected in objective reality and in subjective experience. Globalization implies a departure from the classic sociological idea of "society" as a well-bounded system with distinct political, economic, and cultural implications to a system that concentrates on continuous construction and reconstruction of social life, particularly in organizational contexts across time and space. This will be our point of departure in noting that these new aspects of temporal and economic consequences resulting in the compression of distance and time scales as reflected in the book entitled, *The Death of Distance* (Cairncross, 2001). Globalization has had the following consequences:

- Cultural identities are being strongly altered as a result of the growth of "cultural homogenization" and the development of a post-modern mindset (Govindarajan and Gupta, 2001).
- Nationalistic tendencies, particularly in parts of Europe and Asia (Greider, 1997), and an emphasis on particularistic exchanges (Foa and Foa, 1974) are being strengthened as a result of globalization.

As large scale, network-based organizations evolve and family-based organizations, worker cooperatives, and other traditional forms of organizing begin to give way to modern organizations as a result of globalization, the need for sophisticated cross-cultural research becomes even more acute. This is particularly critical if cross-cultural research is to yield significant knowledge in terms of the definition proposed by Davenport and Prusak (1998) and alluded to earlier. This requires that cross-cultural researchers refrain from conceptualizing behavior in organizations as a static process (Ancona, Okhuysen and Perlow, 2001).

Computer-Mediated Communication

The impact of innovations in communication has been phenomenal. Autonomous business units of multinational corporations are being connected, not necessarily in the context of large physical structures, but in terms of sophisticated electronic networks functioning interdependently. In knowledge-intensive organizations, boundaries will be defined by patterns of knowledge transfer and, in many instances, will not only be fluid or blurred, but nonexistent (Davenport and Prusak, 1998; Leonard-Barton, 1995; Starbuck, 1992; Shenkar and Li, 1999). The consequences of an information intensive economy, with the resultant structural changes required (Child and McGrath, 2001) will play an important role in future cross cultural research.

With the creation of dynamic work environments where tasks are no longer localized in the physical context of the organization, coordination of activities around the globe become significant for managers. Employees of global organizations can be more responsive to the messages they receive through electronic networks than from their co-workers and supervisors. This changes the velocity of decision-making responses to problems and challenges (Adler and Borys, 1996). Ironically, as decisions accelerate the likelihood of their being incorrect increases because decisions are likely to be data- or information-driven rather than knowledge-driven.

In our analysis, we found that research on the impact of technology, particularly innovations in technology in communications and computers, have increased our insights of how global and multinational corporations manage such processes, but there has been little attention as to how new theoretical models and research designs should incorporate important findings from this dynamic and evolving field of inquiry. Unless we develop research strategies to integrate technological innovations, our grasp of behavior in organizations in distinctive cultural milieu that are integrating such technological innovations in their organizational processes will not be complete.

Organizational Culture

In his extensive review, Mitchell (1997) suggested that, for work behavior to be properly understood, one has to diagnose the unique contextual requirements of the organization. Various dimensions of organizational culture reflect the kind of contextual determinants that we are concerned with in Figure 3.3. Issac and Pitt (2001) identified the importance of the strength of organizational culture as a behavioral variable existing at both the organizational and individual levels in the organization. Hofstede, Neuijen, Ohayv, and Sanders (1990) work on organizational culture reveals six dimensions of organizational culture that are relevant for explaining behavior in organizations. These are:

- *Process oriented versus results oriented* Key indicators of this dimension are concerned with the degree to which the organization stresses results versus focusing on relatedness and organizational processes.
- *Job oriented versus employee oriented* This dimension is concerned with the degree to which the organization emphasizes maximal output from its employees as opposed to showing both short and long term concern for them.
- *Parochial versus professional* In parochial organizations, there is greater concern with the behavior of employees in both work and non-work contexts. Furthermore, in terms of selection, social and family background is taken into account along with job competence. In professional cultures, on the other hand, there is more emphasis on job competence in selecting, training, developing, and compensating employees.
- *Open versus closed system* In organizational cultures that are primarily open, there is a greater interaction with the environment. In closed systems, organizations and employees behave in more closed-minded and secretive ways, even among insiders.
- *Loose control versus tight control* Loosely controlled organizations emphasize non-routine processes in the execution of various tasks, and are likely to de-emphasize effects of individual perceptions of deadlines on team performance. Tightly controlled organizations emphasize high degrees of cost-consciousness, punctuality in meeting deadlines and in the execution of various organizational tasks, and members are encouraged to speak highly of

their immediate work environment and employing organization (Waller, Conte, Gibson, and Carpenter, 2001).

- *Pragmatic versus normative* In organizational cultures that are pragmatic, there is a major emphasis on results as opposed to procedures, and customers are highly valued in a transactional sense. In contrast, in normative cultures, employees and customers are valued more than the transactional cost associated with maintaining relationships with these two important constituents.

These dimensions, as proposed by Hofstede, et. al. (1990) and elaborated upon in detail in Hofstede (2001), are of significant value in analyzing behavior in and of organizations. However, the cross-cultural research that we reviewed does not incorporate these dimensions in various situations where they could indeed provide additional insights beyond what was discovered. It is crucial for researchers working in the era of globalization to be sensitive to the relevant dimensions of organizational culture that become more important for predicting behavior in and of organizations in their search for sophisticated patterns in cross-cultural management.

Cultural Syndrome

The next important determinant, which is indeed complex in character, is concerned with the cultural syndrome of the society in which the organization is located. Triandis (1989, 1994, 1995) proposed that the pattern of culturally distinct constructs, when combined in a rational fashion, constitutes the cultural syndrome of a given society. Cultural syndromes are dimensions of cultural variations that can be used as parameters of theories for explaining and predicting behavior in and of organizations (Triandis, 1995). These syndromes reflect a pattern of shared beliefs, categorizations, self-definitions, norms, role definitions, and values that are organized around a theme and reflect a major determinant of behavior in social and organizational contexts. A cultural syndrome can only be shared by a group of people who speak the same language and are located in a distinct geographical region of the world during a specific historic period (Triandis, 1995). Jain's (2001) review of cross-cultural applications in human and organizational development is particularly insightful, giving examples of the effect of cultural syndromes. The cultural syndrome of a country or a distinct geographical region does undergo profound changes over time. It could be argued that globalization is increasing the pace at which such changes takes place placing an even greater premium in incorporating the construct of cultural syndrome in studies of organizational functioning. We conceptualize cultural syndrome as being composed of:

Individualism versus collectivism One dimension of culture that has been found to constitute the "deep structure" of cultural differences among societies is individualism-collectivism (Greenfield, 2000; Hofstede, 2001; Triandis, 1995, 1998). Individualism is a social pattern that consists of loosely linked individuals who view themselves as independent of collectives and are concerned with sustaining their own preferences, needs, rights, and contracts. Collectivism, on the other hand, is a social pattern that consists of closely linked individuals who see themselves as belonging to one or more collectives (e.g. family, co-workers, in-groups, work organizations, tribes, suburban communities). Collectivists are primarily motivated by norms, duties, and obligations which are imposed by the groups they belong to, and they give priority to the collective goals over individual goals, regardless of how they may feel internally. Individualism is found in Western European countries, the US, Canada, Australia, and New Zealand. Collectivism is found in much of the rest of the world, including parts of Eastern Europe, Africa, Asia, and Latin America. Although many researchers feel that this dimension is too simplistic, others believe that it assists as a framework for cultural differentiation (Greenfield, 2000), as do the other dimensions.

Vertical and horizontal relationships   In some cultures, hierarchical relationships are highly emphasized compared to other cultures. These are vertical cultures. In horizontal cultures, found in countries such as Sweden, Denmark, Australia, and Israel, hierarchical relationships are not critical determinants of social or interpersonal behavior.

Cultural complexity   This dimension of cultural syndromes is concerned with the extent to which individuals make a large number of distinctions between objects and events in their social, organizational, and technological environments. For example, the number of distinct occupations that are present in a given country reflects complexity. There are over 250,000 occupations in modern industrial societies (refer to the U.S. Department of Labor *Dictionary of Occupational Titles*). Primitive or tribal societies barely have 20 to 30 occupations. Other indicators of complexity are related to such issues as relative mobility among residents in a given location, the degree of population density, the nature of transactions that characterize them, level of political sophistication, degree of social stratification, and complexities of units of monetary exchanges (e.g., stocks, bonds, treasury bills).

Tightness versus Looseness   Tight cultures (Pelto, 1968) have clear norms that are strictly enforced and deviation from normative behavior results in severe sanctions. Loose cultures, on the other hand, have unclear norms and tolerate deviance from norms rather effortlessly as these norms are not particularly functional in a given locate (Triandis, 1994). Japan, Greece, parts of rural India, and Egypt reflect examples of tight cultures. Loose cultures are found among Lapps of Northern Sweden and the Thais. Loose cultures are often located at the intersections of major distinct cultures that are separated from each other by geography. Sometimes such hybrids reflect instabilities in a given culture, as in the latest turbulent events in many parts of Thailand. Cultural homogeneity, of the kind that exists in Japan and parts of southern Europe, tend to give rise to tight cultures. Interestingly, the US, which is perhaps the most ethnically and culturally diverse country in the world, may be conceived of as tight cultural groups within a loose national culture.

Temporal orientation This dimension of cultural syndrome is similar to Hofstede's (2001, p. 354) long-term versus short-term orientation, but it is not necessarily rooted in Confucius' teachings. Bhagat and Moustafa (2002) suggested that temporal orientation is a function of how the members of a given culture learn to pattern their time related experiences as a function of the dominant cultural themes. Temporal orientation deals with the extent to which an individual considers the past, the present, or the future to have more meaning or significance. Some individuals regard future activities and goals to have more significance than the present, while others are interested in maintaining their current way of life. It can be defined as "the extent to which a person's past and future are psychologically integrated into his or her present life" (Nuttin and Lens, 1985; Lens, 1986).

Triandis (1995) noted that the number of syndromes for an adequate description of a given cross-cultural difference is unknown at present. However, there might be a number of syndromes that could be identified in the future to aid us in providing reliable cultural explanations for why different types of behavior occur in countries that vary along these syndromes.

Taken as a whole, Figure 3.3 depicts that globalization, computer-mediated information, organizational culture, and cultural syndrome, interact to predict behavior in which take place in work organizations in distinctive cultural contexts in the global environment. However, we need a detailed framework that links these four facets with other relevant antecedents that determine behavior in organizations. The socially contextualized model, as described in Figure 3.4, is suggested as a framework for research to enable us to gain a deeper understanding of behavior in global organizations.

The model highlights the importance of several classes of cultural and societal variables from both distal and proximal perspectives. We start with the well-accepted assumptions of cross-cultural psychology and anthropology that societal level distal antecedents are responsible for various organizational level processes. For example, Berry (1980) incorporated multidimensional variables for behavior in his model of social and cultural change. His model noted the interplay of socio-culture and institutional influences with individual dynamics. Oyserman, Kemmelmeier, and Coon (2002) modeled the multiple levels of cultural influences on cognitive, affective, and behavioral outcomes.

In our model, organizational culture, history, and the relevance of computer-mediated communication will be greatly influenced by a combination of:

- *Societal level proximal culture,* reflecting the legal system, the economic system (including globalization), the educational system, socialization practices, and the prominence of the cultural syndrome.
- *Societal level distal culture,* reflecting historical, philosophical, religious, and linguistic traditions.
- *Individual level variables*, reflecting internalized cultural values, social scripts and norms, and cognitive style.
- *Organizational level proximal antecedents,* concerned with organizational history, organizational culture, and the role of computer-mediated

communication in facilitating the speed of organizational processes and interpersonal communication.

- *Individual and group level proximal antecedents,* reflecting the subjective construal of the situation, as selectively perceived by the individual or the group. Cognitive, affective, and behavioral consequences are a direct result of how an individual or group construes a given organizational situation and the level of intensity present in internalized cultural values, social scripts and norms, and cognitive style.

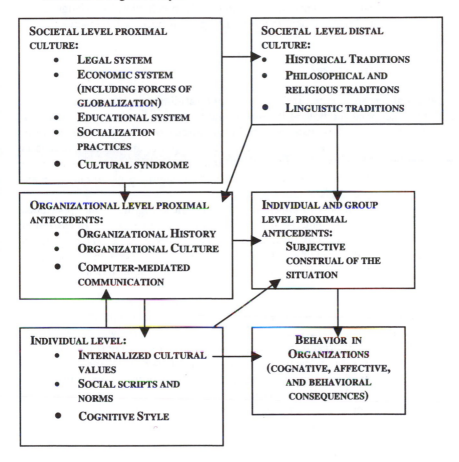

Figure 8.4:   A socially contextualized model of cultural influences on behavior of individuals and groups in organizational contexts

The focus in our chapter is to describe behavior in organizations, which is a function of the five antecedents, as depicted in Figure 8.4. These antecedents collectively create behavior in organizations within a societal context with a distinct cultural orientation and at a distinct point of its evolution in the global economy.

In Figure 3.4, we attempt to present a comprehensive approach to demonstrate that the various antecedents of behavior in organizations should be considered before attempting to generate cross-cultural knowledge regarding a given phenomenon. We realize that it is nearly impossible for a researcher or a team of researchers to be concerned with all of the variables in a given investigation. However, unless an attempt is made to include the variables that are of strong theoretical significance for predicting a given behavior, knowledge in the area of cross-cultural management in the area of globalization will be incomplete.

Where do we go from here?

Cross-cultural research on the influences of cultural dimensions on organizational processes, conceptualized both at the macro and the micro levels, seems to be at a turning point in which key questions are being raised about how to meaningfully recapture the earlier goals and promise. In certain respects, the present situation is indeed exciting. There have been significant improvements in theory construction and high quality data collection in predicting and explaining a given phenomenon of interest at multiple levels of inquiry.

In developing the present paper, we have sought to highlight the importance of other determinants that emerge from the evolutionary process of globalization that have occurred in the last three decades. The Economist (2001) provided a broad map of "how the world has (and hasn't) changed". Perspectives reflected are indeed real and echo many of the concerns raised by both supporters and critics of globalization.

However, as a practical matter, future research designs need to consider the limits of convergence, as discussed by Guillen (2001). He conceptualizes the path to economic development as being different for each society, which has strong implications for global organizations functioning in distinct cultural contexts. His discussions of the various paradoxes that are associated with these paths to development are useful and should be incorporated in future theory building efforts (Guillen, 2001, p. 225). His discussion about conditions for development in Argentina, South Korea, and Spain since 1950, showed that the cultural traditions and ideologies interplay with domestic politics, state structures, international pressures for globalization, etc., in different ways in these three different countries (see Table 2.4, Guillen, 2001, p.36). It is important to consider this recent theorizing on the limits of convergence, which in our opinion, have important consequences. When one considers the perspective that we have provided in Figure 3.3, along with Guillen's approach, what we get is a conflicting view of how cultural changes shape organizational processes, and reflects a more realistic orientation.

Although many authors caution against the automatic use of Western theories of organizational behavior in other contexts, their use continues to be widespread (Jain, 2001). It is important for researchers to examine cross-cultural behavior in and of organizations to determine where universal practices are beneficial and where these should be altered to fit the cultural context (Nath, 1988). Although this has been restated, it seems that few studies have incorporated this view. Increasing globalization means that researchers should consider not only convergence and divergence as possible outcomes of increasing globalization, but also adaptation, rejection, creative synthesis, and, as one of our authors suggests, innovation to fit into the cultural context of the society receiving the input.

- Convergence implies that as nations become industrialized, there is a significant change in values towards common behavioral patterns. It is commonly observed in the area of consumer behavior. With the exposure to global media (dominated by the US companies), teens across different parts of the world, most significantly Japan, behave similar to the American teenagers. The Japanese teens like to dress, and eat and behave similar to their American counterparts.

- Proponents of the divergence approach to the understanding of cross-cultural management argue that national culture, not economic ideology, drives values. For example, despite Western management philosophies taking root in various developing countries, the way elderly people are treated in Asian and Latin American cultures has remained more or less constant. Due to their national cultures emphasizing respect for the elder population, people in these countries tend to respect and revere their elders. Another example is found in the distinctive cultural identities that are evolving between the Palestinians and the Israelis in the Middle East, despite being exposed to similar broader cultural and technological forces.

- Adaptation occurs when one group adjusts an idea, service, or good provided by another to fit its own needs. One example of adaptation occurs with regularity in Egypt. Because the cost of spare automobile parts for foreign made cars are too expensive, special shops of tool and die makers have developed in Cairo to create these car parts. Often the parts are better made than the ones that would have been imported, as each is hand-made to fit the automobile as a replacement. In addition, special adaptations to the parts are often made to meet the special needs of Cairo traffic. Another example is found in India, where drinking water is a precious commodity in many areas. In the case of bottled water, the cost of the package – the bottle – is more expensive than the product (water). Hence, it is common to find drinking water being sold in plastic sachets that are much cheaper. For large quantities of water like a ten gallon can, it is likely to be sold in bottles or cans, but for smaller quantities it is likely to be sold in plastic sachets.

- The rejection of ideas, services, or goods provided by another is not uncommon, and each group gives different reasons for rejection. For example, in many developing countries cheap labor is abundantly available. Hence, the level of automation in factories and offices is greatly reduced. In Western countries, automation is a cheaper alternative to employing costly labor. However, due to the difference in the economies of the labor markets, in developing countries they prefer not to use automation when it would not make a significant performance improvement.

- Ogbor (2000) suggests that creative synthesis is also possible, that is, something beyond convergence and divergence where each group requires the other to complete the creation. In creative synthesis, the result is "actions that succeed in utilizing new or alien norms to serve established ends and values (and vice versa)" (p. 71). This is because the outside idea, service, or good is in line with the indigenous values, beliefs, or norms, quite outside the original intent. It is similar to adaptation, in that the ideas, services, or goods provided by another are used, but not for their originally intended function. One example is where white goods are sold in large cartons with very good packaging to protect the costly appliances. While this concept has been borrowed from Western countries, it is common for the packaging to be sold by appliance dealers in many developing countries. This creates a secondary market for the packaging material that is then recycled for other uses. This also helps the appliance dealer reduce the price on the appliance for the customer as he/she makes some money on the packaging material.

- Innovation is a special case, where a problem faced by several groups is met by a different solution in each group. One example of innovation of this type can be seen in Egypt, where cola bottles are recycled, not to produce cola bottles, but to produce functional and decorative pieces for use in the home. The glass art produced using the cola bottles produces a variegated, air-pocketed glass that is used by the local population in place of more expensive glass tableware and is collected by tourists.

Bhagat and Kedia (1996), in a paper entitled, "Reassessing the elephant: Directions for future research," strongly urge a non-ethnocentric and non-parochial perspective in developing theoretical models and research designs in order to yield higher quality knowledge. We suggest some steps required in current research efforts in order to gain the kind of knowledge that conforms with the major tenets of the definition proposed by Davenport and Prusak (1998):

- There should be a complete moratorium on static group design research, as reflected in Figure 3.1. Bhagat and McQuaid (1982), Bhagat, et. al. (1990), Arvey, et. al. (1991), Triandis (1994), Bhagat and Kedia (1996), Hui and Luk (1997), and Bhagat, et. al. (2003, in press) strongly emphasize the need for more comprehensive theory-building, which goes beyond comparing mean scores of a variable of interest in to different societies and then quickly rush to the cultural explanation. Excessive reliance on static group designs prevented the evolution of knowledge in the cross-cultural research involving management and organizational processes in the 70s and 80s. Such designs were also responsible for findings that were hard to integrate with the mainstream literature on organizational functioning. What we need today are well-conceived studies that will enable us to grasp the diversity of cultural imprints on organizational processes internationally. Along with such studies, which are likely to be somewhat cross-sectional in character, we also need studies depicting the process of culture change. Sophisticated designs, which go beyond the use of simple change scores to more three-dimensional views of change (as reflected in the work of Edwards, 1994), should be incorporated in such culture change studies. As we have argued in this chapter, processes of globalization and computer-mediated communication are driving the process of culture change in some parts of the world rather rapidly. It is important for us to assess the degree to which convergence of cultural syndromes are emerging in various parts of the world, and it is only with the help of sophisticated culture change studies that we can begin to understand the significance of such a phenomenon.

- Processes of globalization and computer-mediated communication should be explicitly incorporated in understanding determinates of behavior in and of organizations. Individuals respond to organizational events by combining their subjective construal with additional considerations from globalizing experiences taking place in their own societies. Consider the case of Hong Kong and Singapore: The economic environments of these countries have long been dominated by extensive participation in the global marketplace, and customers and employees in this part of the world respond to organizational experiences not only from the framework of Confucian teaching, but also from the values derived from the processes of globalization (Thomas, 2002). In a similar vein, connections in the workplace have increased tremendously as a result of computer-mediated communication, which is slowly dissolving cultural isolation that some countries in the Asian might have experienced in the 60s and the 70s. Social historians have observed that the fall of the USSR was primarily due to the diffusion of information and knowledge from the Western economies across the Iron Curtain of communism. Greider (1997) noted that even the ghetto dwellers in San Paulo, Brazil, Bombay, India, and Mexico City, Mexico, have access to television and the Internet. There is no doubt that the various components of the conceptual framework depicted in Figure 3.3 are of importance in future model-building efforts. In developing this conceptual framework, we have sought to go beyond the traditional explanations that most cross-cultural researchers emphasize in their findings. To conduct effective cross-cultural research, it is necessary to possess the virtue of patience and act as a member of an international research team (e.g., MOW research team, 1987), being extremely careful not to be biased by ethnocentric tendencies.

- There is also a need to go beyond the limited *heuristic* value of dimensions such as individualism-collectivism, power distance, and associativeness-abstractiveness and recognize the need for more fine-grained analyses that capture the idiosyncratic outlooks and heterogeneity that exist among and within different cultural communities. In elaborating the significance of individualism-collectivism for advancing cross-cultural insights into human functioning in social contexts, Miller (2002) explained the significance of this issue well. She has argued for greater caution in interpretation of the meaning of subjective construals that individuals undergo in differing cultural contexts. Subjective culture-based interpretations and insights from cultural and indigenous psychology should also be incorporated. By incorporating emic concepts, which are derived from a rigorous understanding of indigenous psychologies, we will be in a better position to frame the interpretations that individuals in different cultural contexts use in reacting and adopting to organizational events and processes.

   Taken collectively, these suggestions should be of considerable help for cross-cultural researchers in creating the knowledge base that we need to live not only comfortably, but also reflectively, in this era of globalization. A journey of a thousand miles begins with a single step.

Note

Ideas in this paper reflect work presented in the symposium, "New Perspectives in Organizational Theory: An Old Turk Perspective," chaired by Rabi S. Bhagat and Kim Cameron, at the 2001 Academy of Management Annual Meeting in Washington, D.C. Rabi Bhagat presented a paper entitled, "Beyond Confucius: The Evolving World of Organizations in the Era of Globalization and Information Technology." In addition, related ideas were presented in a symposium on "The Applicability of Organizational Sciences in the Far East Context," at the 2002 SIOP Annual Meeting in Toronto, Canada.

References

Adler, N.J. (1982), Cross-cultural management research: The ostrich and the trend. *Academy of Management Review, 8*: 226-232.

Adler, P.S. & Borys, B. (1996), Two types of bureaucracy: Enabling and coercive. *Administrative Science Quarterly, 41*: 61-89.

Ancona, D.G., Okhuysen, G.A. & Perlow, L.A. (2001), Taking time to integrate temporal research. *Academy of Management Review, 26*: 512-529.

Arvey, R. D., Bhagat, R. S., & Salas, E. (1991), Cross-cultural and Cross-national Issues in Personnel and Human Resources Management: Where do we go from here? *Research in Personnel and Human Resources Management, 9*: 367-407.

Barrett, G.V., & Bass, B.M. (1976), Cross cultural issues in industrial and organizational psychology. In M.D. Dunnette (ed.), *Handbook of industrial and organizational psychology*. Chicago: Rand McNally.

Berry, J.W. (1980), Social and cultural change. In H.C. Triandis & R.W. Brislin (eds.), *Handbook of Cross-Cultural Psychology*, Vol. 5 (pp. 211-279). Boston: Allyn & Bacon, Inc.

Bhagat, R.S. (1997), The yin and yang of progress in international business: A philosophy of science based perspective. In B. Toyne & D. Nigh (eds.), *International business: An emerging vision* (pp. 651-672). Columbia, SC: University of South Carolina Press.

Bhagat, R. S. & Kedia, B. L. (1996), Reassessing the elephant: Directions for future research. In B. J. Punnett & O. Shenkar (eds.), *Handbook of international management research*, Cambridge, MA: Blackwell Publishers. 521-536.

Bhagat, R. S., Kedia, B. L, Crawford, S.E., & Kaplan, M.R. (1990), Cross-cultural Issues in Organizational Psychology: Emergent Trends and Directions for Research in the 1990's. In C.L. Cooper & Ivan T. Robertson (eds.), *International review of industrial and organizational psychology*, Vol. 5. New York: John Wiley and Sons, 59-99.

Bhagat, R. S., Kedia, B.L., Perez, L.M., & Moustafa, K.S. (2003, in press), The role of subjective culture in organizations: Progress and pitfalls twenty years later. In B.J. Punnett & O. Shenkar (eds), *Handbook of international management research*. Ann Arbor: University of Michigan Press.

Bhagat, R.S. & McQuaid, S.J. (1982), Role of subjective culture in organizations: A review and directions for future research. *Journal of Applied Psychology Monograph*, 67 (5): 653-685.

Bhagat, R.S. & Moustafa, K.S. (2002), How Non-Americans View American Use of Time: A Cross-Cultural Perspective. In P. Boski (ed.), *New Directions in Cross-Cultural Psychology*. Warsaw: Polish Psychological Association, 183-192.

Cairncross, F. (2001), *The death of distance*. Boston: Harvard Business School Press.

Davenport, T. H., & Prusak, L. (1998), *Working knowledge*. Boston: Harvard Business School Press.

Drenth, P.J.D. 1985, Cross-cultural organizational psychology: Challenges and limitations. In P. Joynt & M. Warner (eds.), *Managing in different cultures*. Amsterdam: Universitetsforlaget, A.S.

Economist, The (2001), How the world has (and hasn't) changed. October 27th.

Edwards, J.R. (1994), Regression analysis as an alternative to difference scores. *Journal of Management*, 20: 683-689.

Foa, U.G. & Foa, E.B. (1974), *Societal structures of the mind*. Springfield, IL: Charles C. Thomas Publisher

Govindarajan, V., & Gupta, A.K. (2001), *The quest for global dominance: Transforming global presence into global competitive advantage*. San Francisco: Jossey-Bass.

Greenfield, P. (2000), Three approaches to the psychology of culture: Where do they come from? Where can they go? *Asian Journal of Social Psychology*, 3: 223-240.

Greider, W. (1997), *One world: Ready or not*. New York: Crown Business.

Guillen, M.F. (2001), *The limits of convergence: Globalization and organizational change in Argentina, South Korea, and Spain*. Princeton, MA: Princeton University Press.

Haire, A. Ghiselli, R. & Porter, L. (1967), *Managerial thinking: An international study*. New York: John Wiley.

Hofstede, G. (2001), *Culture's consequences: Comparing values, behaviors, institutions, and organizations across nations* (2nd ed.). Thousand Oaks, CA: Sage

Hofstede, G. (1991), *Cultures and organizations: Software of the mind*. London: McGraw-Hill.

Hofstede, G. (1980), *Culture's consequences: International differences in work-related values*. Beverly Hills, CA: Sage.

Hofstede, G., Neuijen, B., Ohayv, D.D., & Sanders, G. (1990), Measuring organizational cultures: A qualitative and quantitative study across twenty cases. *Administrative Science Quarterly*, 35: 286-316.

Hui, H., & Luk, C.L. 1997), Industrial/organizational psychology. In J.W. Berry, M.H. Segal, & C. Kagitcibasi (eds.), *Handbook of cross-cultural psychology*, Vol. 3, p. 371-412. Boston: Allyn & Bacon.

Issac, R.G. & Pitt, D.C. (2001), Organizational culture. It's alive! It's alive! But there's no fixed address! In R.T. Golembiewski (ed.), *Handbook of organizational behavior*, (2nd ed.) (pp. 113-144). New York: Marcel Dekker.

Jain, U. (2001). Transcending cultural boundaries for human and organization development: Experiences of international exchanges between India and the United States. In R.T. Golembiewski (ed.), *Handbook of organizational behavior*, (2nd ed.) (pp. 737-756). New York: Marcel Dekker.

Joynt, P. & Warner, M. (eds.) (1985), *Managing in different cultures*. Amsterdam: Universitetforlaget.

Kerr, C., Dunlop, J.T., Harbison, C.A., & Myers, C.A. (1960), *Industrialism and the industrial man*. Cambridge, MA: Harvard University Press.

Lens, W. (1986)., Future time perspective: A cognitive-motivational concept. In D.R. Brown and J. Veroff (eds.), *Frontiers of motivational psychology*. New York: Alfred A. Knopf, Inc.

Leonard-Barton, D. (1995), *Wellsprings of knowledge: Building and sustaining the source of innovation*. Boston, MA: Harvard Business School Press.

Malpass, R.S. (1977), Theory and method in cross-cultural psychology. *American Psychologist, 32*: 1069-1079.

Miller, J.G. (2002), Bringing culture to basic psychological theory – Beyond individualism and collectivism: Comment on Oyserman et. al. (2002), *Psychological Bulletin, 128* (1): 97-109.

Mitchell, T.R. (1997), Matching motivational strategies with organizational contexts. *Research in Organizational Behavior, 19*: 57-150.

MOW International Research Team. (1987), *The meaning of working*. New York: Academic Press.

Nath, R. (1988), *Comparative management: A regional view*. Cambridge, MA: Ballinger.

Negandhi, A.R. (1983), Cross-cultural management research: Trend and future directions. *Journal of International Business Studies, 14*: 17-28.

Nuttin, J. & Lens, W. (1985), *Future time perspective and motivation: Theory and research method*. Leuven, Belgium: Leuven University Press.

Ogbor, J.O. (2000), Implication: Creative synthesis in organizational change across cultures. *International Journal of Cross-Cultural Management*, 10 (1): 71-73.

Oyserman, D., Kemmelmeier, M., & Coon, H.M. (2002), Cultural psychology, a new look: Reply to Bond (2002), Fiske (2002), Kitayama (2002), and Miller (2002). *Psychological Bulletin, 128* (1): 110-117.

Pelto, P.J. (1968), The difference between "tight" and "loose" societies. *Transaction, April*: 37-40.

Roberts, K.H. (1970), On looking at an elephant: An evaluation of cross-cultural research related to organizations. *Psychological Bulletin, 74*: 327-350.

Ronan, S. & Kuman, R. (1986), Comparative management: A developmental perspective. In B.M. Bass, P. Weissenberg & F. Heller (eds.), *Handbook of cross-cultural organizational psychology*. Beverly Hills, CA: Sage.

Schneider, S., & Barsoux, J. (1997), *Managing across cultures*. London: Prentice-Hall.

Shenkar, O. & Li, J. (1999), Knowledge search in international cooperative ventures. *Organization Science*, 10: 134-143.

Starbuck, W.H. (1992), Learning by knowledge-intensive firms. *Journal of Management Studies, 29*: 713-740.

Thomas, D.C. (2002), *Essentials of international management : A cross-cultural perspective.* Thousand Oaks, CA: Sage Publications.

Triandis, H. C. (1998), Vertical and horizontal individualism and collectivism: theory and research implications for international comparative management. In J.L. Cheng & R.B. Peterson (Eds.), *Advances in international comparative management, 12*: 7-35.

Triandis, H. C. (1995), *Individualism and collectivism.* Boulder, CO: Westview Press.

Triandis, H. C. (1994), *Culture and social behavior.* New York: McGraw-Hill.

Triandis, H.C. (1989), The self and social behavior in differing cultural contexts. *Psychological Review, 96* (3): 506-520.

Waller, M.J., Conte, J.M., Gibson, C.B. & Carpenter, M.A. (2001). The effect of individual perceptions of deadlines on team performance. *Academy of Management Review, 26* (4): 586-600.

Index